THE
UNLIKELY
DISCIPLE

THE
UNLIKELY DISCIPLE

A SINNER'S SEMESTER
AT AMERICA'S
HOLIEST UNIVERSITY

KEVIN ROOSE

GRAND CENTRAL
PUBLISHING

New York   Boston

Unless otherwise indicated, all scripture quotations are taken from the HOLY BIBLE, NEW INTERNATIONAL VERSION®. Copyright © 1973, 1978, 1984 International Bible Society. Used by permission of Zondervan. All rights reserved.

Scripture quotations marked NASB are taken from the NEW AMERICAN STANDARD BIBLE®. Copyright © 1960, 1962, 1963, 1968, 1971, 1972, 1973, 1975, 1977, 1995 by The Lockman Foundation. Used by permission.

Scripture quotations marked NLT are taken from the Holy Bible, New Living Translation, copyright 1996, 2004. Used by permission of Tyndale House Publishers, Inc., Wheaton, Illinois 60189. All rights reserved.

Scripture quotations marked NKJV are taken from the New King James Version. Copyright © 1982 by Thomas Nelson, Inc. Used by permission. All rights reserved.

Scripture quotations marked KJV are taken from the King James Version.

Grand Central Publishing
Hachette Book Group
237 Park Avenue
New York, NY 10017

Visit our website at www.HachetteBookGroup.com.

Printed in the United States of America

First Edition: March 2009
10 9 8 7 6 5 4 3 2 1

Grand Central Publishing is a division of Hachette Book Group, Inc.
The Grand Central Publishing name and logo is a trademark of Hachette Book Group, Inc.

Library of Congress Cataloging-in-Publication Data
Roose, Kevin.
   The unlikely disciple: a sinner's semester at America's holiest university / Kevin Roose.—1st ed.
       p. cm.
   ISBN: 978-0-446-17842-6
   1. Liberty University—Students—Social life and customs. 2. Church college students—Virginia—Lynchburg. I. Title.
   LD3071.L33R66 2009
   378.755'671—dc22   2008037866

Book design by Giorgetta Bell McRee

AUTHOR'S NOTE

The events in this book are true as depicted. However, with the exception of certain public figures and individuals who agreed to be identified, all names and personal details have been changed. Some bits of dialogue have been slightly rearranged, and some events appear out of sequence.

To Mom and Dad,
who would kill the fatted calf for me any day.

CONTENTS

Do not forget to entertain strangers, for by so doing some people have entertained angels without knowing it.

HEBREWS 13:2

Prepare Ye

It's midnight at Liberty University, and I'm kneeling on the floor of my dorm room, praying.

This is not a particularly unusual event. Any night of the week, a quick stroll through Liberty's campus would reveal hundreds of students in the same position, making the same kind of divine appeal. At this school, we pray for everything: good grades, a winning football season, religious revival in America, chicken fingers in the dining hall. Our God is a workhorse God, and as the Bible instructs, we petition him without ceasing. Put it this way: if prayers emitted light, you'd see us from space.

Our chancellor, the Reverend Jerry Falwell, always tells us that prayer is the key to a productive Christian life. And, well, he should know. In 1971, Rev. Falwell felt God calling him to start a Christian college in his hometown of Lynchburg, Virginia. He answered the call, and over the next thirty-six years, while organizing the Moral Majority, shepherding one of America's largest megachurches, and establishing himself as the father of the Religious Right, he found time to transform that Christian college into what it is today: the world's largest evangelical university, a ten thousand–student training ground for America's conservative Christian youth. "Bible Boot Camp," he calls it.

1

It's a tongue-in-cheek name, but a fairly accurate one. Like a West Point drill sergeant, Rev. Falwell prides himself on discipline. His field manual, a forty-six-page code of conduct called "The Liberty Way," governs every aspect of our lives and dispenses concrete punishments when we veer off course. Such as:

- Possession and/or use of tobacco: 6 reprimands + $25 fine
- Improper personal contact (anything beyond hand-holding): 4 reprimands + $10 fine
- Attendance at, possession or viewing of, an R-rated movie: 12 reprimands + $50 fine
- Spending the night with a person of the opposite sex: 30 reprimands + $500 fine + 30 hours community service

Rev. Falwell envisioned Liberty as a Christian safe haven where young evangelicals could get a college education without being exposed to binge drinking, pot smoking, sexual experimentation, and all the other trappings of secular coed culture. He planned to make it the evangelical equivalent of Notre Dame or Brigham Young, a university where every student would be trained in the liberal arts, fortified in the evangelical faith, and sent out into the world as a "Champion for Christ."

That plan must have worked, because today, our school is still a bastion of sparkling Christian purity—sort of the anti-Animal House. On this campus, you'll find girls who are saving their first kisses for marriage, guys whose knowledge of the female anatomy is limited to the parts you can show on basic cable, and students of both sexes who consider it a wild Friday night when their Bible study group serves Cheetos *and* Chex Mix.

Of course, you'll also find Liberty students who aren't so sheltered, who don't walk around campus humming hymns and speaking in parables. Like any other religious community, Liberty has its fair share of nonconformists. A few Liberty students, in fact, choose to live relatively normal collegiate lives, even when it means violating "The Liberty Way." That's why I'm praying on the floor of my room tonight—because my friend Dave is in trouble.

It started last Friday afternoon when Dave, a brawny, goateed shot-putter on Liberty's track team, approached his friend Wayne with an idea.

"Let's get out of here for the weekend," he said.

Dave explained that one of his high school friends, a non-Christian girl named Jessie, had invited both of them to a special party at her secular college, three hours away from Lynchburg.

"A *lingerie* party," he said. "Wayne, she invited us to a lingerie party. Like . . . a party . . . where the girls wear lingerie."

Wayne chuckled. "Naw, man. You know we can't do that."

He was right. Attending a party of any type is forbidden under "The Liberty Way," but a lingerie party would be off-the-charts sinful. Still, as Dave talked more about the party and how many beautiful, scantily clad girls would be there, he felt his resistance weakening. *I mean, I haven't been off campus all semester. And what harm could one night do?* By the time Dave finished his pitch, Wayne's mind was made up: he wanted to go. The party wouldn't be holy, but it wouldn't be the worst thing in the world, either. So the two friends signed out on the campus log sheet—to the off-campus apartment of an older Liberty student they knew—and drove to secular school instead.

The party was wilder than they'd expected. Girls in sheer negligees and lacy bustiers floated around the room, grinding lustily with each other while loud hip-hop music blared over the rowdy yells of beer pong players. Dave had gone to some parties in high school, but Wayne was relatively new to the scene, and getting comfortable took three or four cups of a beverage he'd never heard of ("jungle juice," was it?).

After an hour of drinking, Dave and Wayne felt loose enough to unveil their big surprise: two pairs of special underwear, purchased in advance for the occasion. Dave stripped down to a black man-thong, and Wayne, a bit more reserved, wore a pair of SpongeBob SquarePants boxers. They drank and danced and cavorted with the secular students until the wee hours, using Dave's digital camera to snap the photos he would eventually post, for posterity, on his MySpace profile.

That was the fatal step, of course, and no one can quite understand why Dave did it. Did he really think his secrets were safe on the Internet? Was he *trying* to get kicked out?

These are the questions that have circulated through our dorm for the past week. By now, we've heard all the stories. We've heard how, a few days after the party, Dave found an urgent e-mail from the dean of men waiting in his inbox. How, when he was brought in to the dean's office, Dave tried to make the case that he hadn't been at a party. How the dean had pulled from his desk a stack of photos, culled from Dave's MySpace page, that proved otherwise. How some of the photos had been shockingly lewd, including one of Dave in his man-thong, holding a bottle of liquor in each hand while looking up a girl's skirt. How Dave had broken maybe half the rules in "The Liberty Way," including "Attendance at a dance," "Sexual misconduct and/or any state of undress," and "Possession or consumption of alcoholic beverages." How he was served with the biggest punishment on our hall—and maybe at Liberty—all year: seventy-eight reprimands, a $650 fine, and thirty hours of community service. How, at that point, adding up Dave's punishments was a matter of procedure, like sentencing a serial killer to twenty-three consecutive life sentences, because the alcohol alone was enough to expel him.

In short, the guy needs a lot of prayer.

After rising from my knees, I walk to Dave's room. He's in there with Wayne and a few other friends, still discussing his dean's office debacle. Dave is still waiting for the official news of his punishment, but he seems to have made peace with the fact that, barring a miracle, he'll be gone by next week.

"I should have done more bad stuff while I was at it," Dave says, chuckling as he picks at a bag of popcorn. "I mean, they can't kick me out twice, right? I could have snorted some coke or something."

"Come on, Dave," says Joey, a Jersey-born freshman who lives at the end of the hall. "At least try to be serious about this."

"I can't, dude," Dave says. "When I get serious, I feel pain in my heart."

Wayne is in better shape, it seems. There were no photos of him on Dave's MySpace page, just photos of their car ride together. His meeting with the dean of men is tomorrow, and he's planning to say that he dropped Dave off and went somewhere else, skipping the party altogether.

"Are you positive he doesn't have any pictures of you at the party?" Joey asks.

"No, not positive," Wayne says. "But there are none on the Internet. He would have to have another source."

"If he catches you," Dave says, "you should bust out a Jesus quote."

Wayne's eyes widen. "What?"

"Jesus hung with sinners and tax collectors, dude. If he can hang with sinners, you can, too."

"Yo, that's a pretty good idea."

"You guys are retards," says Joey. "Jesus hung with sinners, but he didn't sin with them. It's not like the tax collectors had a lingerie party and said, 'Yo, J.C., you gotta get over here, it's off the hook!'"

We're screwing around, but in truth, this is no laughing matter. Dave, our friend and hallmate, is about to be expelled from school, and Wayne may go with him. Our dorm has hosted its share of controversy this semester, but no one expected this. What Dave and Wayne did was against the rules, of course, but some of us wonder whether, in this case, the punishment truly fits the crime.

"I heard about a guy who got more reprimands than you, Dave," says Wayne.

"No way. More than seventy-eight?" says Dave.

"Yeah. A few years ago. This guy got triple digits. Broke every rule in one night. He went to a few parties, smoked weed, had sex with a girl, went dancing, destroyed some property. I think he might have even done some homosexual stuff, too."

Joey sweeps his eyes around the room.

"Pretty much what secular kids do every weekend, huh?"

I used to be a secular kid. Still am, I guess. It's hard to tell sometimes. These days, I go through the motions of a model Liberty student. I attend prayer groups, I sing in the church choir, I spend my Friday nights at Bible study. When it comes to socializing, I follow the old

Baptist moral code: "Don't drink, smoke, or chew, and don't go with girls who do."

But what Dave, Wayne, Joey, and the rest of my friends at Liberty don't know is this: I haven't always lived this way. In fact, everything I do here—the Bible study, the choir, the clean-cut morality—it's all part of a borrowed life.

Three months ago, I was a student at Brown University, a school known for everything Liberty is not. In fact, it wouldn't be unfair to call the schools polar opposites. Liberty was founded as a conservative Christian utopia, and by those standards, Brown, with its free-spirited student body, its grades-optional academic scene, and its active chapter of the Young Communist League, is a notch or two above Sodom and Gomorrah.

If such a thing exists, I considered myself a fairly typical Brown student. I studied English lit, drank fair-trade coffee, attended the occasional anti-war protest, and sang in an a cappella group.

This semester, I transferred to Liberty precisely because it was so different—not just from my old school, but from anything I'd ever seen before.

I grew up in the tiny college town of Oberlin, Ohio, a crunchy liberal enclave plopped down improbably in the middle of the Lake Erie Rust Belt. My parents are Quakers, a rather free-spirited sect of Christianity whose members (called Friends) spend a lot of time talking about peace and working for social justice. But despite our affiliation, our house was practically religion-free. We never read the Bible or said grace over our meals, and our attendance at Quaker services was spotty—though we did visit a small Baptist church once a year to sing Christmas carols. (To be clear: this is the kind of Baptist church where the pastor swaps out the gendered language in the carols, like in "Lo! How a Rose E'er Blooming" when "as men of old have sung" becomes "as *those* of old have sung.")

When high school came around, I left home to attend a boarding school in the Philadelphia suburbs. It happened to be a Quaker boarding school, but going there was hardly a religious decision. In fact, during high school, I wasn't sure what I thought about my parents' religion, or about religion in general. I liked learning about the Quaker moral tenets—simplicity, peace, integrity, and equality—but when the subject of God came up, I always found myself lagging behind. Quakers talk about God as an "inner light," and while I understood that position intellectually, I couldn't bring myself to think that there was a divine being who existed independent of the human mind, who guided our decisions and heard our prayers. To put it in Quaker terms, my inner light flickered a lot, like the overhead fluorescent at a Motel 6, and sometimes, it burnt out altogether. The closest I came to consistent faith was during my senior year religion class, when we learned about the Central and South American liberation theology movements and I became briefly convinced that God was a left-wing superhero who led the global struggle against imperialism and corporate greed. Sort of a celestial Michael Moore.

You can probably guess, then, how I felt during college, when by virtue of a job I had taken as a writer's assistant, I found myself standing in the lobby of Jerry Falwell's twenty thousand–member Thomas Road Baptist Church, which occupies the entire northern end of Liberty's campus.

My boss, the journalist A. J. Jacobs, had taken me to Thomas Road on a research trip for his book, *The Year of Living Biblically*. I had never been to a megachurch before, and there was something thrilling about the idea of seeing Jerry Falwell in action. Like many non-evangelicals, I knew Rev. Falwell only as the arch-conservative televangelist with the least effective brain-to-mouth filter in the English-speaking world. I remembered that he had gone on TV to blame the terrorist attacks of September 11, 2001, on feminists, homosexuals, abortionists, and the ACLU, among others. I had seen some of his other inflammatory remarks, like when he told CBS's *60 Minutes* that the prophet Muhammed was "a terrorist," or when he said that AIDS was "God's punishment for the society that tolerates homosexuals."

But Jerry Falwell in theory and Jerry Falwell in practice are two very different things, and by the time I was standing in Thomas Road's cavernous lobby on a mild Sunday morning in July, watching a few thousand Falwell devotees mill around, my thrill had turned into stomach-clenching anxiety. My inner monologue was going a mile a minute: Who are these people? Do they really love Jerry Falwell? Do they believe 9/11 was caused by gay people, too? How is that even possible? And what's a coffee shop doing in a church lobby?

When A. J. left to take notes on another part of the church, I chatted up a group of Thomas Roaders I found in the lobby, two girls and a guy who looked to be around my age. I introduced myself, told them why I was visiting, and asked how long they'd been coming to Thomas Road.

"We come here every week," they said. "We go to Liberty."

I wasn't sure whether "go to Liberty" was some sort of coded religious language, like "walk the path" or "seek the kingdom," so I asked. I had to chuckle when they told me that "Liberty" meant Liberty University, a Christian liberal arts college founded and presided over by Rev. Falwell. I mean, come on. A liberal arts college run by Jerry Falwell? How about an etiquette workshop run by Courtney Love?

But I wanted to give them the benefit of the doubt, so I asked them to tell me more about their school.

"Oh, I love Liberty!" said one of the girls, an effusive blonde in a green sundress. She spent five minutes making an enthusiastic pitch, which included statistics about Liberty's recently opened law school, its top-ranked debate team, and its Division I athletic program. She told me that Liberty has grown at a rate—from 154 students in 1971 to nearly 25,000 in 2007 (including more than 15,000 taking courses via the Internet)—that few colleges, secular or religious, have ever matched.

It was impressive stuff, but it wasn't quite what I wanted to know.

"So, what do you guys do for fun?" I asked.

They looked at each other quizzically, then back at me. The blonde stammered, "I mean, we do different . . . things. I don't really know what you're asking."

This wasn't getting me off on the right foot. Maybe I needed to break the ice.

"Any good parties around here?"

But I got no chuckles, only blank stares. The guy, a long, lean boy-band type with jutting platinum hair, squinted and peered down his nose.

"Do you know Christ?"

I was new to evangelical argot, so I didn't know that if a Liberty student has to ask this question, he probably knows the answer already. The way I saw it, I could (a) tell him I did know Christ, which might not go so well if he decided to follow up, (b) try to deflect with sarcasm again, something like, "Yeah, he's a friend of a friend. We don't really hang out much," or (c) admit that I was a foreigner.

Too scared for (a) or (b), I chose (c). I told him I didn't know Christ, and after he spent five minutes explaining why I should consider meeting him, I said, as gently as I could, that I wasn't interested in converting.

"Please don't be offended," I said. "It's just not my thing."

They glanced at each other, all three a little mystified. Not my thing? How could it not be my thing? They didn't browbeat me, but I had definitely made them uneasy. We made a little more small talk, and then, since church was starting, we parted ways with nods and hesitant half-waves.

On the plane ride back from Virginia, I replayed those fifteen minutes over and over in my mind. Every time, I got more frustrated with myself. Why wasn't I able to hold down that conversation? I mean, I've heard of the God Divide before, in a thousand *Newsweek* articles and one-hour CNN specials. I'm aware that a tree-hugging Brown student isn't supposed to be able to talk to a Bible-thumping Liberty student. But why not? Aren't we all part of the Millennial generation? Don't we all carry the same iPhones and suffer from the same entitlement complex?

One recent study showed that 51 percent of Americans don't know any evangelical Christians, even casually. And until I visited Thomas Road, that was me. My social circle at Brown included atheists, agnostics, lapsed Catholics, Buddhists, Wiccans, and more non-observant Jews than you can shake a shofar at, but exactly zero born-again Christians. The evangelical world, in my mind, was a cloistered, slightly frightening community whose values and customs I wasn't supposed to understand. So I ignored it.

After my visit to Thomas Road, though, I was hooked. I started reading up on Liberty and other evangelical colleges, and the more I read, the more I began to realize the importance of knowing about my Christian peers. This isn't a fringe culture, after all. According to the Barna Group, an evangelical polling firm, a full one-third of America's teenagers self-identify as born-again Christians. Liberty has almost ten thousand students living on its campus, and it's just one of hundreds of evangelical colleges across America. Alumni of evangelical colleges run blue-chip corporations, work in big media, and sit in elected office. If I ever get a real job, my cubicle might well be next to a Liberty graduate's.

As a college student who doubles as a journalist, what fascinated me most about Liberty was its student culture. I still had so many unanswered questions. Like, what do Champions for Christ learn in class? Do they date? Do they use Facebook? What exactly do they believe? And are we really that different? I also felt intuitively that there was something limiting about being an outsider in the evangelical world. When I told the Liberty students at Thomas Road that I hadn't accepted Christ as my savior, the entire dynamic of the conversation changed. It began to feel distant and rehearsed, like a pitch for Ginsu knives. So how could I, a curious non-evangelical, get the inside scoop?

Several months after my Thomas Road visit, while browsing Liberty's website one morning, it clicked: What if I spent a semester at Liberty as a student? What if, instead of speculating about Christian college life from afar, I jumped over the God Divide and tried to experience it myself?

These days, it seems like all my college friends talk about is study abroad, the modern rite of passage in which students spend a semester in Paris, Barcelona, Munich, or any of the other first-world cities with low minimum drinking ages. The appeal of these programs—at least from a school's perspective—is that experiencing a foreign culture firsthand makes us more informed global citizens. But what about American citizens? Here, right in my time zone, was a culture more foreign to me than any European capital, and these foreigners vote in my elections! So why not do a domestic study abroad? If I enrolled at

Liberty for a semester, I'd get to take the same classes, attend the same church services, and live under the same rules as my evangelical peers. And maybe I'd be able to use what I found to help bridge our country's God Divide, or at least to understand it better.

Of course, I had to ask myself: was I ready to live the life of an evangelical college student?

On a practical level, clearly not. As I said, I grew up with no religious training. At my Quaker boarding school, I acted in a musical about the Garden of Eden, so I knew the basics of the Genesis story (Adam names the animals, Eve bites an apple, and we all break into jazz squares). I could probably have named the four Gospels if you gave me a minute or two, but that's where my Bible knowledge ended. So how would I be able to hang with lifelong Sunday schoolers?

Obviously, I had some decisions to make.

First, what would I tell Liberty students about myself?

Naturally, I wanted to be as honest as possible. I wasn't eager to sneak around like a spy, and I didn't want the mental burden of juggling a double identity, so I decided to stick to my guns: regular old Kevin Roose from Oberlin, Ohio. No alias, no faked documents, no lies about my past. If people asked, I'd tell them that I came to Liberty from Brown, and if they asked why, I'd say, "I wanted to see what Christian college was like."

Which was true. I did want to see what Christian college was like, with as little prejudgment as possible. I knew that wouldn't be easy—you can't neutralize a lifetime of bias overnight—but I wanted to try my best. So my second decision was: no cheap shots. If I went to Liberty, it would be to learn with an open mind, not to mock Liberty students or the evangelical world in toto. For starters, that task is far too easy to be interesting. The satirist P. J. O'Rourke once compared making fun of born-again Christians to "hunting dairy cows with a high-powered rifle and scope." That was a few years ago, before names like Ted Haggard and movies like *Jesus Camp* came on the scene. Now, it's more like hunting the ground with your foot.

My next decision was harder, because even though I wanted to use my real identity at Liberty, I was nervous about what would happen if I told people certain things about myself—namely, that I wasn't an evangelical Christian. I wanted to be able to portray the Liberty experience in a way that was authentic and fair, but that meant I had to avoid the sorts of guarded interactions I had during my first trip to Thomas Road.

So I decided: I would do whatever it took to blend in with Liberty students. I'd pray when they prayed, sing when they sang, and take exams when they took exams. If anyone ever asked, I'd say that I was a Christian (strictly true), but if the questions got more specific—say, if someone asked me how I felt about homosexuality—I'd have to be more evasive. I had to stay on the inside of the community, even if it meant holding back my true feelings.

Staying on the inside also meant withholding the fact that I was planning to write about my time there. This gave me much more pause than blending in, even though my goal was to be open-minded. But in the end, I decided that although I didn't like the idea of writing in secret, I had to do it. It was the only way I'd be able to get the unfiltered story of life at Liberty.

So, on a Tuesday night in early October, I logged onto Liberty's website to fill out the application for admission, a short form that required little more than a few biographical details and a brief essay. Liberty's application doesn't include a mandatory statement of faith, but to complete the essay prompt—"Describe how your perspectives of life and morality will enable you to contribute to Liberty University's mission"—I had to read a few dozen Christian articles and sermons online and wrangle some of the buzzwords into a three-paragraph response. (I won't reprint the whole thing here, but it included sentences like "The path to righteousness is not an easy one.") I filled in a few more blanks, clicked "Send," and my application tumbled through the ether to Liberty.

Next, I met with Brown's dean of students, who stared at me with wide eyes when I asked him if I could take a semester's leave to study at Liberty. "I don't think anyone has ever asked me that," he said. "Actually, I'm sure no one has." But I left his office with good news. If I wanted to take a leave of absence, I would have a spot to come back to.

After getting permission from the dean, I had to get permission from my parents, a much more nerve-wracking proposition. My mom and dad—a college administrator and a lawyer, respectively—are staunch, proud left-wingers, and I don't think they ever imagined their youngest son asking to study under Jerry Falwell's tutelage. They both worked as Nader's Raiders in the 1970s, and my dad still keeps a "Buy Blue" list in his wallet to make sure he only shops at stores owned by Democrats. And technically, they still had veto power. When I first floated the idea, they were opposed. But after I told them about my intentions, they seemed to soften. After a few hours of coaxing and prodding, they caved and gave me a reluctant green light.

The reactions I got from my friends at Brown were also largely positive, if confused. The prevailing attitude seemed to be: *well, better him than me.* When I told the guys in my a cappella group why I wouldn't be singing with them during the spring semester, they asked a few questions to make sure I was serious, and then the jokes began. My friend Jimmy's response was typical: "A semester with no sex? And this is different how?"

My friend Laura was the only person with lasting concerns. Remember when I mentioned that I had no evangelical Christians in my social circle? Well, I actually had one. I always forget that Laura, a sweet, curly-haired brunette who went to boarding school with me, grew up in a conservative evangelical family in rural Pennsylvania. You wouldn't necessarily know it by talking to her, but she's got a church deacon dad and two decades of Sunday school under her belt. Real Christian street cred.

"Oh man," she said, when I told her my plan. "You're in trouble, Kev."

Laura explained that while she thought I had a good idea, it wasn't going to work. "Christian culture is not just something you pick up," she said. "These kids are going to know you don't belong there."

She was right, of course. Did I really think I was going to learn everything as I went along? How cocky is that? Luckily, Laura threw me a life preserver. If I came to her apartment in Baltimore, she offered to give me a last-minute crash course before my evangelical immersion began.

"I won't be able to teach you everything," she said, "but I can get you some of the way there."

So I went to Baltimore, and for three days, Laura became my evangelical Yoda. She drilled me on biblical characters, famous scripture verses, and common errors among non-evangelicals (like calling the last book of the Bible "Revelations" instead of "Revelation"). She taught me worship songs, told me to read the apocalyptic novel *Left Behind*, and lent me her collection of *VeggieTales*, the Christian cartoon series that stars Bob the Tomato and Larry the Cucumber in oversimplified Bible reenactments. (My favorite: the "Josh and the Big Wall!" episode, in which the little Israelite vegetables take down the walls of the Canaanite vegetable city. In the biblical story, the Canaanites are killed in a gruesome massacre, but in the *VeggieTales* version, they just walk around sulking.)

On the last day of my training, Laura and I sat in an Irish pub in Baltimore's Inner Harbor, eating fish and chips and doing some last-minute review. As we finished, she put down her Bible and looked at me.

"So, do you think you're ready for a semester of Christianity?" she asked.

"Yeah, I think I remember most of what we talked about," I said. "I'm doing better on my Bible stuff, and I got the C. S. Lewis books you recommended."

"No, that's not what I mean," she said. "I mean, are you *spiritually* ready?"

She took my silence as a no.

"Kev, places like Liberty are designed to transform skepticism into belief, and you're not going to be immune to that. You have to be open to the possibility that this semester is going to be bigger than you think."

Laura wasn't the only one who warned me about the danger of being changed. In talking with my friends and family members about my Liberty project, the question had come up several times: what if you convert?

I always admitted that it was an outside possibility—that was the definition of keeping an open mind, after all—but I didn't really believe myself. My mind told me that I had enough built-up resistance to Falwell-style Christianity to avoid internalizing the experience. How could I possibly convert? My parents wouldn't disown me, but it would certainly change our relationship. In fact, becoming a conservative evangelical would change all of my relationships. What would I say to my gay friends at Brown? How could I tell the guys in my a cappella group that I couldn't go out drinking with them anymore? How could I go back to my old world at all?

A few days later, the thick envelope came in the mail.

"Congratulations!" the letter read. "You have been accepted to Liberty University for Spring Semester 2007."

Inside the envelope was a Liberty lanyard and a letter thanking my parents for considering a biblical education for their son. The letter said I could start at the beginning of the semester, in mid-January. Now, with permission from my school, my parents, and Liberty, the pieces were all in place. I was ready.

And so, three months ago, armed with a box of Christian books and a silver Jesus fish affixed to my car bumper (a friend's suggestion), I packed my Providence dorm room into duffel bags and boxes and made the move to Lynchburg to begin my semester at Bible Boot Camp. I was nervous, of course, but I consoled myself with the fact that at the end of the semester, after my evangelical sojourn was over, I'd be returning to life as usual.

Three months ago, I thought that was how it worked.

Come and See

In the beginning was the word, and the word was God, and the word was inappropriate.

"Dear God, this place is huge," says my dad. "Did we accidentally take the Disneyland exit?"

"Honey, you can't say that here."

"Disneyland?"

"No, God. You can't say 'God' unless you're talking about church. It's taking the Lord's name in vain. Right, Kev?"

As my parents and I walk into Liberty's front entrance for the first day of new student orientation, I begin to think that having two church-phobic Quakers drop me off at Bible Boot Camp might not have been my best idea.

It wasn't my idea at all, in fact. I planned to set off for Liberty alone, but about a week before I was scheduled to leave, my parents announced that they wanted to come along to see the place for themselves.

My mom has become increasingly nervous about my project. After the news sunk in, she seemed to realize what going to Liberty would mean for me, and it tripped her wires of maternal concern. She's scared that Jerry Falwell will find me out as a non-evangelical, and I'll end up on my knees in front of a roomful of Christian thugs, getting acquainted with the business end of a bullwhip. For the past few weeks, she's been not-so-subtly suggesting other things I could do with my semester. Don't I want to travel in Europe? What about an internship?

My dad, on the other hand, is excited to see Rev. Falwell in the flesh. In the know-thine-enemy vein, he has been digging up Falwell-related trivia on the Internet and has recently developed a curious fascination with the man. Most nights at the dinner table, he peppers me with new findings. Did I know that Falwell is reported to have financial ties with the Moonies? Had I heard that he once outed a Teletubby?

Bottom line: they both wanted to see me off, and after a little hemming and hawing, I decided it wasn't worth a fight. So early this morning, we prepared for the road trip. I made it clear that in order to come along, they would have to make themselves passable as evangelical parents. Which they took to mean, "Please dress like the Cleavers." My dad dug a navy suit out of his closet, and my mom put on makeup and shaved her legs (both blue-moon events, she said). We packed our Honda to the ceiling with my belongings and set off down Interstate 77 toward Lynchburg, Virginia.

Liberty sits atop a five thousand–acre foothill in Virginia's Blue Ridge mountain range, and my dad is right about the size of the place. Perched on its hill, the campus towers over Lynchburg in a way that seems almost oppressive. There's a domed stadium that looks like it was plucked from Epcot Center, an arrestingly large brick building with tall Jeffersonian columns, and, of course, the Thomas Road Baptist Church, which has swollen to the size of two or three conjoined IKEAs since the last time I was here. The whole campus looks nice in a generic, recently-power-washed way, but it doesn't scream Christian. In fact, other than the small white chapel in the middle of campus and the electronic billboard advertising an upcoming "Prayer Summit," the physical space looks a lot like any other big university.

In keeping with the boot camp theme, dorms at Liberty are numbered, not named. My assigned dorm, number 22, is a boxy three-story near the center of campus. First observation: the word "MEN" is painted over the front door in large, white letters. Liberty, like many other evangelical colleges, has single-sex dorms with strict no-visitation policies. According to "The Liberty Way," "entering the residence hall of the opposite sex or allowing the same" gets you eighteen reprimands, a $250 fine, and eighteen hours of community service.

My room, number 205, is near the middle of a dimly lit hallway as narrow and long as two bowling lanes laid end to end, with glossy blue floors and sterile cream-colored walls. When I open the door, a lanky, crew-cutted guy is sitting on his bed unpacking a black suitcase.

"You must be Kevin," he says, rising to shake my hand. "I'm Eric, your roommate."

Eric is a second-semester freshman from Michigan who, like me, is arriving at Liberty for the first time. He tells me that we have a third roommate named Henry, also a transfer student, who arrived yesterday and who has already chosen a bed for himself. Eric and I will be sleeping on a set of bunks—him on bottom, me on top. "If that's cool with you," he adds.

It's cool with me, and after a little unpacking, my parents and I head over to the first orientation event, the Mid-Year Kickoff. Several hundred transfer students have come to Liberty this semester, and all of us are getting the red-carpet treatment. As we walk into the field house where the kickoff is held, we're treated to a laser light show and a silhouetted cityscape projected on the wall. Red and blue balloons fill the air, and a student jazz band in the corner is playing what sounds like a Weather Channel background loop.

When the music stops, an LU administrator comes to the stage to introduce our chancellor, president, and spiritual leader: "Dr. Jerry Falwell" (Falwell has no earned doctorate, but at Liberty, he uses the title from three honorary degrees he's received).

"We've heard a lot about Martin Luther King's very famous speech, 'I Have a Dream,'" the administrator says. "Well, thirty-five years ago, Dr. Falwell had a dream."

At this, my dad chortles. My mom's eyes bulge, and we glare at him.

"You have a role model here in Dr. Falwell," the administrator continues. "I have the privilege of working with Dr. Falwell every day, and I can tell you that this visionary leader has had the most fantastic impact. He has changed the way politics have worked in this nation. He has changed the world."

After a little more grandiloquence, Dr. Falwell (I might as well start with the title now) struts out to a roaring ovation. He's a behemoth of a man, and he carries himself proudly, wearing a black suit with a red tie and beaming as he crosses over to the lectern.

"Welcome to all of my new students for the spring semester!" he says. His voice is booming and deep with a slight southern accent, somewhere between James Earl Jones and a guy who records radio commercials for Chevy dealerships. For the next half hour, the assembled parents listen eagerly as he explains Liberty's history. He tells the story of Liberty's first class: 154 students meeting in a Sunday school room in the fall of 1971. There was no jazz band then, no gymnasium or dormitories, or even much of a curriculum. All they had was a vision: "Through producing doctors, lawyers, businesspeople, pastors, evangelists, and athletes, we wanted to take the gospel of Christ to the world."

It might sound trite now, but in the early 1970s, Falwell's idea was novel in the world of conservative evangelicalism. Liberty's predecessors, schools like Bob Jones University and Oral Roberts University, were founded primarily to train pastors, theologians, and missionaries. Falwell had attended a school with a similarly narrow focus—Baptist Bible College in Springfield, Missouri—but he wanted to extend his reach for his own school. He wanted a fully accredited, academically rigorous liberal arts institution where Christian kids could learn the skills and values they would need to take on the secular world in all walks of life.

Dr. Falwell also had a political mission. As one of the nation's leading conservative voices, he wanted Liberty to be "as far to the right as Harvard is to the left." That meant clearly articulating the school's political views to all incoming students. (One promotional brochure I received touted Liberty's "strong commitment to political conservatism, total rejection of socialism, and firm support for America's economic system of free enterprise.") It also meant exposing Liberty students to prominent conservatives, an objective reflected in the list of guest speakers: Karl Rove, George H.W. Bush, FOX News pundit Sean Hannity, and most recently, Senator John McCain, who came to Liberty to mend fences with Dr. Falwell after calling him an "agent of intolerance" during his 2000 presidential campaign.

"When you say you're a Christian university," Dr. Falwell continues, "it doesn't just mean you're religious. It means that every one of the faculty members believes the Bible is the infallible word of God. We also believe that if we profess to be Christian, our lives ought to reflect that. This is a drug-free zone. We do not permit the use of alcohol, illegal drugs, or anything like that. None. Period. We have no coed dorms. We catch a boy in a girls' dorm, we shoot him."

The parents around us guffaw and slap the tables. My dad slow-claps.

"America's colleges and universities, I'm sad to say, have become breeding grounds for immorality and drugs, and worse than that, an attitude that is anti-Christian and often anti-American. Very frankly, we are conservative. We don't have a single socialist on our faculty. Not one. We don't have a single liberal working on our campus, either. We're trying to build a university that brings America back to God and to the faith of our fathers. And I'm glad you've joined us in that mission. Students, welcome to Liberty!"

After the kickoff, my parents make a beeline for the car. Seems they've seen enough of Liberty. In the parking lot, my dad tells me sotto voce that the campus has "a distinct totalitarian feel to it." My mom looks close to tears as she hugs me goodbye. As I watch their car pull out of the lot, my head starts to spin. Having my parents here has been havoc on my nerves, but also comforting. With them goes the last remaining link to my old life. Now, it's me and Bible Boot Camp, alone for the long haul.

I walk around for a while, getting my bearings. It's an unsettling experience, because Liberty looks normal enough that its peculiarities are all the more striking. I walk into a campus bookstore that looks fairly unremarkable until I see the T-shirts lining the walls, with screen-printed mottos like "LIBERTY UNIVERSITY: POLITICALLY INCORRECT SINCE 1971" and "TEAM JERRY." The men's bathroom outside the bookstore looks like any other public bathroom until I see the graffiti scribbled in black marker above the toilet paper dispenser:

If God is omnipresent, was Jesus necessary?

(Below it, a response in red pen: *YES, B/C OF SIN!!*)

At dinnertime, I check out the dining hall—a large, industrial building with long tables in neat rows spanning the room. I take a helping of spaghetti from the nice-looking woman behind the counter and plop myself down at one of the center tables.

I sit for an hour, watching the Liberty students cycle in and out. They look happy enough, laughing and giving each other high fives and fiddling with their iPods. You could be forgiven for thinking this was the dining hall at a secular school. As I'm finishing, an elderly female custodian begins wiping down tables, readying the room for closing. Her cleaning cart is decorated with Bible verses written on manila folders and one catches my eye: "In all your ways acknowledge him, and he will make your paths straight."

On the evening of Day One, Dorm 22's Resident Assistants call a meeting for the new transfer students. (Most returning students aren't back from winter break yet.) My RAs are two Liberty juniors named Trevor Stubbs and Anthony Fox. Stubbs is a long, lanky biblical studies major with dirty blond hair and trendy rectangular glasses, and Fox is a spike-haired communications major with a soul patch who would make a good front man for a mid-1990s pop-punk band. Together, they're the hall deputies, the only students authorized to dole out reprimands and fines to other students.

When I arrive in their room, I do a double take. On Stubbs's desk, beside his laptop, is a Jerry Falwell bobble-head doll. Dr. Falwell is mounted on a clay platform, dressed in a black suit, clutching a Bible and gazing straight ahead. When he sees me ogling his doll, Stubbs flicks the head, sending it in motion. "So cool, right?" he says. "I got it in the bookstore. It's a limited edition." It occurs to me that Stubbs and I have led vastly different lives.

Soon, six or seven other new guys file into the room. There's Paul, a football player from South Carolina; Kurt, a computer programmer from Delaware; Ryan, a filmmaker from Nevada; and a few more whose names I miss. When we're seated on the floor, Stubbs explains the organization of Dorm 22's leadership. Below the RAs, he says, are two Spiritual Life Directors (SLDs), upperclassmen who serve as hall chaplains. Below the SLDs are eight Prayer Leaders, who lead our weekly small-group prayer sessions.

At Liberty, Stubbs says, dorms aren't just collections of rooms under a roof. They're spiritual teams, and each hall decides on its own theme, a motto that guides its religious life for the year. Our theme is "Beyond Mediocrity."

"We're trying to transcend averageness on this hall," he explains. "We don't want to be average in our walks with the Lord. We don't want to be average in how we treat ladies, and how we spend time with God. Every day, we try to remind each other to live beyond mediocrity."

Next, Fox picks up a copy of "The Liberty Way" and holds it aloft.

"You've probably noticed that we have some rules here," he says. "And whether we agree with them or not, they're set in place for a reason. So let's have a chat, boys."

He opens to the first page: "Stubbs and I will inspect your rooms every Monday, Wednesday, and Friday. Your bed has to be made, things have to be picked up, trash has to be emptied, and your sink and mirror have to be clean. You'll get four reps, or reprimands, if everything's not in proper order."

Fox continues: "As far as social . . . well, I'll just be blunt. As far as interacting with *girls*, hand-holding and hugging are the only official displays of physical affection allowed at Liberty. And hugging is allowed only for a three-second maximum."

One of the new guys raises his hand. "So wait, we're not allowed to kiss? What if she's our girlfriend?"

"Do you want the answer Dr. Falwell would give?" Fox says, the corners of his mouth creeping into a smile. "Technically, there's no kissing allowed, anywhere. But I'll let you guys find out on your own what really happens."

There are some fist pumps and high fives. Now we're talking.

Fox rattles off the rest of the rules at an auctioneer's clip: "No alcohol, no tobacco, no R-rated movies, no risqué posters on your walls, curfew is strictly enforced, men's hair must be cut short—can't touch the collar, can't cover the ears—facial hair should be neatly trimmed, no earrings, no studs, no body piercing (tattoos are fine). Keep a modest dress code—that means no Speedos at the pool, guys—collared shirts and pants are required at all times, jeans may not have rips or tears, shorts are never acceptable, overnight guests must pay $10 a night and be signed in, you may not leave campus for more than four consecutive days, and you must sign out with the RA to go off campus overnight, but you may not sign out to an unmarried person's house unless you're twenty-one . . ."

By the end of the list, filmmaker Ryan is rubbing his temples and breathing heavily.

"Now, I know you guys are probably thinking, what did I get myself into?" Stubbs says. "But it's really not that hard."

Fox adds, "You just have to go in with a positive attitude. If you think, 'Oh man, these rules are such a drag,' you're going to miss out on a lot. We see the rules as a way to maintain our focus on God. They give us freedom to concentrate on the things that really matter."

Over the next two days, this becomes a leitmotif. I attend workshops, faculty panels, and campus tours, all of which emphasize the point: "The Liberty Way" is, quite literally, a way to liberty. Less canoodling means more time for spiritual growth, more time to pray and read scripture and become a Champion for Christ. Once you get used to the rules, Liberty is, as more than one professor put it, "the world's most exciting university."

On Friday of orientation week, I'm told to attend Keeping It Safe, which I assume is some sort of workshop. The orientation packet doesn't elaborate except to say that two simultaneous sessions will be held, one for each gender. (This point is apparently fiercely important: the sessions are labeled "MALE Students ONLY" and "FEMALE Students ONLY.")

I get to the designated male classroom a few minutes late. When

I walk in, a man is shrieking. "It's too *easy,* guys! Too easy to *sin*! You need to be *godly men*! The most important thing in a young woman's life—in her *life*!—is her purity!"

In front of the room is a bald, stout pastor whose job it is to steer us clear of sexual immorality—the definition of which, as Stubbs and Fox told us, covers everything from full-on intercourse right on down to Eskimo kisses. During a lull in the lecture, a freshman pipes up to ask why Liberty bans kissing and long-form hugging. The pastor explains that although no verse in the Bible specifically prohibits either act, Liberty sees them as gateway sins. "Say you hug a young lady," he says, "and then suddenly you feel the urge to kiss her. And then when you kiss her, all of a sudden your hands start to wander, and then you're tempted to do more. You've already compromised your purity."

Our pastor has tips to help us stave off temptation: "If you're out on a date with a girl, and you're feeling sinful desires growing inside yourself, get out of there. Go to a coffee shop, a bookstore, somewhere public. Take her home if you need to. But don't be caught alone in the dark, where temptation can strike." He talks for a few more minutes about the dangers of STDs, reiterates the need for abstinence, and dismisses us.

On the way out of the lecture hall, I see the all-female Keeping It Safe being dismissed from the classroom next door. It's an amazing sight. The first five girls who pass me are stunningly beautiful, and then the next five, and then the five after that. They just keep parading by—a phalanx of fit, well-groomed, pearl-wearing girls, all of whom would be right at home in a J. Crew catalog.

As it turns out, I'm not the only guy who notices. From my all-male session, six or seven of us have leaned against the wall to watch the girls going past. "Thank you, Lord," says the guy next to me. Another guy leans over to whisper that *Playboy* once ranked Liberty's girls second-hottest among all American colleges, "right behind UCLA."

I'm not sure that's true, but it wouldn't surprise me. These girls are all very good looking in that non-threatening, morning show–host way—the sort of girls that might end up in *Playboy* if it weren't for, you know, morals. It's sort of cruel, if you think about it. Here these pious

Christian guys are, trying to stave off lust at a college where thousands of world-class women stroll the halls. It'd be like going to Willy Wonka's chocolate factory with a wired jaw.

After Keeping It Safe, I'm browsing the shelves in the campus bookstore when I come across *Give Me Liberty,* a thin instructional booklet designed to orient incoming Liberty students to campus life. I could use a little more orientation, so I pick up a copy, perch myself on a green couch in the school library, and begin to read. *Give Me Liberty* is filled with faculty-penned essays about various aspects of Liberty life—filling out a financial aid form, calculating a GPA, learning to use the library catalog—and none of it is very interesting until the end, where I see a chapter called "Where Visions Go to Die." It begins:

> As we consider Dr. Falwell's vision . . . it is important to realize that we are not the first school to seek these lofty goals. Harvard, Yale, Princeton, and Brown were all started by churches that wanted to train students to serve Christ. . . . However, over time the priorities of these colleges shifted, and they started to focus on increasing the perceived quality of education rather than the spiritual life of the campus. Eventually, these schools achieved their academic goals, but they did so at the expense of their original Christian purposes. . . . Will Liberty fall into the same trap that these universities did, abandoning our Biblical worldview in the name of contemporary academics?

This passage echoes Dr. Falwell's speech the other day, in which he talked about the delinquent morality plaguing American colleges, and it reminds me that there are really several kinds of purity Liberty cares about. The first two, as Keeping It Safe demonstrated, are the sexual and spiritual purity of its students, concepts that seem to be fairly intertwined. But third, and arguably more important, is the emphasis on institutional purity. Liberty takes great pride in defining itself as the Christian university that has held itself staunchly upright, remaining true to its evangelical mission while the colleges around it are blown about by the changing winds of culture—so much so that Dr. Falwell has instructed Liberty alumni to come back and burn down the school if it ever turns liberal. What Liberty fears most, in other words, is not losing its accreditation or seeing its endowment shrink. It's turning into Brown.

Speaking of which, I haven't told anyone about my old school yet. A few people have asked me where I transferred from, and my stock answer ("a school in Rhode Island") has done the trick so far. We'll see how long this streak lasts.

When I walk into church on Sunday morning, it feels like I've just reached the front of the line for Jesus: The Ride. It's pitch-black inside the Vines Center, Liberty's ten thousand–seat basketball arena, and a full-scale laser light show rages while two fog machines pump wispy cirrus clouds over the first ten rows of seats.

This is Campus Church, a service led by Pastor Andy Hillman, the twenty-four-year-old wunderkind of Liberty's preaching staff. On Sundays, some Liberty students go to Dr. Falwell's Thomas Road services and a sprinkling attend other area churches, but a good five or six thousand pile into the Vines Center to hear Pastor Andy. Campus Church is the "spiritual heartbeat of campus," as one guy on my hall put it.

At the beginning of the service, a five-piece student band is playing a worship song from the stage. I think this song is called "How Great Is Our God," but I'm just guessing from the lyrics:

> *How great is our God*
> *How great is our God*
> *How great*
> *How great*
> *Is our God*

Immediately upon glancing around the arena, the first of my stereotypes is shattered: the buttoned-up, "Sunday best" evangelical. I read a *Washington Post* article from a decade or so ago that mentioned the "well-scrubbed Pat (or Debby) Boone look" of Liberty students. That article as my guide, I filled my suitcases with penny loafers, khakis, and monochrome button-downs—the stuff I wear to my grandparents' retirement home. But apparently times have changed, even where church attire is concerned. In fact, with the exception of the collared shirts and short haircuts on men, Liberty students I've seen are basically indistinguishable from secular college students. In my row, there's a guy wearing a loose-fitting hoodie, a girl in a black polo, and a pair of guys in rugby shirts. The longer I look around, the more self-conscious I get about the clothes I chose this morning: a red V-neck sweater and pressed chinos. Here I am at an arena rock concert, and I'm dressed like a caddy.

After three or four songs from the praise band, the fog clears and Pastor Andy takes the stage. He's a Ryan Seacrest look-alike, and he's got a nice, down-to-earth vibe about him, more a superspiritual older brother than an overexerting youth pastor. Ten minutes into Andy's message on prioritizing, I can see why this guy is a campus legend. He's disarmingly open, with no fire and brimstone in sight.

"I'm going to be real with you," he says. "The most difficult thing about my life is trying to serve Jesus while doing tons of other things. I multitask entirely too much sometimes, and my life gets out of priority, and suddenly here I am, a minister of the gospel, and I can get so busy—just like you guys—that my relationship with Christ gets put to the side."

At the close of his sermon, Andy prays, and the praise band kicks in for another set. As they play, the guy sitting beside me steps into the aisle and kneels, aiming both hands straight overhead. All around the arena, people shift into worship mode, and arms begin to rise. Soon, the arena is awash in passion. Some sway, some jump in place, others stand still and look straight up. One guy runs to the front of the arena, right beside the stage, and falls to his knees in prayer.

Damn. I've seen evangelical worship before, but always in photographs and movies, where it seemed sort of disjointed and melodramatic. But in person, it's enough to send a chill down your spine. I didn't grow up in a church where people cried out with religious fervor; and even though it could be more foreign—they could be speaking in tongues or handling snakes—the sight of all these students giving up bodily control is a little frightening.

What's most overwhelming, though, is how monolithic this school still seems. Presumably, every student in here agrees with Liberty's official doctrinal statement, which says, among other things, that people can get to heaven "only through the work of Jesus Christ, through repentance of sin and by faith alone in Him as Savior," that those who remain unsaved are "subject to eternal punishment, under the just condemnation of a holy God," that the Bible is "inerrant in the originals and authoritative in all matters," and that "the return of Christ for all believers is imminent." And coming from a world where individualism reigns, where you could never get an arena full of students all thinking, feeling, and believing the same things, the level of unified passion in this building pushes some sort of atavistic panic button in my brain.

But once scenes like this become familiar, I hope I'll be able to take a more nuanced view. Find some shades of gray in the black and white. After all, no community adheres completely to its stereotype. Even though Brown had a reputation for liberal politics and loose morals, we still had our nonpartiers, our religious groups, even our (tiny, tiny) chapter of the College Republicans. So there must be some ideological diversity in this building. Unless I'm off base here, these can't all be Falwells-in-training.

On the night before classes start, Dorm 22 is a bustling metropolis of returning students moving back in after the holiday break. I've been ambushed by fifty-five new hallmates, all of whose names I'm expected to remember. Perhaps unsurprisingly, there are lots of Lukes, Matthews, and Pauls.

I spent some time tonight talking to my roommates, Eric and Henry. Eric is an all-American guy, athletic and personable, with a portrait of his girlfriend next to his computer monitor. He tells me that he transferred to Liberty from community college at the urging of his dad, who leads a large evangelical church in Lansing. This makes him a PK, he says, or Pastor's Kid.

Henry, the other roommate, is more enigmatic. He's a wiry guy with a shaved head who hails from just outside St. Louis, and he hasn't been in the room much, so we haven't been properly introduced. He doesn't seem like a big talker, but tonight, I manage to extract the following information: Henry just transferred to Liberty, he is a history major, and he's twenty-nine years old.

"Twenty-nine?" I ask.

Yes, he says, he is a decade my senior, and when I ask whether this is because he performed some sort of military service before coming to college, he looks at me oddly and says, "No." Was he beginning a second career, then? "No." How about a recent conversion? Was he a new Christian trying to learn more about the faith? "No. It just took me longer to get here."

I'd ask more questions, but honestly, I'm too tired to play detective right now. I've whizzed through the past week on pure adrenaline, and I think my body is catching up to me. There's just so much to think about. Every hour of the day is filled with hundreds of chances for error. I'm scared to talk for fear of saying something immoderate. I'm scared of eating in a group for fear of praying the wrong way before my meal or violating some biblical silverware law I don't yet know about. I'd be nervous enough if I were starting classes at a new secular school, but starting at Bible Boot Camp is frankly terrifying.

Before I fall asleep, I lie in bed with *Give Me Liberty,* trying to pick up some last-minute tips before my semester begins. On page 3, I come upon this passage:

> Scripture tells us that we are to be "anxious for nothing" (Philippians 4:6, NASB), that is, we are not to be consumed with worry over things in this life. The reason is that we have resources to help us through difficulties, and you need to realize that you will not be facing the challenges of Liberty University alone.

It's a small comfort, but I'll take what I can get.

Stranger in a Strange Land

Last night was the worst sleep I've had in years. I think it was the after-hours worrying that did it. Or maybe it was the fact that while I brought many things to Liberty: picture frames, a John Ruskin anthology, two brands of dental floss—you know, useful things—I forgot to bring sheets. I haven't managed to find Lynchburg's Bed Bath & Beyond yet, so for the past week, I've been sleeping on a bare mattress in sweatpants and a jacket, using a rain poncho as my comforter. It works in a pinch, but it's hardly comfortable. Cold, sore, and a little cranky, I begin the climb down from the top bunk.

"Good morning," comes a voice from below. It's my roommate Eric. He's sitting on his bed cross-legged, staring intently at the pages of his thick leather Bible.

"You ready for the first day of class?" he asks. "What are you taking?"

It's a good question. I had an incredibly hard time making my academic schedule this semester. My dilemma was this: Liberty offers hundreds of courses you'd find at any other American college—English, business economics, psychology. About 60 percent of the course catalog has nothing to do with Christianity, as far as I can tell. But Liberty also has a slate of courses you won't find elsewhere. Most colleges don't offer Basics of Christian Womanhood or Intro to Worship Music. Very few have a Department of Youth Ministry.

So which route should I go? Take the secular-sounding classes? Or follow my curiosity and go for the Christian ones?

Perhaps luckily, I didn't end up having a choice. I found out during orientation week that Liberty's required core curriculum includes most of the classes on my strange/intriguing list. So I signed up for six core classes in an effort to replicate the average Liberty freshman's schedule.

My first class of the day is Contemporary Issues, which is abbreviated as GNED by absolutely everyone. GNED, I learn, is short for General Education, so named because it's Liberty's foundational course in Christian ethics. As a result, the class is quite large—over two hundred students in my section. I walk into the amphitheater-style lecture hall and take a seat in the back, next to a few guys from my dorm.

After the class has filled, Dr. Parks welcomes us. He's a midforties man with a tidy brown goatee, a starched red button-down tucked into his Dockers, and a cell phone clipped to his belt. Sort of the State Farm agent look. Dr. Parks spends the first ten minutes of class telling us how he worked as a full-time pastor in Maryland until he felt God calling him to teach. After that, he left the pulpit to pursue a doctorate, and then came on as a professor at Liberty.

"I'm here for good now," he says, "and I cannot think of anything I'd rather do than help you all live your lives for Jesus Christ."

Before beginning, Dr. Parks bows his head. Every class at Liberty, no matter the subject, starts with prayer led by the professor. He speaks softly into his microphone:

> Lord, thank you for bringing these students to my class. You have them here for a reason, God, and I pray that you'll allow me to say the right things. Anoint my teaching, Lord, and pour out your blessing on these students as they enter the new semester. In Jesus' name, Amen.

From what I can tell, GNED seems to be about half Western philosophy, half Christian reactionary training. The syllabus puts it thusly:

"This course is designed to aid the student in the development of a biblical worldview. This will involve an introduction to critical thinking, an evaluation of contemporary moral philosophies, and an affirmation of absolute truth." We'll be learning about moral philosophies like nihilism, relativism, and utilitarianism, Dr. Parks says, but mostly as opposition research. We'll discuss where they appear in American society, then learn how to combat them from the Christian perspective.

"Let me give you an example," Dr. Parks says. "How many of you have seen *The Italian Job*?"

A few hands go up.

"It's a neat movie. A bunch of thieves get together to pull off a gold heist, and it works. They get the gold. But then one of them turns out to be a double-crosser, and he steals the gold from the group. So the rest of them have to find this guy and steal the gold back. And the weird thing is, the good guys in the movie are thieves! You find yourself rooting for them. Now, what's wrong with that?"

A small girl in the second row raises her hand. "We're rooting for sinners? I mean, the Bible says, 'Thou shalt not steal.'"

"Exactly! Now, I'm not telling you not to watch that movie. But when you watch it, make sure it's not forming the way you think. When you see something, you have to critically analyze it."

A lot of what we'll be doing in GNED, Dr. Parks says, is dismantling the harmful worldviews we've already developed unwittingly in the secular world. Liberty draws a majority of its students from public high schools, and GNED is one way of getting everyone on the same page, both spiritually and politically. "We'll talk about things your friends have said and things other schools have taught you," he says, "many of which are opposed to the biblical worldview."

It's time to go, but Dr. Parks puts one final slide on the board as we pack our bags to leave:

> *Don't let anyone capture you with empty philosophies and high-sounding nonsense that come from human thinking and from the spiritual powers of this world, rather than from Christ. (Colossians 2:8, NLT)*

"Oh, I almost forgot," he says. "We will have a quiz next class over today's material."

The class groans.

"And remember: Can you cheat on a quiz in this class without me seeing you? Yes, probably. It's a big class. But can you cheat on a quiz without God seeing you?"

He chuckles. "I'll let you consider that one on your own."

Next up is History of Life, the introductory survey course in Liberty's Creation Studies Department.

"My name is Dr. James Dekker," says the professor, "and I am a real scientist."

He looks like one, anyway. With his lanky frame wrapped in a white lab coat, his gold-framed spectacles, and the frizzy tuft of brown hair atop his head, Dr. Dekker could have been shipped in from Central Casting as a movie extra, perhaps Chemist # 4. The only thing that doesn't quite fit is the novelty tie slung around his neck. On the tie is a picture of the solar system, captioned with five words written in flowing white script: *"In the Beginning God Created . . ."*

Liberty's science program, I should explain, is slightly fraught. In 1982, in response to pressure from the ACLU, a Virginia state education board ruled that biology graduates from Liberty University (then called Liberty Baptist College) were uncertifiable as public school teachers, since Liberty's undergraduate biology program was based in creationism. In response, university higher-ups made a quick fix, shuffling the creationism courses out of the Biology Department and into a new department called Creation Studies.

Liberty has since gotten teacher certification approval for its biology program, and the school now teaches courses in both evolution and creationism—sort of. All Liberty students are required to take a creation studies course, while only biology majors are required to learn evolution-based science. And even those evolution courses are sort of Fair and Balanced™, if you get my drift. As Dr. Falwell said in 1982, before the Virginia board ruling: "We, with God's help, want to see hundreds of our graduates go out into the classrooms teaching creationism—of course they'll be teaching evolution—but teaching why it's invalid and why it's foolish, and then showing the proper way and the correct approach to the origin of the species."

That approach, of course, is young-earth creationism. Every biology professor at Liberty teaches that God created the universe about six thousand years ago in six literal, twenty-four-hour days, pretty much the way it looks now. This is the most extreme version of creationism, the most literal of the literal, and it makes no compromises. Carbon dating that has revealed scores of million-year-old fossils? Defective. Noah's Flood? As historical as the 1985 World Series.

Before beginning class, Dr. Dekker spends five or ten minutes enumerating his scientific credentials: BA from Michigan State, PhD in neuroscience from a top-flight research university, published in "over a dozen" peer-reviewed journals.

"When I was looking for jobs," Dr. Dekker says, pacing the stairs of the lecture hall, "I thought, well, I'm a creationist, and I want to teach biology. There must be a ton of Christian colleges that will hire me. Boy, was I surprised."

According to Dr. Dekker, only about a dozen American colleges still teach young-earth creationism. Many evangelical colleges now teach intelligent design, a newer, arguably sleeker origins model that posits a creator of the universe without specifying who that creator is. Even the conservative Christian schools have moved to a "creation compromise" that allows for an old earth, like the day/age theory (each day in Genesis represented a geological age) or the gap theory (an unwritten gap of billions of years separated the earth's formation and the rest of the Genesis narrative).

Dr. Dekker blames the lack of young-earth creationism in Christian academia on its media portrayal as a pseudoscientific movement. Christian teens, he says, are scared to sign onto young-earth theories for fear they'll be called irrational and backward. Hence the importance of classes like History of Life. "As Christians," he says, "we need to be equipped with reasons for our faith. We need apologetics."

The word *apologetics*, he explains, comes from the Greek *apologia*, meaning "defense." It's the same word found in the book of Acts, when

Paul is being brought to trial—he gives his *apologia* in front of the judge. Technically, History of Life is an apologetics course, not a science course. We will study science throughout the semester, but only as needed to accomplish the course's primary objective, which, according to our textbook, is to "equip students to defend their faith and give answers to common questions" raised by people for whom "the Bible is just a book of fairy tales rather than the Word of God."

Next, Dr. Dekker reads a verse from his thick black Bible:

> Thou shalt love the Lord thy God with all thy heart, and with all thy soul, and with all thy mind. (Matthew 22:37, KJV)

"Do you hear what that says? 'With all thy mind'! Christianity is a reasoned faith! We have reasons for the doctrines that we believe." He smirks. "You don't hear much about *Islamic* apologetics. Or *Mormon* apologetics. But Christians know that it's important to be able to prove, for example, that Adam and Eve were real people."

History of Life is part of Liberty's core curriculum, Dr. Dekker says, because all Christians need to know how to defend creationism, not just biologists. "Any future pastors in here?" he asks. "I guarantee that one day, someone from your church will come to you and say, 'Hey, Pastor, CNN said someone found this dinosaur that dates to sixty-five million years, but you said creation happened six thousand years ago. What's up with that?' You'd better have the answer. Future lawyers, you'll have to defend public school teachers who lose their jobs because they say they don't believe in evolution. And to everyone who plans on having kids—which I assume is all of you—when your kid comes home and says, 'My teacher told me that we came from monkeys,' you'd better know how to correct them."

Dr. Dekker spends the rest of the class going over grade policies and attendance requirements (the syllabus includes cheeky notes like "Your salvation is a free gift from God; your grade is based solely on works"), and dismisses us for the day.

After History of Life, I shove my notebook into my backpack and hurry over to my next class, Evangelism 101. This class is taught by

Pastor Andy Hillman, the guy who led the Campus Church service yesterday.

Pastor Andy spends the first few minutes of class going over logistics. Our study of evangelism, the practice of converting non-Christians, will occupy only the last half of the semester. Until then, we'll be doing a unit called "The Christian Life." Our textbooks, he says, are *The Purpose-Driven Life*, the mega–best seller by evangelical pastor Rick Warren, and the Bible ("any translation will do"). Pastor Andy's lectures will cover topics like "Jesus, the Centerpiece of Civilization" and "God's Word Brings Life." Like my other classes, Evangelism 101 is popular, maybe three hundred students piled into a hall with stadium-style seating.

Evangelism 101's first lecture/sermon is on the topic of purpose. "Regardless of how convinced you are that God exists," Andy says, "someday you'll lay your head on your pillow at night and wonder: What is my purpose in life? Even atheists ask themselves that question. And when I meet atheists, I tell them, 'Hey, I respect your views, and you don't have to believe me, but I think somewhere in your heart is a desire for God. I think you were made by God, for God, and that when you discover God's purpose for your life, you'll be living life at its fullest.'"

As far as sermons go, Pastor Andy's seem pretty inoffensive. Still, while he's talking, I find myself thinking back to Dr. Dekker's creationism class. Even before today, I knew taking History of Life would be bad for my open-mindedness at Liberty. As a guy who gives evolution two opposable thumbs up (to quote a bumper sticker I once saw), hearing a PhD-toting professor espousing young-earth creationism bothered me on multiple levels, not the least of which was Dr. Dekker's ultra-sarcastic, oddly defensive delivery. (He kept tugging on the lapels of his lab coat and saying, "Look! A real scientist!")

I almost didn't take History of Life because I thought it would make me too cynical. But I had to. After all, it's central to the Liberty experience. Not only is creationism taught in science classes here, it's also a foundational part of the theological and moral architecture. Spending a semester at Liberty without taking Dr. Dekker's class would be like going to West Point and ignoring the whole army thing.

It brings up something my high school friend Laura said during our evangelical crash course. Namely, Liberty is not a middle-of-the-road Christian college. As Dr. Dekker said, only a dozen schools still teach young-earth creationism, and the number of schools with Evangelism 101 classes can't be a whole lot higher. Laura said that speaking as a Christian, she wished I were ramping up to this experience somehow. Maybe going to a more liberal Christian school, then to somewhere moderate, and then to Liberty. She thought going from the extreme left to the extreme right would give me ideological whiplash, and I'd be left feeling alienated and confused.

She might have been onto something.

Back in Dorm 22, I'm slowly adjusting to life on the hall. My hall-mates are an eclectic bunch. In the past few days, I've met a guitarist from Cape Town, a chef from New Jersey, a graphic designer from Norfolk, and a guy from the Bronx who tries to sell those Amway-type Quixtar products to everyone on the hall.

Then there's Zipper, my next-door neighbor, who comes bounding in through my open door tonight yelling, "Kevin Rooooose! Want to come to Pancake Night?"

Zipper, a short, moon-faced sophomore from the Philadelphia sub-urbs, introduced himself to me the other day. He's a Prayer Leader on the hall, and he may be the happiest person I've ever met. Even in win-ter, Zipper (birth name: Charles Ziparo) wears Hawaiian shirts and a pair of big, wide-rimmed Ray-Bans with a neon green bungee cord to secure them around his neck. He uses phrases like "super-duper" and "all-righty," and his face carries a perpetual look of glee, like Mister Rogers after a few whippits. Even his breaths seem to have exclama-tion points.

Here's one thing I can say so far: Liberty students are the friendli-est college students I've ever met. They're much friendlier than the students at my old school. Or maybe a different type of friendly. A more overt friendly. The past week has been a constant deluge of "Great to meet you!" and "I can't wait to show you around!" Zip-per, within two days of meeting me, has volunteered to help me pick classes, shop for textbooks, take me out to dinner—everything except tuck me into bed.

Tonight, he's inviting me to Pancake Night with the sister dorm. Every hall at Liberty is paired with a hall of the opposite sex, and the two halls plan occasional joint activities. Lynchburg's local pancake house has a half-off deal for Liberty students on Tuesday nights, so Dorm 22 and our sister dorm, Dorm 33, have made it a regular meeting place. I decide to go along.

At Pancake Night, I meet a few girls from the sister dorm. They're all at least moderately attractive, at least moderately personable, and seemingly normal. In fact, that's the thing that strikes me hardest: this is not a group of angry zealots. I knew I'd see a different side of Liberty students once I resolved to blend in among them, but I thought it would be a harsher side. I had this secular/liberal paranoia that when evangelical students were among themselves, they spent their time huddled in dark rooms, organizing anti-abortion protests and plotting theocratic takeovers. But that's not true at all. In fact, a lot of the time, the conversations I hear at Liberty are pretty banal. Over pancakes, girls from the sister dorm ask guys from my dorm about their vacations. They complain about their expensive textbooks and gossip about a couple who broke up over break. There's a long discussion about the merits and drawbacks of one of Dr. Falwell's latest construction projects—an eight-acre LU monogram being built on the side of Liberty Mountain. Some people think it's a good marketing tool, others think it's a waste of their tuition money. But that's about as heated as the conversation gets.

After saying goodnight to the girls, Zipper and I head back to campus. Most nights, we're allowed out until midnight, but on Tuesdays, curfew is moved up to ten to accommodate our weekly hall meeting. When all sixty Dorm 22 residents are back on the hall, Fox and Stubbs have us all sit on the floor.

"McGrath, will you start us in prayer?" Stubbs asks, looking at a tanned, strapping guy next to him.

McGrath takes off his Cubs hat. "Lord, thank you for the new guys on the hall. Help us all get to know each other. Help this hall grow in continuity, and help us grow closer to you. In Jesus' name, Amen."

A small black guy named Dylan cackles. "Continuity! That's a big word for you, McGrath!"

McGrath socks Dylan in the stomach, drawing laughs from everyone. "Shut up, queer."

Fox and Stubbs make some general announcements about mission trips, upcoming sports games, and disciplinary issues on the hall. Then, it's time to break into prayer groups.

My prayer group is led by a varsity baseball player named Matthew, a military-looking guy with one arm in a sling from a recent in-game injury. Matthew brings the five members of my prayer group into his room, where I meet my new prayer partners: a soccer player from Virginia named Eddie, a freshman from Bolivia named Carlos, a drummer from New York named Tim, and a shot-putter from Oklahoma named Dave.

"Prayer requests," Matthew says. "Let's hear 'em."

Tim says that a man in his home church has leukemia, and we should pray for his recovery. Eddie's little brother broke his arm playing basketball the other day, and he's in a lot of pain. Carlos's mom has a job interview this week, and she really needs this job, so could we pray for her? Dave wants to get a 4.0 GPA this semester, and "that will take a lot of help from the Big Man."

When it comes around to me, I hesitate. I didn't grow up in a praying family, and I have trouble getting my mind around the idea that God actively works to give us better grades or new jobs. The closest I've ever come to real, ask-and-ye-shall-receive prayer is the occasional request for my safety during airplane takeoffs and landings. But I decide to participate in this prayer group regardless. If I'm going to be living with these guys for a semester, I should get used to opening up to them, no matter what I believe about the efficacy of prayer.

Plus, there's been a traumatic incident in my family recently, and I could use the moral support. My eighty-seven-year-old grandfather had a massive heart attack a month ago, and survived only with a risky quadruple bypass operation that even my secular family called a miracle. He pulled through in the end, but he's not completely well yet, and we're all still pretty shaken up.

When I tell the guys about Grandpa Roose, they look genuinely pained. They're all leaning in, asking concerned questions. Is he okay? How's the rest of the family? Is there anything we can do?

"Let's all pray for him extra hard this week," Matthew says. The rest of the guys nod in agreement. Then, Matthew tells us to stand up. "This is our group's tradition," he tells me. "Just follow along."

We form a close circle, arms draped over each other's shoulders. And then, with no preamble, the guys all close their eyes and start praying out loud for each other, all at once, all for different things. Only partial phrases emerge from the mix:

"Dear Lord, thank you for . . ."
"Father, I pray for Tim's . . ."
". . . with leukemia and I pray that you would heal . . ."
". . . Kevin's grandfather, Lord, just that you would . . ."
". . . and give Carlos the wisdom to get . . ."

As the guys pray—one minute, then two—the voices blend together and a sort of white noise hum rises from the circle. Slowly, the prayers taper to silence.

. . . according to your will . . . God, I just . . . thank you for giving me the str . . . Eddie's brother and that he might . . . grades this semester, Lord . . . Jesus' name, amen . . . amen . . . Jesus' name, amen . . . in your name I pray . . . amen . . . amen.

The group remains in place for several seconds and then gently breaks huddle.

"Thanks guys," Matthew says. "See you next week."

As we gather our things, Dave from Oklahoma slaps his knee.

"You know what always amazes me?" he says to no one in particular. "God just heard our prayers through all that chaos. He knows every word we said!"

He throws back his head and laughs. "Man, God is a stinkin' baller!"

The next night, I have my first big scare. At dinner, one of the guys in Dorm 22, a bulky Virginian named Judd, is telling a story to a half-dozen guys sitting around the table. He was driving on the highway during Christmas break, he says, when he skidded on ice, rolling his Ford F-150 into a ditch. The truck flipped seven times, but he was unharmed.

"That's crazy!" I say. "Holy shit!"

All eyes zoom to me. Audible gasp from Judd.

"I mean, holy . . . shoot."

When I was training for my Liberty semester with my friend Laura, I asked her what the biggest tip-off to Christian teens would be, which gaffe would automatically peg me as an outsider. Without blinking, she responded: cursing.

It was bad news. Like a lot of secular college students, I curse as a way of life. In my old world, epithets were dropped into everyday speech as liberally and mindlessly as "uh" or "like." But according to Laura, cursing is a serious no-go in evangelical circles. And according to "The Liberty Way," each slip-up here will earn me "12–18 reprimands + corresponding fine." Luckily, no RAs were sitting at our dinner table tonight, so unless someone reports me, I'll be okay. But after an excruciatingly long dinner filled with wary looks from my hallmates, I jog back to my room and head straight for my bookshelf.

After Laura told me that I'd have to give up cursing, I bought a Christian self-help book in an airport bookstore called *30 Days to Taming Your Tongue*. It's a tiny thing, maybe forty pages in total, but I've never managed to get through it entirely. I thought I could quit cursing cold turkey, through sheer willpower. But now, it's clear that my sin is too deeply ingrained.

So tonight, I read through the book on my bed, marveling at the percentage of my vocabulary I'm going to have to give up if I want to remain inconspicuous here. My four-letter words will have to go, of course, but also my third commandment violations—"Oh my God,"

"Jesus Christ," and the like. (The author suggests replacing them with Christ-honoring exclamations, like "Glory!") In addition, the book says that all negative speech—including exaggeration, gossiping, and cynicism—must be jettisoned for true righteousness.

I'm a little worried for what these Christian language rules are going to do to my social life. Telling a Brown student he can't be cynical is a little like telling Monet he can't paint water lilies. Without cynicism and cursing, what will I say to people? What if I want to make a snide comment about a professor? What if I stub my toe on a dresser? Until I get adjusted to evangelical speech, my conversations are going to sound like a censored version of *Letters to Penthouse:* a few conjunctions and a lot of blank space.

On Friday, I check my private e-mail for the first time. I read in "The Liberty Way" that all Internet activity on campus is monitored by university administrators, so I decided to keep two accounts, one for Liberty e-mail and one for everything else, and access the outside account only from off campus.

After my morning classes, I drive to a Panera Bread with free Wi-Fi just down the road from campus, laptop in tow. From the e-mails I got, you'd think I spent the last week in the Hanoi Hilton. One friend from Brown wrote: "Oh my God, I've been so worried about you. Is everything okay?" Another friend put it more bluntly: "I can't believe you're there and breathing and haven't been burned at the stake."

The loudest reaction came from my family. I called my mom a few days ago to give her a brief update on Liberty. I summarized my classes, my church experiences, and my burgeoning social life. She sounded slightly reassured, though she told me that my trip to Liberty had inspired lots of interesting conversations among family members. (She said "interesting" very gingerly, the way Brian Williams might tell Mahmoud Ahmadinejad his thoughts on America's foreign policy are "curious.")

Somewhere near the end of the conversation, I told my mom that I still winced whenever one of my hallmates called someone a "fag" or "queer." I said that not even Jerry Falwell uses those words anymore, and then made a joke along the lines of "I think Falwell is actually the campus moderate." My mom, bless her heart, called my entire extended family to pass on this joke. It didn't go over well, especially with my lesbian aunts Tina and Teresa.

Tina, my dad's older sister, is one of my favorite relatives—a retired librarian with short salt-and-pepper hair and kind eyes. Teresa, her longtime partner, works as a massage practitioner and psychotherapist in their hometown of Olympia, Washington. Tina and Teresa are dedicated gay-rights activists, and they spend lots of weekends visiting pride parades around the country. At these parades, they dye their white standard poodle the colors of the rainbow and lead her around on a bright purple leash, a stunt that has made them minor celebrities in Olympia's gay community. They've even given themselves a joint name, "T-n-T," to go with their "dynamite activist" personas.

T-n-T was split over the news of my first week at Liberty.

Teresa responded with sympathy. "I am so glad to hear from you and relieved you made it through the first week," she wrote. Tina responded that she, too, was glad to see I was alive. Then, she continued: "I confess to sadness and anger at your hallmates' comments about homosexuals. Falwell may sound more moderate, but I don't believe that for a minute. He blamed 9/11 on feminists and homosexuals. I believe he encourages hate and violence while perhaps trying to sound more moderate."

Aunt Tina knows I'm not a Falwell fan. She's not worried that I'll be writing home on his stationery at the end of this semester. But she does worry that I'm taking the issue of homophobia too lightly. She sent me three follow-up e-mails with links to gay-rights websites about hate crimes perpetrated by fundamentalist Christians and CC'd my entire family.

She's not wrong to assume that Liberty is home to more homophobic language than your average college. And so far, the way I've been dealing with the intolerance is by lying to myself. Someone will call someone else a faggot during a late-night video game session, and instead of thinking about how Liberty students almost certainly vote for ballot measures that disenfranchise people like Tina and Teresa, or how the remnants of a society that still uses a word like *faggot* to mean "idiot" have made gay people's lives a lot harder, I just allow myself to be deluded. It's just a word, I say. Just an unfortunate cultural holdover. No harm meant. Of course, that's not true, and my moral gerrymandering probably isn't helping anyone.

After seeing Tina's response, my mom wrote me a stern e-mail: "I hope you don't scare anyone with your updates. The scene at Liberty is VERY different from what anyone in the family has ever seen."

She's right, and I feel awful for sending shock waves through my family. They're already dealing with the fact that I'm at Bible Boot Camp. So I'm thinking about sending less frequent updates and being careful what kinds of things I include in them. They don't need to know everything that happens here, and I don't need to do any long-term damage.

O Sing Unto the Lord a New Song

Every Monday, Wednesday, and Friday at 10:00 AM, all of Liberty's resident students pack into the Vines Center for convocation ("convo" for short), the mandatory chapel service at which schoolwide announcements are given, worship music is played, and sermons are preached. At today's convo, Dr. Falwell takes the stage. He welcomes the Reverend Billy Graham's daughter, who is visiting her son, a student here. He asks us all to pray for the fifteen-year-old daughter of one of Liberty's senior administrators, who was badly injured in a car accident. Then, he begins his sermon: "If I were to ask you today to write down on a piece of paper your dream for the life that is ahead of you, I would get about ten thousand different answers. But then, I would ask you: Do you plan to do it of your own energy and proficiency? Or do you plan to tap into the anointing of God's spirit?"

Dr. Falwell slips into his message on "the anointing" by way of a few autobiographical anecdotes. He tells a story of his first Christian job— a Sunday school teacher in a Missouri Baptist church, with an eleven-year-old boy as his lone pupil. Through prayer, determination, and a bit of guerilla marketing, Dr. Falwell grew that one-student class into a cadre of fifty-six within the first year. Soon, he branched off and started his own church, with thirty-five charter members meeting in an old bottling factory in Lynchburg. That congregation, Thomas Road, grew over two decades into a twenty-four thousand–member juggernaut with a worldwide TV audience numbering into the tens of millions.

This story sounded somewhat familiar, because yesterday, I took my first trip to the Jerry Falwell Museum. The museum occupies one wing of the DeMoss Hall Atrium, smack-dab in the middle of campus, and it's free for visitors six days a week, so I spent an hour there between classes. It's an amazing place. Among the highlights:

- Dr. Falwell's first Bible
- A copy of his first sermon at Thomas Road
- A life-size replica of his father's Model T, with a wax replica of the elder Falwell inside
- A screening room with his A&E *Biography* special on continuous loop
- A stuffed brown bear, "just like the one Dr. Falwell's father kept in his study!"

The first thought I had while walking through the museum was: Wow, this place really is a personality cult. What other living college president has an entire museum dedicated to him? I was slightly reassured when I read that Dr. Falwell didn't build the museum himself—it was a gift from his sons on his seventieth birthday. But still, it's an odd thing to have.

My second thought was: Man, what a tragic career arc. Before coming to Liberty, I never knew how influential Jerry Falwell was at his peak. I assumed he'd always had the role in American civic life he does now—a crotchety televangelist who appears on cable news shows as a token arch-conservative. But he actually used to be quite a civic star, beloved by vast swaths of America. He was the Moral Majority's golden boy, the man who was almost single-handedly responsible for corralling America's evangelical population into a motivated political bloc. *Time* magazine once called him the "force of fundamentalism." A 1983 *Good Housekeeping* poll named him the second most-admired man in the nation, behind only Ronald Reagan.

The museum leans heavily on the Moral Majority years, and it's easy to see why. The Jerry Falwell of the 1980s was a commanding presence, a preacher who had worked his way up to prominence, who hobnobbed with America's political elite but retained his humble Lynchburg roots. It would have been exciting to be a Thomas Road parishioner back then; Christians were on the move, and Dr. Falwell was leading the charge. In the museum, I saw a row of TVs playing looped Thomas Road sermons from those years, and his charisma oozed from the screens.

The past week has taught me some good, humanizing facts about Dr. Falwell. I never knew, for example, that in addition to Liberty and Thomas Road, he also founded a Liberty Godparent Home for unwed mothers and a home for recovering alcoholics. I never knew that he has eight grandchildren, all of whom call him Poppy, or that he still takes time out of his schedule to visit sick Thomas Road members in the hospital. You don't get to be a religious icon without touching some lives, and it's clear there are more sides to Dr. Falwell than the red-faced demagogue.

Of course, in the interest of fairness, I should mention that the museum omitted certain biographical details, and it's those details that have largely defined Dr. Falwell's public persona in recent years.

For example, the museum's collection doesn't include the controversial February 1999 issue of Dr. Falwell's *National Liberty Journal*, which contained an article called "Parents Alert: Tinky Winky Comes Out of the Closet." The article wrote of the beloved purple Teletubby: "He is purple—the gay-pride color; and his antenna is shaped like a triangle—the gay-pride symbol."

Also not seen anywhere in the museum: *The Clinton Chronicles*, an eighty-minute conspiracy film that Dr. Falwell promoted and distributed on his *Old-Time Gospel Hour* TV show in 1994. The video accused then-President Bill Clinton of cocaine use, drug smuggling, money laundering, involvement in the murder of Vince Foster, and sexual harassment, among other offenses. It was immediately debunked, but sold a reported 150,000 copies anyway.

And, of course, there was no mention of the pièce de résistance, the speech Dr. Falwell gave on *The 700 Club* on September 13, 2001, while smoke was still rising from the World Trade Center: "The abortionists have got to bear some burden for [the attacks], because God will not be mocked," he said. "And when we destroy forty million little innocent babies, we make God mad. I really believe that the pagans and the abortionists and the feminists and the gays and the lesbians who are actively trying to make that an alternative lifestyle, the ACLU, People for the American Way—all of them who have tried to secularize America— I point the finger in their face and say 'you helped this happen.' "

Since I first decided to come to Liberty, I've been interested in seeing what Liberty students think about Dr. Falwell. I can understand why conservative evangelical students would find him appealing, but surely, I reasoned, they couldn't agree with his most controversial statements. You couldn't find ten thousand college students in the twenty-first century who supported Dr. Falwell's 9/11 remarks, which Walter Cronkite called "the most abominable thing I've ever heard."

Well, I've got to say—and I'm reserving my final judgment for a time when I've met more Liberty students—if they disagree with Dr. Falwell, they do a great job hiding it. No one seems to object to the portraits of Dr. Falwell hung in high-traffic areas around campus, to the prayer room decorated with quotes from his autobiography, or to the ubiquitous bobble-head dolls. Simply in quantity, the Jerrymania seems, if not idolatrous, at least a little North Korean.

After today's convocation, Stubbs the RA puts his arm around my shoulder.

"Well, Roose, welcome to Liberty. You've heard the 'one little boy' story. It's official now."

"He tells that story a few times a semester," Fox says.

"Yeah," Stubbs says. "He has about four speeches. Let's see . . . there's that one, the 'I walked every inch of this mountain' one . . . what else?"

"The one about when he learned to tithe," Fox adds.

"Oh yeah, that's a great story."

In a 1971 book called *Church Aflame*, Elmer Towns, Liberty's cofounder, recalled a conversation he had with a young Falwell follower named Danny Smith. Towns quoted Danny as saying, "The greatest compliment in life is to be called a man of God. The second is to say I am like Pastor Falwell." There's little doubt in my mind that Danny's adoration is shared by the Liberty students of today, though his language has been updated for the twenty-first century. Outside the Vines Center on my way to lunch, I spot a guy walking hand in hand with his girlfriend. His T-shirt announces: JERRY IS MY HOMEBOY.

Among the Falwell fans on campus is my roommate Eric, the pastor's kid from Michigan. Eric wants to follow his dad into the ministry, and yesterday he listed Dr. Falwell as one of his biggest professional inspirations. "I just like the way he preaches," he said. "All his jokes and stories and stuff. I could learn a lot from him."

Eric is the closest thing I've seen to a model Liberty student. He plays Christian rock on his stereo, wakes up early every morning to read his well-thumbed leather Bible (embossed in gold with his name), and speaks reverently—if a little warily—of his parents. "If I cursed at home, I'd get in so much trouble," he told me. "Oh my gosh, I don't even know what they'd do."

I haven't learned much more about Henry, the third resident of room 205. I still haven't figured out why he's starting at Liberty at age twenty-nine or what the rest of his story is, but he seems like a decent guy. He's a bit of a neat freak, and he tidies the room several times a day, but as a guy who tends to neglect things like cleanliness and basic hygiene, it's probably good for me to have a scrupulous roommate.

The only other notable thing I've learned about Henry is that he's very socially conservative. In fact, he may be the most conservative person I've ever met. Before bed tonight, he tells me about his old school, a state university in his home state of Missouri.

"There was just no morality on campus," he says. "All this partying, all these girls who dressed like *prostitutes*. I had to get out of there."

Henry sips his Mountain Dew (he drinks four or five cans a night) and turns to me. "So, what about you? Where did you transfer from?"

"A school in Rhode Island," I say, using my tried-and-true minimal revelation strategy. Unfortunately, Henry isn't satisfied.

"Which school?"

"Brown."

"You went to Brown?" he says, his eyebrows arching.

I nod.

"Wow," he says, exhaling through rounded lips. "It must be terrible there. I wouldn't go to any of those schools. Yale, Harvard, Princeton. No way. I heard they have naked parties there. Lots of sinful behavior. And you can't go there without accepting their point of view."

After a few seconds of silence, he says, "So, how did you realize that Brown was morally corrupt?"

I decide to reframe his question slightly: "Well, you probably wouldn't have liked all the partying there."

"And what about the professors? I mean, what do they teach about how man was created?"

"I mean, I haven't taken any biology classes," I say. "But I'm pretty sure they teach the evolutionary model."

He laughs. "Yeah, and *they're* supposed to be the best and brightest . . ."

I've had the Brown conversation with ten or eleven guys on the hall so far, and Henry's is the first openly hostile reaction. The more common response has been sympathy. Most of the Liberty students I've met came from secular high schools and chose Liberty because of the ideological sanctuary it gave them. They assume I fled Brown to escape its atmosphere of secular hedonism. I get a lot of "Man, Liberty must be such a breath of fresh air for you."

I'm not sure breathing fresh air is the best metaphor for how I feel so far. If we're sticking with the respiration theme, it's more like violent, post–Boston Marathon panting. Everything I do here serves to remind me how out of place I am, from the conversations with Henry to the Bible mistakes I'm still making (when talking with Eric this morning, I mentioned that I liked the book of Philippians, pronouncing it "Phillip-PIE-uhns." He looked at me askance and said: "You mean Phil-LIP-pee-uhns?").

During orientation week, blending in with Liberty students gave me a subversive thrill. Every time I did something right, I'd get a little head rush, like I'd just placed a dinner order at a Parisian restaurant and the waiter hadn't made a funny face at the way I pronounced *filet de boeuf.* Even my cursing slipup was exciting in its own way. But now that the novelty has worn off, maintaining this kind of verisimilitude is just tiring. My mom asked me on the phone today if I missed my friends at Brown. And I know this sounds awful, but I honestly hadn't thought much about them. I'm too busy to exist fully in one world right now, never mind two.

A Bible that is torn and tattered usually belongs to a person who is not. This is Dr. Harold Thompson's daily devotion. It's projected in large letters on the whiteboard as we enter the lecture hall. Last class, it was: "The road to Hell is paved with good intentions."

Old Testament Survey, which meets three times a week in the early afternoon, is an intimidating course. For one, Dr. Thompson is a severe man with frizzy, unkempt hair and very little humor about him, an archetypal grumpy teacher out of a Roald Dahl book. But my main issue with this class is practical: I'm just not sure how I'm going to pass. As any casual Bible reader will attest, the Old Testament is no walk in the park. There's all that Israelite geography, all those genealogies and lists of high priests with sixteen-letter names who appear for a page or two and then disappear forever.

Luckily, I don't think I'll have to tackle the tough parts for at least another few weeks. We'll be going through the books of the Old Testament in order, beginning with the more familiar Genesis. And there's more good news: from what I can tell, Old Testament Survey isn't going to require a massive amount of background knowledge. In fact, Dr. Thompson seems mostly concerned, like Dr. Dekker in History of Life, with teaching us how to defend the authority of the Bible in the face of skepticism.

I got this feeling on the first day of class, when Dr. Thompson spent fifty minutes proving that Moses wrote the first five books of the Bible, also called the Pentateuch (or, in Judaism, the Torah). Secular religion scholars have largely abandoned this view, and the current prevailing theory says that the Pentateuch was composed of four separate literary strands over about five hundred years. Even most conservative theologians now admit that Moses didn't write all of the Pentateuch, though they maintain he may have had a hand in compiling it.

But as a literalist, Dr. Thompson considers it paramount that Moses himself, and only Moses, penned the five books. It's a tricky stance to substantiate—perhaps the biggest obstacle being that Moses' death is recorded in Deuteronomy, a book literalists believe he wrote. But Dr. Thompson has an explanation for this: "God gave Moses a prophetic vision of his own death, and he was able to write his own obituary into scripture."

This is shaping up to be his MO—finding parts of the Old Testament that require fancy footwork to be taken literally and working out a plausible solution. Today, for example, he brings up a theological roadblock posed in the Genesis creation story, when God rests on the seventh day.

"Why would God need to rest?" he asks. "He's God! He doesn't get tired!"

This verse bothered him for years, but he eventually came up with a fix. The word for "rested," he says, can also be translated from Hebrew as "refreshed himself." So when God rested, he wasn't worn out—he was "breathing a sigh of appreciation."

Or consider Noah's Flood, one of the hardest literalizations in the Bible. Dr. Thompson raises a series of common objections to the Flood narrative and then provides his own explanations.

Objection: There isn't enough water in the atmosphere for a flood that covers the whole earth, like Genesis says it did.

"Well, not now there isn't, but that doesn't mean there wasn't enough in Noah's time."

Objection: There couldn't have been enough space on the Ark for all the food the thousands of animals would need.

"Well, that's simple. The animals would have been in estivation, a semicomatose state that happens to animals when they're traumatized. It's sort of like hibernation. In this state, animals on the Ark wouldn't require much food."

Dr. Thompson's defensive maneuvering is one way to deal with contradictions and textual problems in the Bible. The other way is to gloss over them entirely. This is the favored method of my New Testament Survey professor, Dr. Elmer Towns. Dr. Towns—Liberty's co-founder and longest-serving professor—teaches Sunday school at Thomas Road, and much of New Testament Survey is conducted in the same folksy, lay-audience tone, with little pause for analysis or critique. Consider this piece of yesterday's lecture about a star that appeared in the sky before the birth of Jesus: "I think—and this is just my conviction—that the star was supernatural. I think the wise men could see the star, and most other people looked up and didn't see it. If you saw the movie *The Nativity*, the star was there, and they think it was the merging of two planets. Now, many Christians have thought that over the years, but I don't happen to agree with that interpretation."

On the whole, I enjoy my Bible classes, even though my secular up-bringing puts me miles behind my classmates. It's a little bizarre when the material gets hyper-literal, like in the last Old Testament class, when Dr. Thompson spent ten minutes teaching us why Adam and Eve didn't have belly buttons. (Correct answer: Adam was formed from dirt, and Eve was formed from Adam's rib, so neither of them needed umbilical cords.) Or when Dr. Towns, in an effort to keep us awake, tries to inject teen-speak into his New Testament lessons. ("Right here in Luke, when it talks about Jesus meeting a trollop, that's another word for . . . what do you guys call it these days? A ho. She was a ho.") But most of the time, the classes deal with scriptural nuts and bolts. Stories from the Gospels. The lineage of Israel's patriarchs. Things that will be useful to know, even outside of Liberty.

In fact, I'm finding enlightenment in even my non-Bible courses. Like Theology. My professor in that class, a warm, soft-spoken guy in his midthirties named Mr. Watson, spends each class telling us about the history of Christian doctrine. It's by far the hardest class in my schedule, with homework questions like "What is the semi-Pelagian view of predestination?" and "What did the Council of Trent decide regarding man's will and God's grace?" And, like Old Testament, I'm not sure how I'm going to pass. But I'll give it my best shot, and who knows? Maybe there's a Christian scholar inside me yet.

I will say this: it's good that History of Life, my creationist sci-ence class, is held late in the afternoons, when I usually have almost twenty-four hours to wipe my mind clean of cynicism before my other classes. That class is still hard for me to sit through, and so far, I've only come up with one strategy to make it easier: I tell myself that by going, I'm learning things that will help me empathize with my new friends at Liberty. By listening to Dr. Dekker's vituperative anti-Darwin lectures and filling in blanks like "Outcomes of an Evolution View: Racism, Forced Sterilization, Abortion, and Euthanasia," I'm putting together the pieces of the creationist worldview. It's an hour of pain, but like childbirth or going to the dentist, it's productive pain.

It's Friday night, and I'm watching my roommate Eric play his twenty-sixth consecutive game of computer solitaire.

"There's nothing to doooooooooo," he says. "And it's only seven thirty. I'm so bored."

During the week, Dorm 22 is a fairly happening place. The enforced curfew brings all sixty residents back on the hall by midnight, where they hang out en masse until guys start to go to bed around 2:00 or 2:30 AM. Those two-ish hours are always filled with video game battles, push-up contests, and other thoroughly masculine activities. Last night, a bunch of guys decided to stage a poker tournament. (Proverbs warns against making "dishonest money" through gambling, but apparently doesn't come down either way on playing for Fritos.)

The weekend is a different story, though. Students who live locally tend to go home, and aside from the occasional Christian concert, the university's weekend calendar is usually empty. So without the option of partying, those of us who remain on campus are left to our own devices. Earlier tonight, I took a trip to Staples to buy an ink cartridge for my printer, then went back to my dorm, where I installed the cartridge and played two games of Crazy Eights with my next-door neighbor Zipper (who calls it "Crazy, Crazy, Crazy Eights").

A few minutes after eight, my hallmate Paul Maddox comes into my room carrying his Bible.

"Roose, you want to come to Bible study? I need . . . what do you call it . . . a wingman."

Paul and I bonded during orientation week. He's a tall, buff, light-skinned black guy with a wide, pearly smile and triangular shoulder muscles that climb halfway up his neck. Paul is a fellow transfer student, and like me, this is his first time in an all-evangelical environment. He came to Liberty from a historically black college in South Carolina, partly for the Christian atmosphere and partly because he hopes to make the Liberty football team as a walk-on. Tryouts are next week, and he's been furiously preparing, lifting weights twice a day and running wind sprints late into the night.

But tonight, Paul has a romantic agenda. He wants to meet a Brazilian girl who is rumored to attend a certain Bible study group on Friday nights.

"I saw her the other day at the gym," he says. "She stopped me dead in my tracks, man."

It's a novel idea—Bible study as singles mixer. And since the alternative is to watch my roommate play solitaire until he claws his eyes out, I decide to go along.

The Bible study is held at the off-campus house of an older Liberty student named Jeremy. Every Friday night, a dozen or so students sit on the couches in Jeremy's basement to discuss scripture and drink Caffeine-Free Diet Coke. And as Paul promised, there is at least one very attractive Brazilian girl present, a tanned, brown-haired beauty with come-hither eyes and a thick accent that makes "God" into "Goad." Jeremy leads us through the book of Ephesians, stopping periodically to discuss important passages. Paul and I are both relatively silent during the whole process—in my case, because I don't know anything about Ephesians, and in his case, because he's busy trying to sneak glances at the Brazilian girl (whose name, we learn, is Mariana).

After an hour of Bible study, Paul and I go upstairs to "fellowship" with Mariana. I didn't know what that verb meant when Paul suggested doing it, but judging from context, *fellowship* is Christian-speak for "hit on unsuccessfully." Paul is trying his best, alternating between laughing too hard at everything she says and telling his own stories with too much gesticulation, but it's hard to watch.

After a while, Mariana's friend Anna comes over to talk. Anna is a tall, slender girl with long dark hair pulled into a ponytail, wearing a form-fitting green sweater and smart-looking glasses. Very cute, sort of a young Tina Fey.

When I introduce myself, Anna gestures to Paul and Mariana.

"Let's leave those two to flirt awkwardly in peace," she whispers.

I nod, and we amble over to the couch in the corner, where we sit and talk by ourselves. Ten minutes into our conversation, I am nursing a small-to-medium crush. Anna is an elementary education major from Delaware, a charming girl with a quick, playful wit. When I tell her I'm a transfer student, she talks candidly about her distaste for our school's strict rules ("Liberty is a pretty ironic name for this place, huh?") and gives me good advice on getting settled, including "never, ever eat at the dining hall," and "if you don't have time to clean your room before morning inspection, just throw your dirty clothes under your blanket."

After half an hour, I see Paul motioning toward the door. His efforts with the Brazilian girl haven't gone so well, and he's giving up. Strangely, I could swear I'm feeling a little chemistry with Anna.

"I should get going," I tell her. "But if you're not busy sometime . . ."

"I could show you around campus," she interrupts. "You need someone to stop you from screwing up."

I laugh and grab my things, following Paul out the door.

"Ugh, this was such a bad night," he says, dragging his feet in the driveway.

"Really?"

"Well, maybe not for you," he says. "You looked like you were doing well over there."

I'm not exactly sure how I did, honestly. That chemistry with Anna may have been a figment of my imagination. All I know is that tonight exceeded my expectations by several notches. I wouldn't say it was a crazy, crazy, crazy night—maybe two-thirds of a crazy—but not bad at all.

When I wake up at 7:45 on Sunday morning, I expect to feel much worse. It's 7:45 on Sunday morning, after all. I sit up in bed and pat my torso like a sci-fi movie character after being teleported, checking to see if everything is in working order. And man, is it ever. My parts are loose and limber, like I could run a few consecutive 5Ks before breakfast with no real trouble. My mind is razor sharp, and my eyelids are defying gravity.

This is a relatively new phenomenon. Last semester at secular college, I spent a good number of my Sunday mornings in bed with head-splitting hangovers. I'd roll out of bed around noon, reach for the Advil, and spend the rest of the day in biological repentance. But today, I feel great. And it's a good thing, too, because I'm going to be on TV this morning.

A week ago, I was browsing Liberty's course offerings on the student website, looking for another class to add to my schedule when I came across a half-credit course called TRBC Choir. I read the description, and it was exactly what it sounded like: an invitation to join the Thomas Road Baptist Church choir for class credit. I couldn't believe it.

Thomas Road, of course, is one of America's largest and most legendary churches, sort of the St. Peter's of evangelicalism. It was among the first handful of American churches to host a television broadcast, and during its halcyon days, its services were seen in one of every four American homes. With Dr. Falwell in the pulpit, Thomas Road's congregation has always wielded tremendous political clout—it used to be said that no Republican could get to the White House without first passing through Jerry's House. Today, the church remains influential, averaging fifteen thousand attendees every Sunday and a TV viewership in the millions. It's the crown jewel of the Falwell empire, the institution that made all the rest possible.

Even before coming to Liberty, I wondered what being on the creative end of a Thomas Road worship service would feel like. Was it any different than viewing it from the congregation? Was there any secret backstage drama? And now, I was being offered a chance to join the choir, where I'd have an all-access pass to Thomas Road's inner workings in exchange for an hour of my time every week. How could I refuse? So I signed up.

I make my first blunder right away. I was told to arrive at church half an hour before the service for warm-up. I assumed this meant the nine o'clock service. When I get to the Thomas Road lobby at eighty-thirty, an elderly man working as an usher informs me that, in fact, the choir does not perform at the early service.

"Only eleven o'clock," he says. "You must be new. You made a new guy mistake."

I am, and I did. So with two hours to kill before warm-up, I take the time to case out Thomas Road.

Thomas Road, I should explain, is only partly a church. Yes, it has a sanctuary, a pulpit, a baptismal pool, and slots on the back of each seat containing tithing envelopes. But to call it a church is really to miss the point. Thomas Road is located in a million-square-foot former cell phone factory, which Jerry Falwell obtained in 2004 and whose renovations have cost $24 million to date. Even in its semifinished state, the building already serves as a home to a staggering number of outfits. There's the Liberty School of Law, the Liberty Theological Seminary, a campus fitness center, a bookstore, an ice cream parlor, a doctor's office, an Olympic-size indoor track, and the Liberty Christian Academy, which serves more than 1,500 students in pre-K through twelfth grade.

Thomas Road's main sanctuary is a pristine, lavishly decorated Boeing hangar of a room. It seats six thousand on two levels, has a production booth in the balcony, a pair of giant Jumbotron screens flanking the stage, and two soundproof glass-walled "cry rooms" in the back for screaming babies and their mothers. Outside the sanctuary is main street, a shiny-floored hallway the size of an O'Hare runway. All along the hall, shelves of evangeli-kitsch cry out for attention. On offer are copies of *Falwell: The Autobiography*, baskets of "Jesus First" lapel pins, DVDs of Dr. Falwell's old sermons. At the end of main street, the Lion and Lamb Café, an ersatz Starbucks, doles out muffins and cappuccinos to the pre- and postchurch crowds.

As I'm staring at the Kids' Cove, a rubber-floored play area with a fiberglass Noah's Ark as its centerpiece, I look at my watch. It's time for choir.

I walk into the choir room just as Linda, the choir manager, is assigning robes to the Liberty students gathered around her. Thomas Road's choir is composed of about half Liberty students, maybe 120 students out of three hundred total singers. I stand in line in front of the rolling metal racks, and eventually get a purple polyester robe thrust at me. The tag identifies it as number 308.

As I slide it over my shoulders, I realize that it's far, far too big—an XXXL, at least. I'm pretty sure robe number 308 was designed to be worn on the body, but at this size, it could also be used to catch people jumping from burning buildings. I swallow my pride and take an empty seat in the back row. A big, burly man comes over to me almost immediately and introduces himself as Perry, the tenor section leader.

"I'm sorry young fella, but this is Frank's seat," he says. "He's been sitting here almost thirty years."

Perry suggests I take one of the seats in the front row.

Front row? He can't be serious. I was given a CD with the choir's repertoire a few days ago, and I've listened to it four or five times, but that hardly qualifies as rehearsing. Until I got up to speed, I planned to stand in the back and make myself inconspicuous. I tell Perry I'm nervous about being in front.

"It's my first week," I say. "I like to take my cues from other people."

He points me to a chair in the center of the front row and gives me a little push on the small of my back.

"Don't worry, son. There's a prompter in front of the stage. You'll be fine."

Within a few minutes, three hundred robe-clad singers are lined up in straight rows, ready to enter the choir loft. Section leaders pass out black folders with the morning's music. Our first song is "Days of Elijah," choir director Al announces. Al is a huge, rotund guy with a wide porcelain smile and a fair bit of pep in his step—think John Candy, but with the complete opposite disposition.

"Let's pray and get out of here, folks," he says. A few chatty sopranos shush each other, and all heads are bowed.

"Lord, may we sing today with such enthusiasm that people's hearts and minds are renewed, that they are reminded that you are the immutable, unchanging God. Blend our voices, Lord. I pray people would be directed to your son Jesus today. In his name we pray. Amen."

Al snaps his head up. "Okay folks, we're moving!"

We file down the back hallway of Thomas Road, climb the stairs leading up to the loft, and take our places. A purple curtain separates us from the audience, but I can hear the instruments tuning up on the stage below.

At 10:59 AM, Al pokes his head through the curtain to make sure we're ready. Then, three . . . two . . . one . . .

"Good morning folks, and welcome to Thomas Road!"

The curtain peels apart, the klieg lights come flooding down, and there they are—six thousand parishioners.

Before I know what's going on, I'm swept into action. The choir sings at full volume, accompanied by a fifteen-piece band:

> *Behold he comes, riding on a cloud,*
> *Shining like the sun at the trumpet call.*
> *Lift your voice, it's the year of jubilee*
> *And out of Zion's hill salvation comes!*

As advertised, there's a TelePrompter in the front row of the congregation with song lyrics in large yellow letters, so I'm playing a little game of karaoke that would be sort of fun if I weren't on national TV.

After I mumble my way through a few more songs and after the ushers come through the aisles to take the offering, Dr. Falwell pushes himself out of his chair and makes his way to the pulpit with his penguin-like shuffle—leading with his hips and sort of waddling behind them. He's wearing his trademark black suit and red tie, and from the back, I can make out the line behind his ears where his stage makeup ends.

"Today," he says, "I want us to take another step—moving to another level. For you as a believer, for you as a Christian family, and for us as a local church."

As he preaches, a clock on the prompter tells him how much time remains in the broadcast. Video cameras whiz around on mechanical arms, flying in for shots from all angles. From my seat, I can see the team of engineers in the production booth jostling around frantically, making sure everything goes smoothly.

"God has great things in mind for each of us. God wants to use you and bless you even more than you want to be used or blessed."

Thomas Road's televised service bears almost no resemblance to the shrieking, crying, miracle-healing church services most outsiders associate with televangelism. The cameras play background roles here, and you'd hardly notice them if you weren't looking. Dr. Falwell works with no notes, and there's nothing on the prompter during his sermon. He stands and delivers calmly, sometimes shifting back on his heels, sometimes slipping his hands in his pockets.

When the clock on the TelePrompter begins running down (0:33 . . . 0:32 . . . 0:31), the piano player sprinkles in a soft background melody, and Dr. Falwell winds up for the altar call.

"Life is so short, and God has big things for us to do," he says. "God has something for *you* to do today. Let's bow our heads and pray. While our heads are bowed, our pastors will position themselves at the head of every one of these aisles. If you need to be born again or confess your sins and get started over again or join Thomas Road Baptist Church, come down the nearest aisle."

While choir director Al sings the invitation song, Dr. Falwell watches the aisles closely and prods his congregants to respond, growing a little harsher each time.

I'm forgiven . . .

"Come on down the aisles right now."

. . . because you were forsaken.

"Step out and come."

I'm accepted, you were condemned.

"Sing the next stanza, Al. Come on to the Lord right now."

Sitting in the choir, watching this spectacle of convincement, I get a throbbing adrenaline rush. It hits me: I'm in Jerry Falwell's choir, on national TV, in the middle of one of the world's most famous church services, as probably the only non-evangelical ever to sit in this choir loft. It's a thrilling notion, and a slightly terrifying one.

After church, I'm back in the choir room, hanging my enormous robe back on the rack, when section leader Perry comes over to me.

"How was your first day?" he asks.

"Really interesting," I say. "I learned a lot."

He puts his hand on my shoulder. "Buckle up, kid. You're in for the ride of your life."

As my second week at Christian college winds down, I'm making my home in Dorm 22. I'm a little nervous about being too social too soon, mostly because I'm still breaking in my sanitized Christian vocabulary, but it's hard to be anonymous with this crowd. Every night, guys come into my room after curfew, introducing themselves and inviting me to various hall activities. Most of them have decided to drop my first name—I'm now Roosey, K. Roose, or Rooster—which probably has nothing to do with Christianity, but sort of makes me feel like I'm back on my high school soccer team.

Speaking of my Christian vocabulary, I want a refund for that *30 Days to Taming Your Tongue* book that was supposed to teach me how to speak to evangelicals in their own language. After reading it, I went around for several days saying things like "Mercy me, that was a doozy of a class, wasn't it?" But instead of credibility, I mostly got looks of pity. As it turns out, although it's true that most Liberty students don't curse, they don't walk around saying "Glory!" or "Good heavens!" Instead, they use network TV versions of standard curses. Nerf curses. "Darn" and "crap" seem to be popular. While watching an NFL game with the hall's jock crowd tonight, I discovered some new options:

"What a gee dee kick return!"
"Bump you, ref!"
"Catch the *ball*! Son of a friggin' *biscuit*!"

Another surprise: although evangelicals are usually stereotyped as earnest and humorless, the guys on my hall seem to deploy sarcasm just as well as your average secular nineteen-year-olds. Last night, Stubbs the RA told a guy named Luke that he needed to cut his skater-length hair to comply with Liberty's dress code. They haggled about it for a few minutes, and then Luke said, "Hmm . . . you know, Stubbs, I seem to remember reading about a guy in the Bible who had long hair. What was his name again? Started with a *J*, I think. . . ."

All in all, the Liberty students I've met are a lot more socially adjusted than I expected. They're not rabid, frothing fundamentalists who spend their days sewing Hillary Clinton voodoo dolls and penning angry missives to the ACLU. Maybe I'm getting a skewed sample, but the ones I've met have been funny, articulate, and decidedly non-crazy. They play pickup basketball, partake in celebrity gossip, and gripe about homework just like my friends in the secular world. In fact, I suspect a lot of my hallmates at Liberty could fit in perfectly well at a secular college.

Of course, Liberty students depart from the mainstream in fairly obvious ways. Politically, for example, your average secular student is somewhere left of center, whereas your average Dorm 22 resident is somewhere right of Alan Keyes. And I haven't even started plumbing their specific religious beliefs. But already, I'm seeing some more surprising, deeper differences at work.

Last week, I was walking to the gym with Zipper, my ultra-happy next-door neighbor. Zipper (whose outgoing voicemail message starts, "You've reached the magical world of Zipper's phone!") told me about his most recent prayer walk, and the thoughts it had inspired.

"I was walking around the parking lot, and out of nowhere, I had this crazy realization: As a follower of Christ, I should be known by my actions, not my words. I need to show Christ's love to the world in everything I do. Because I want people to see something different in me, so they'll ask where it comes from. And then I can tell them, well, there's this dude, see? And he lives inside me, right? This guy, he rose from the dead! He transcends mankind! And if I didn't have him, I'd be just an ordinary guy!"

While Zipper was talking, I was trying to figure out why he was giving me this spiritual soliloquy. Was it because he didn't think I was saved? What was he playing at here?

In the last few days, though, I've learned that at Liberty, it's perfectly socially acceptable to pour your soul out to everyone within earshot. There's no such thing as TMI. Today, after church, I had coffee with James Powell, one of the two Spiritual Life Directors on my hall. Powell is a slim, faux-hawked pastor's kid from Georgia. We're both fans of the Drowsy Poet Café, a popular gathering place just outside Liberty's campus, so when our visits coincide, we sit and chat.

Today, Powell was talking about an awesome church service he attended this morning, and he uttered the phrase, "Man, I love being a Christian," which prompted me to ask him why. He paused, put down his coffee, and rubbed his chin.

"Roose, my whole life, Christianity came easy to me," he said. "And for a long time, I was totally self-centered, especially when high school came around. The car I drove, the girls I dated, my clothes, my grades—I had to have the best of everything. It was all about me. And then one day, I realized: I'm not alive because of me. I'm here because God wants me to live for him. For years, I couldn't pick myself up when I was going through hard times. But I realized that if I rely completely on God, if I give my life completely over to his service, he'll pick me up. He'll see me through. And now, I feel really, truly alive for the first time in my life."

I'm still adjusting my mind to all the earnest God talk I'm hearing at Liberty. From time to time, it still feels like I walked onto the set of a Lifetime movie. But one thing has become clear: these Liberty students have no ulterior motive. They simply can't contain their love for God. They're happy to be believers, and they're telling the world.

The philosopher William James once wrote that although he himself was not religious, seeing believers who were transformed by their faith made him feel "washed in better moral air." And so far, I think I see what he meant. It's hard to watch Liberty students singing along to worship songs during convocation, raising their hands and smiling beatifically, and not wonder whether they've tapped into something that makes their lives happier, more meaningful, more consistently optimistic than mine.

I still don't get what that something is, or how it changes them, or how it can coexist with the sorts of socio-political beliefs that have made Jerry Falwell one of America's most reviled public figures. It still feels like everyone on this campus is tuned in to a radio frequency I don't get on my antenna. But with the help of my hallmates, I'm starting to piece things together.

Let Us Learn Together What Is Good

Recently, I've been spending some time on Facebook, the annoyingly ubiquitous social networking website that wastes the time of secular and religious college students alike. I still have my account from Brown, but I hadn't thought about signing up for a second one until I was advised by my friend Janine, who writes me weekly e-mails from Brown, that not having a profile in Liberty's Facebook network would probably rouse some suspicion among my Christian classmates. Actually, the way she put it was, "You should just carry a sign that says: I'M A JOURNALIST."

Fair enough. So I signed up for an account with my liberty.edu e-mail address. I don't have many Facebook friends at Liberty yet, but I've been enjoying a page called Network Statistics, which compiles the most listed items in a given college's network. For example, among Liberty students, the most popular books are three solid Christian classics: the Bible, *Redeeming Love* by Francine Rivers, and C. S. Lewis's *Mere Christianity*. In Brown's network, on the other hand, those spots go to Harry Potter, *The Great Gatsby*, and *Lolita*—which concern witchcraft, bootlegging, and pedophilia. (Sadly, this Network Statistics page is confirming more stereotypes than it breaks—Liberty's most listed interest is God, and Brown's is Ultimate Frisbee.)

Whatever you think of it, Facebook is the perfect tool for the kind of amateur ethnography I'm doing here. How else could I keep track of a hundred Liberty students' lives with a few clicks? If social networking sites had existed in Margaret Mead's day, she wouldn't have had to do all that messy field research in the South Pacific. She could have logged on to the Samoa network, browsed some profiles, poked the chieftains, and formed her conclusions, all from her neighborhood Starbucks.

The most surprising thing about Facebook at Liberty is that in the safe space of the Internet—or the perceived safe space of the Internet—Liberty students air all the grievances they don't feel comfortable airing in public. In fact, with the exception of a few up-with-Liberty Facebook groups like "Jerry's Kids" (not to be confused with the muscular dystrophy support group), a lot of the content on Liberty's network is downright subversive.

Consider the Facebook group "You Know You Went To Liberty If . . . ," which contains submissions like:

. . . *You know all three verses of "Victory in Jesus."*
. . . *You've learned more about tithing than your major.*
. . . *After you tell people where you went to college, you follow it up with the phrase "It wasn't that bad."*

Or the groups formed as send-ups of the most byzantine rules in "The Liberty Way":

Couples Who Kiss At LU (12 members)
I Hug For 3 Seconds, Sometimes 4. (73 members)

The second surprise about Liberty's Facebook network is the massive amount of faith-related content it contains. I mean, I probably could have predicted that Liberty students' profiles would be heavy in Christian sentiment, but I never expected this much. Liberty students post wall messages to share inspiring Bible verses with each other. They fill the Religious Views section of their profiles with sentences like "I desire for my life to be modeled after Christ" and "Jesus Christ is the only truth I've found." And of course, there's the Facebook status, which is used at Liberty as a moment-to-moment indicator of spiritual well-being—sort of a Reuters for the soul. Just now, on the first page of my Friends list, I see:

Status: Chris is in need of prayer.
Status: Sam is finding security in Christ.
Status: Bethany is enjoying some good coffee! Praise the Lord!
Status: Brittany is so happy that she has a GOD who LOVES HER!!
Status: Sean is happy, and praising Jesus even though he's feeling a little sick.
Status: Caroline is completely and totally in love with Jesus. Every waking moment is illuminated by his grace.

Spending all of this time on Facebook raised the question: what should I put on my Liberty profile? I don't think I can pull off anything like "every waking moment is illuminated by his grace," but I should probably have some identifiably Christian details on there. As it is, my personal information is blank, and my default photo is a big blue question mark. It might work at a Unitarian school, but at Liberty, I'm not so sure.

So tonight, I craft my Facebook identity. First, I settle on a photo. I fill out my hometown, my date of birth, my mailbox number. I set my Religious Views to "Christian" and my Favorite Books to "the Bible, *Mere Christianity*, and *East of Eden*" (which are the last three books I read, but close enough), and I write a short personal paragraph for my About Me section.

Starting a Facebook account from scratch is an unexpectedly gratifying experience. This new profile feels somehow cleaner, more virtuous than the old one. All the photos from sweaty frat parties are gone. No more wall posts from my ex-girlfriend. I've never really reinvented myself, so this micro-makeover gives me a little head rush. I'm feeling so good, I even post a status update: "Kevin is a new man!"

Five minutes later, I find myself looking at the profile of a tanned, long-haired blonde who lives in Dorm 17, who enjoys "music that glorifies the Lord!" and who went to Jamaica over Christmas break, judging from her photo albums. Hold on. Is that a bikini I see? Then I realize: I'm back to my old ways—trolling for girls on Facebook. Old habits die hard, I guess.

When I walk into Old Testament on Wednesday morning, an acrostic is written on the whiteboard in large, blocky letters:

> For God so lo**V**ed the world,
> that He g**A**ve
> His on**L**y
> begott**E**n
> So**N**,
> **T**hat whosoever
> believeth **I**n Him
> should **N**ot perish,
> but have **E**verlasting life. —John 3:16, KJV

Today, Liberty is celebrating two holidays. Since it is, in fact, February 14, campus is filled with the traditional Valentine's Day hoopla. Heart-shaped boxes of chocolate and long-stemmed roses are everywhere, and people are eating those conversation hearts that taste like sweetened sidewalk chalk.

But at Liberty, romance has its limits, because today also doubles as the National Day of Purity, a conservative Christian holiday designed to promote abstinence before marriage. On Valentine's Day 2003 Mat Staver, the dean of the Liberty School of Law, started the holiday as a way to give Christian teens the opportunity to make a public declaration of their chastity by wearing plain white T-shirts. Here at Liberty, the administration loosened the dress code for the day to allow students to wear their purity shirts to class.

Two days ago, Dean Staver, a minister turned lawyer, spoke at convocation to explain the Day of Purity.

"God created sex for good," he told the assembled undergraduates. "Sex is the capstone of intimacy. But sex cannot produce intimacy apart from love and commitment. In Chernobyl, when radioactive material was contained in the reactor, it produced power, light, and heat. But as soon as the reactor broke and melted down, it produced destruction and death. The nuclear reactor that God created is husband and wife, committed to each other in a lifelong commitment. And when sex is contained within that reactor, it produces unity and intimacy. But when it is taken outside, it results in abortion, disease and death, harm and hurt. It tears apart husbands and wives and damages children."

Dean Staver flitted between all kinds of social conservative talking points—everything from the dangers of pornography to the sinfulness of homosexuality to the liberal redefinition of gender boundaries— before landing on sexually transmitted diseases.

"Think about your wedding night, guys," he shouted. "Do you want to know that you're going to be *killing your wife* by not knowing you're carrying an incurable STD?! You don't *ever* want to go down that way!"

I've been thinking a lot about sex this week. Or, more specifically, about Liberty's sexual climate. On the surface, this school's sexual mores seem completely pure and innocent. Many of the Liberty students I've met have freely admitted that they're virgins, and a lot of the girls on campus wear some form of abstinence jewelry—purity rings, "Love Can Wait" bracelets, and the like. Last week, a girl named Dayna explained the symbolism of her purity ring to me. Pointing to the three large diamonds on top, she said, "This one represents my dad, and this one represents my mom. They're the people holding me to purity. And this big one, the one in the center, that represents God."

So, yes, most Liberty students take abstinence seriously. But here's the confusing part: while Liberty isn't a sexual place in the same way most college campuses are, it's certainly sexual*ized*. Liberty girls might be virgins and they might not wear two-piece bathing suits to the pool, but they do wear thigh-hugging jeans, clingy blouses, and dresses that leave some, but not all, to the imagination. On the male side, while sex is clearly frowned upon, talking about sex is completely de rigueur. There was a heated debate in my dorm the other night about which sexual positions are best for stimulating the G-spot. Probably wouldn't shock Larry Flynt, but it seemed pretty racy for a bunch of Baptists.

Then there's the Day of Purity, which I must admit I don't understand at all. If the day is a celebration of premarital abstinence, as Dean
Staver said, then why was 50 or 60 percent of his convocation speech
about homosexuality and the redefinition of gender boundaries? What
does that have to do with not having sex? Is the implication that if gay
marriage is legalized, Christian boyfriends and girlfriends will turn
to each other, shrug their shoulders, and say, *Well, gee, might as well*?
From what I can tell, not a whole lot of forethought has gone into the
holiday.

The best evidence for this comes this afternoon, when I walk out of
the dining hall after lunch. Outside, I see six guys from my hall huddled
on the sidewalk, snickering to each other in a circle. They call me over,
and a guy named Ben whispers in my ear: "Don't make it obvious, but
look at that girl."

With his eyes, he motions to a very attractive blonde standing behind him. She's wearing tight jeans and a white Day of Purity T-shirt,
leaning back against the building and talking on her cell phone.

"What about her?"

"Just . . . look."

Swiveling around slowly, I laugh out loud. White T-shirts? In thirty-
degree February? What was Liberty thinking? The blonde stands un-
aware, gabbing into her phone while six godly men stare at her nipples,
poking through her shirt like a pair of Cupid's arrows.

After curfew, a hallmate named Rodrigo comes into my room. He
plops himself down on my bed while I'm doing my New Testament
homework.

"Roose, right? Just thought I'd come say hi. You know, meet the
new guy."

Rodrigo is a short, wiry sophomore from Mexico City. He's gregari-
ous and friendly, and he offers to help me with my work, since he's a
religion major. We talk for a while about the Religion Department, he
helps with a few of my short-answer questions, and then, before leaving, he leans in close to my face.

"So, Roose," he says. "Tell me about your relationship with Christ."

I've come to anticipate this question. It's been foisted on me, in some form or other, by a different hallmate almost every day this week. First, it was Eric, my roommate, who asked me about my salvation while we were getting ready for bed. Then, the next morning, I got it from Zipper, my next-door neighbor, on our way to convocation.

I planned from the very beginning to be truthful when Liberty students asked about my faith. I wasn't going to mention the word *Quaker,* but *Christian* would suffice, I thought. However, I've learned that *Christian* is a narrow category at Liberty. To be considered a true Christian, you must have experienced a moment of salvation in Christ, you must believe the Bible is the infallible word of God, and you must place at least some emphasis on bringing nonbelievers into the faith. According to evangelical theology, this means that lots of people who think of themselves as Christians, such as Catholics, Episcopalians, and mainline Protestants (including Quakers), are still considered lost or unsaved.

"You know," Rodrigo says, "when I came to Liberty, I was a Catholic. I grew up in a Catholic family, went through confirmation, all of that. And then I got here, and my roommate started talking to me. He showed me that I wasn't saved, even though I had been going to church all my life."

When I found out how strictly Liberty defines its theological in-group and how much flak I'd catch for being outside it, I decided I had no choice but to craft a testimony, the story evangelicals tell about their conversion. My fictional testimony is as bare-bones as I can manage: I say I got saved six months ago, when a friend brought me to a church service in Providence. (The six-months-ago twist was my friend Laura's suggestion—my unfamiliarity with the Bible is a lot easier to explain if I don't paint myself as a lifelong Christian.) It's not an iron-clad story, but it seems to satisfy Rodrigo.

"So you've been growing in Christ since then?" he asks.

I nod.

"And you believe the Bible is the word of God?"

I nod again.

"Well, tell me about your devotions."

Devotions is the name given to a Christian's daily Bible reading, and it serves as an approximate spiritual barometer among believers. If you do an hour of devotions every morning, you're probably growing in your faith. Ten minutes twice a week? You'll get prodded to pick up the pace. I tell Rodrigo the truth—I've been reading the Bible for about half an hour every morning, though I forget some mornings and cut others short by a few minutes.

Rodrigo smiles. "Good, good."

At first, I was almost offended by the nonchalance with which people probed my soul. Within five minutes of meeting a new hallmate, I've been asked how often I pray, which is not something I'm used to. But after answering enough of these questions, I'm starting to realize that in the evangelical world, prying can be an indicator of compassion. In Liberty's theology, there are only two categories of people: believers and nonbelievers, people headed to heaven and people condemned to hell. So Rodrigo's attempt to suss out my faith isn't intended to be obnoxious. He just wants to make sure I'm safe.

The next day, campus gossip revolves around two questions: who got engaged on Valentine's Day, and how did they do it?

I guess I should explain that outside of Jane Austen novels, nowhere is marriage a more frequent topic of conversation than at Christian college. Since arriving here, I've heard hundreds of jokes about the Liberty wedding frenzy—the "ring by spring" race, going to school for your MRS degree, and on and on. Three weeks into the semester, it's already crystal clear: this school wants marriages like Ohio State wants football championships.

Girls are typically considered the driving force behind Liberty's marriage hysteria, but guys get swept up in it as well. Last week, a junior named Lucas came back to our hall from a successful first date screaming, "I'm goin' to the chapel, boys!!! Who wants to be the best man?!?! *Who wants it?!?!*" Even Dr. Falwell got in on the cheerleading in convocation the other day. "Listen up, students," he said. "Now, I made sure there were five thousand girls here on campus, and five thousand boys. I don't know how much more I can do. Folks, we need more Liberty babies for Christ. Let's get going!"

I've never felt particularly rushed about getting married (probably because I've never taken an abstinence pledge), but when you're surrounded by nuptial-crazed Christians, it forces the issue. Every few days, I hear about another Liberty guy who popped the question, and I spend a few minutes feeling panicked. I'm almost twenty! Shouldn't I at least have someone in mind?

My new friends think so. For a few days now, my hallmates have been badgering me to ask out Anna, the brunette from Bible study. Earlier this week, Paul sat me down, speaking solemnly and deliberately, like an oncologist telling me I had six weeks left to live.

"Listen, man," he said. "You have to make your move."

I flinched. I'm not ready to start dating at Liberty. For one, I'm still breaking in my Christian lifestyle. I've been hanging out mostly in groups, where I can be a wallflower, and one-on-one conversation is still a little past my comfort zone. Also, I'm not sure where to draw the ethical line. Given my circumstances, is going on a date at Liberty wrong?

I used to think so, but the reality of Liberty's dating scene is making me reconsider. Liberty's strict rules about physical contact mean that most dating here takes place well within platonic bounds. (As one guy on my hall put it, "At Liberty, hand-holding is third base.") So if I can keep it casual, I think going on a date will help me understand young Christian romance. Plus, it might be fun.

There's only one problem: I don't know how to go on a date. Until this semester, I lived in a post-dating world where chivalry and traditionalism had long gone the way of the porkpie hat. My mom, a proud second-wave feminist, never stressed the importance of holding doors or pulling out chairs. Liberty, on the other hand, is the kind of place where guys show up with corsages on the first date, where they really lay their jackets in puddles.

I told Paul I wasn't feeling up to the task of old-time courtship. He assumed it was because I'm from the North, so he spent some time tonight priming me on the basics.

"Okay, first step," he said, "You have to ask her on a date in person. None of this Facebook, MySpace, text message junk. I want you to go up to her and say, 'Anna, will you go on a date with me?' And when you go on that date, all you have to do is follow one rule: pay, pray, and say."

According to Paul, this is a man's role on a date: pay for the whole thing, pray before the meal, and lead the conversation (or, since "lead" doesn't rhyme, "say" the conversation).

"And never, ever try to make a move on the first date," he said.

I get my chance tonight, after a Liberty basketball game. Anna is standing with a group of her girlfriends at the front of the arena, and Paul and I go over to join them. After a few minutes of small talk, I catch Paul staring at me intently, looking a little annoyed. So I step into action.

"Man, I'm hungry!" I sigh. "Whew. Maybe I'll go out for a burger."

No one hears me. So I try again, this time with a little more oomph.

"I'm going to get a burger. Anybody want to come?"

Anna looks at me. "I'm hungry, too, actually."

"Well, uh, should we go get some food?" I say.

"Sure."

No way. Did that actually just work?

Anna says goodnight to her friends, Paul gives me a behind-the-back fist pound, and just like that, I am on my first Christian date.

As we walk to my car, I bolt around to the passenger side to open her door. It feels a little strange and anachronistic, like I'm stuck in an Archie comic, but I carry it off without incident. We make our way to a drive-in restaurant just past Liberty's back entrance, the kind of place where the waitresses wear roller skates and the milk shakes come with maraschino cherries. When our food arrives, I take out my wallet to pay. She pretends to protest, but I know better. Next, I pray over the meal, keeping it short and sweet: "Dear Lord, bless this food, and bless our time together. In Jesus' name, Amen."

So far, so good.

For the next hour, Anna and I sit in my car, eating our burgers and talking. And about twenty minutes in, I confirm my suspicion: there is something very different about this girl. She's virginal and pure like you'd expect from a girl who was raised in a conservative evangelical home and schooled in a Christian academy, but there's an edge behind the sugar. When we get on the subject of Liberty's rules, she complains about her least favorite restrictions: the curfew system and the single-sex dorms.

"I guess I understand why Liberty would have those rules," she says. "They should at least give us some orange jumpsuits, though. Round out the inmate vibe."

Even her extracurricular interests are puzzling. Her favorite author, she says, is Chuck Palahniuk, the proudly vulgar *Fight Club* scribe. She's read the whole Harry Potter series, and her band of choice is the Beatles, who have been personae non gratae in evangelical circles ever since John Lennon made his infamous bigger-than-Jesus comment.

I don't quite get how a girl like Anna ended up at Liberty, but I'm not complaining. She laughs at my jokes, even the lame ones, and she seems impressed by my fumbling attempts at chivalry. (When I hold the door for her, she says "Wow, a real man.") By the time we finish our food, drive back to campus, and pull up in front of her dorm, I'm drunk with optimism.

"Could I . . . call you again?" I ask.

She giggles, writes down her number on the burger receipt, steps out of my car, and waves goodbye. Success! This date might not have been perfect, but it clearly could have gone much worse. As I drive away, I can't stop grinning.

Back in Dorm 22, Paul, his friend Wayne, and Wayne's roommate Jeremy pull me into Wayne's room for a breathless recap.

"You took her to burgers?"

"Yep."

"You paid, right?"

"Mhm."

"And you remembered to hold the doors for her?"

"Of course."

"Please tell me you didn't make a move."

"Nope, nothing. Just told her goodbye as she got out of the car."

Paul lets out a nervous chuckle. "Heh. You mean after you walked her to the door, right?"

I hesitate a beat too long.

"You didn't walk her to the door?!"

And just like that, the guys explode in laughter. Paul pounds the desk. Jeremy lets out a high-pitched howl.

"You mean to tell me you took her out for dinner, you *got her number,* but you didn't walk her to the door?" Paul says.

"You didn't tell me I had to!"

He mimes shooting himself in the temple. Wayne shakes his head.

"Man, you thought you were riding high," Paul says. "You're a fool, man. Freaking northerners."

Midway through my third week at Christian college, I'm realizing that this semester is going to be an exercise in balance.

On one hand, I'm settling into my classes, I'm fitting in much better on my hall than I expected to, and I've been pretty effective at battling homesickness. Making it through the whole semester doesn't seem so far-fetched anymore, especially now that I've got a love interest. On the other hand, I'm seeing a fair number of foreign, sometimes frightening things here, and I'm seeing them regularly enough that it keeps Liberty from feeling comfortable for more than a few hours at a time. A few revelations of note from the past week:

- Liberty students aren't allowed to hold demonstrations. This Orwellian twist isn't widely publicized, and it didn't come up during orientation week, but I was browsing "The Liberty Way" the other night, and that's what I saw: "Student participation in on campus demonstrations, petitions, or picketing" without university permission is punishable with twelve reprimands and a fifty-dollar fine. There are several other rules Liberty doesn't tell you about during orientation week. For example, a girl found to have had an abortion is subject to thirty reprimands, a $500 fine, thirty hours of community service, and possible expulsion. The same penalty awaits a Liberty student found guilty of "involvement with witchcraft, séances or other satanic or demonic activity."
- I went to a Love4Life relationship conference at Thomas Road

last weekend, which turned out to be a bad idea. Although it was advertised as an event for singles and married couples alike, I was one of maybe a dozen bachelors in attendance and was forced to sit through seminars like "Time-Starved Marriages" and "The DNA of Commitment." About half of the conference was spent denouncing same-sex marriage efforts, with representatives of conservative lobbying groups like the Family Research Council handing out books like *Outrage: How Gay Activists and Liberal Judges Are Trashing Democracy to Redefine Marriage.*

- During my History of Life class yesterday afternoon, we spent some time learning about the precise physical dimensions of Noah's Ark. According to Dr. Dekker, the Ark was 73 feet wide and 437 feet long with a gross tonnage of 13,960 tons and the freight capacity of 533 railroad stock cars. "This thing had space for 125,280 sheep-size animals," he said. "It was basically a floating skyscraper."

- Last night, my hallmates told me about Scaremare, a famous Liberty attraction. Every October, Liberty sets up a massively popular haunted house (twenty thousand people attended last year) that features various frightening characters and gory death scenes. After making their way through the house, visitors see a bloody, agonized Jesus hanging from a cross—"the ultimate death scene"—and are taken into white tents, where Liberty students counsel them on how to accept Christ as their savior and avoid the fate that awaits them when they die. As one hallmate put it, "Most haunted houses try to scare the hell out of people. We try to scare people out of hell."

The weird thing is, I already feel myself becoming numb to Liberty's oddities. Last night, I was at the gym with some guys from Dorm 22, and someone called someone else a faggot. I made a mental note of it, but it didn't make me wince. Dr. Falwell gave a convocation sermon about Christian missionaries the other day, and although I recognized that some of what he was saying was dangerous (e.g., "what the developing world needs is not food or water, but the word of God"), it didn't faze me like it should have.

A few days ago, a friend e-mailed me a *New York Times* article about a science professor at Liberty named Marcus Ross. Ross, who is also a PhD candidate in geoscience at the University of Rhode Island, wrote his dissertation on mosasaurs, a type of marine reptile that went extinct about 65 million years ago. The hook of the article is that Ross doesn't believe the earth is 65 million years old. Like Dr. Dekker, he believes in a six-thousand-year-old earth created by God in six days. When asked how he reconciles his creationist beliefs with his secular doctoral work, Ross says that he does his secular research within one framework (mainstream scientific consensus) and his creationism work within another framework (the Bible).

When I first read the article, I was confused. How can you work with ancient fossils and then turn around and claim that God made them five thousand years ago? It seemed intellectually dishonest, if not downright fraudulent.

I still don't know how Ross does it, but I have realized this: the mental compartmentalization he talks about is a real thing. Over the past two weeks, I've felt it happening in my own life. I still feel very connected to my secular self, and it still responds quickly whenever I hear about something like Scaremare or the no-demonstration rule. But I can feel myself carving a second, smaller self out of the first, sort of a religious version of W.E.B. DuBois's double consciousness. And the Christian slice of my brain is more apt to give these things a fair shake. I hear Dr. Dekker talking about a 437-foot Ark, and most of me says "no way." But a little part—maybe 5 or 10 percent—wants to be allowed to toy around with the possibility that it actually was a floating skyscraper.

This is probably not something I should tell my family.

On Friday night, nearly everybody on campus heads over to the Vines Center for Coffeehouse. Coffeehouse is a massively popular student talent show that occurs once a semester, and unlike other talent shows I've seen, this one is audition-only, which might explain the ridiculously high level of talent. When I walked in, I steeled myself for a few hours of cut-rate student schlock. But from the interpretive dance set to the Mighty Mouse theme song to the country band called Derek and the Hee-Haws, every act is professional quality. Well, almost every act. There are one or two patchy spots, like the guy who does an *SNL*-style Robert Goulet skit that sounds more like a laryngitic Robin Leach. But everything else is top-notch.

Every Coffeehouse features one or two professional Christian musicians brought in to give the event some gravitas. Tonight, the featured performer is KJ-52, a well-known Christian rapper. KJ-52 comes to the stage to huge applause. He's a lanky, goateed white guy, wearing a white sleeveless T-shirt, a baseball hat flipped backward, and a bandana around his neck. KJ-52 fashions himself as the evangelical Eminem and has even written songs comparing himself to the secular rapper. (One such song, in which KJ-52 offered to pray for Eminem, was featured on a VH1 show called *40 Least Hip-Hop Moments*.)

KJ-52—or Five-Tweezy, as he calls himself—explains that his name does not stand for King James as his Christian fans all assume. In fact, it's a combination of his old stage name, King J Mack, and the numbers five and two. "Not fifty-two," he raps, a giant gilded crucifix swinging like a pendulum from his neck. "It's five-two, and it means five loaves, two fishes, baby."

Five-Tweezy's performance is actually not terrible, considering that most of rap's usual subjects—money, drugs, loose women—are off-limits to him. He drops verses like:

> *Back in the day when I was a teenager*
> *I was only fifteen when I just met my savior*
> *And he came in straight in my heart and he just changed the*
> *Way I used to live in ill behavior.*

After he finishes, a hip-hop group composed of Liberty students comes on to close out the concert. They're not bad either, and they have the distinction of providing my new favorite rap lyric:

Tryin' to find purpose in life without Christ
Is like findin' Wesley Snipes in the dark with no flashlight.

For me, the biggest surprise of the night wasn't the fact that Christian rap exists, or that a Christian rap group made a Wesley Snipes reference. It was the fact that all the Liberty students in attendance knew exactly who they were talking about.

When I came to Liberty, I expected to find ten thousand students who had been reared entirely on Christian pop culture. I expected to hear a lot about Michael W. Smith and *VeggieTales* and nothing about Eminem and *Entourage*. But nothing could be further from the truth. In fact, aside from the prayer that kicked off the evening, everything about tonight's Coffeehouse, from the Wesley Snipes reference to the montage of 1990s TV clips that played at the beginning of the night (*Full House! Doug! Saved by the Bell!*), was steeped in secular pop culture.

Of course, there is some Christian pop culture on campus. In addition to KJ-52, my hallmates listen to artists like Chris Tomlin (the evangelical John Mayer) and tobyMac (think Kid Rock plus Justin Timberlake plus Stryper). They play video games like *Left Behind: Eternal Forces*, and the other night, a few of us watched a DVD of Christian stand-up comedy called *Thou Shalt Laugh*, which contained an amazing number of jokes about parenting.

But more often, the pop culture I see around campus is secular. In Dorm 22, Jack Johnson and Dave Matthews make much more frequent appearances on iTunes playlists than BarlowGirl, and for every copy of *Thou Shalt Laugh*, there are two or three *Sopranos* box sets. In fact, some of my friends here are more in touch with secular pop culture than I am. Last week, I kept hearing a new catchphrase being tossed around—something about "give me a chicken sandwich and some waffle fries." I thought it was a Christian in-joke I didn't get, but when I asked my roommate Eric, he pointed me to a viral YouTube video called "Unforgivable," which features a very angry black man saying things that are definitely not found in *30 Days to Taming Your Tongue*.

Liberty used to take a stricter approach to secular pop culture. The 1976 student handbook prohibited "rock music, country-western music, songs with anti-biblical or anti-American words or any Christian music which without the words sounds like rock music." But today's Liberty students are urged only to "choose music that honors the Savior and is in harmony with God's word," with no specific genres or artists prohibited. Secular TV shows, video games, and non-R-rated movies are permitted, though university-sponsored events are often held to higher standards. Last week, I got an e-mail invitation to a student screening of *Nacho Libre,* the PG-13 Jack Black comedy about a Mexican priest who moonlights as a masked wrestler. The e-mail said: "You can dress up like Nacho Libre, except you'll have to wear Liberty Way-appropriate nonspandex pants, and you'll have to wear a Liberty Way-appropriate shirt. Other than that, you can dress up like Nacho Libre!"

I'd guess that Liberty has loosened its prohibitions on secular pop culture partly because the Internet age has made enforcing those sorts of rules nearly impossible. But I suspect it also has to do with the changing tastes of students. Some of my hallmates, for example, don't just prefer secular pop culture—they actively dislike the Christian stuff.

The other day, I hung out with James Powell, the SLD from Dorm 22. Powell was telling me about GodTube, a new Christian website (Motto: "Find Your Purpose") that purports to be the evangelical equivalent of YouTube.

"It only allows Christian videos," he said. "There's a site called My-Praize, too. Have you heard of that? It's the Christian MySpace. Started by a Liberty grad."

"That's awesome," I said.

"Are you kidding me?" he said. "Ugh, I hate that stuff."

Powell proceeded to explain that although he understands why Christian pop culture exists and although he thinks there's some good Christian music out there, he doesn't like it when Christians simply co-opt elements of secular pop culture, rename them, and claim them as their own. He calls this "cheesy Christianity," and he claims that nothing irritates him more.

"I think it gives us a bad name," he says. "And really, why should we want to create a separate culture? It makes no sense. God tells us to be the salt of the earth, and we're afraid to interact with the world on its own terms. When I see something like MyPraize, I just want to shake whoever created it and tell him, 'Brother, if you think creating a Christian MySpace and giving it a corny, clichéd name is the best way you can possibly honor God, something is very wrong.'"

Powell's seems to be the dominant view on my hall—Christian pop culture can be worthwhile if done well, but bad Christian pop culture isn't redeemed merely by the fact that it's Christian. My hallmates would rather chance it in the secular world than listen to Michael W. Smith warble his way through "Our God Is an Awesome God."

At the same time, while some Liberty students don't totally identify with Christian pop culture, they recognize the dangers lurking in secular pop culture. There's a process of discernment, of partaking in the secular world cautiously while keeping one eye on your soul.

Last night, I walked into Powell's room as his roommate, a guy named Jake Myers, was deciding whether or not to watch the new James Bond movie playing at the Lynchburg multiplex. Jake, who serves as the second SLD in Dorm 22, had enlisted the help of a website called Kids in Mind. The website rates thousands of movies on a one-to-ten scale in three categories— sex and nudity, violence and gore, and profanity— and provides detailed descriptions of the more salacious scenes. For the PG-13 Bond movie, the warnings included:

> "A man and a woman exchange flirtatious barbs in a couple of scenes."
>
> "A man and a woman kiss passionately, they pull each other's clothes off (nothing is visible), they kiss, lie on a bed, and they roll over and fall out of the bed and onto the floor (it is implied that they have sex)."

Jake read the scene descriptions out loud, mulled it over for several minutes, emitted a little sigh, and decided to switch to a movie about cartoon penguins, which was rated PG and which got much lower rankings in all three categories. "This one's better," he said. "I think it'll be good."

While he was deciding on movies, I asked Jake where he draws his line. Is one topless scene enough for him to cross a film off his list? What about curse words? Is the F-bomb a deal-breaker?

"I dunno," he said. "I guess it depends how I'm doing in my walk with the Lord at a given point in time. You know, I like action movies as much as the next guy, Roose, but I work too hard at this holiness stuff to stumble just because of one lousy movie. Why not just keep myself pure?"

We All, Like Sheep, Have Gone Astray

Even in its weather patterns, Lynchburg, Virginia, is a fundamentalist city. Unlike the fickle New England winters I came from, where snow, sun, fog, and rain operate on a twenty-minute loop, Lynchburg in late February has good days and bad days, and nothing in between. On a good day, the temperature hovers around fifty, the sun never dims, and you can get away with short sleeves. On a bad day, the wind is piercing and cold, and it thunderstorms from sunrise till dusk.

Today is a good day, so I'm working outside. Behind DeMoss Hall, there's a courtyard with a dozen picnic tables and a decently scenic view, so after classes, I took my books there, kicked my feet up, and began to study for my two favorite classes: Theology and Old Testament.

In Theology, we're learning about the rift between the Calvinist and Arminian views of salvation. To condense two dense and nuanced philosophies into a paragraph: John Calvin and Jacobus Arminius, two sixteenth-century theologians, disagreed on several points of Christian doctrine, the most contentious of which was the doctrine of election. Calvin believed that God chooses, or "elects" people to be saved before their birth (this is also known as the Reformed view). Arminius, on the other hand, believed that people are able to choose whether or not to be saved (the free will view). Even more simply, Calvinists believe that God chooses people, and Arminians believe that people choose God.

Surprisingly, not everyone at Liberty agrees. Dr. Falwell takes a free will approach to salvation. But Liberty has a large and vocal Calvinist population, and they've formed their own Facebook groups, like "Reformed and Proud of It." Naturally, the Arminians have fought back, with groups like "Calvinists Have Cooties" and mocking T-shirts like "CALVINISM: THIS SHIRT CHOSE ME." It's this school's version of a Red Sox–Yankees rivalry, and until this week's Theology lecture, I had no idea what everyone was arguing about.

My Old Testament class has stopped being so defensive, and we're diving into the rest of the Pentateuch. It's fascinating, difficult stuff. For example, most people know that God loosed ten plagues on Egypt in the book of Exodus, but did you know that each of those plagues was targeted to parallel and discredit a specific Egyptian god? The plague of frogs was based on the Egyptian goddess Heqt, who had the head of a frog. The plague that brought disease to Egypt's livestock was an affront to Hathor, a cow-headed goddess that was the symbolic mother of the Pharaoh. When Pharaoh had to ask Moses to petition God to remove the plagues, he was in effect conceding that the god of Israel was more powerful than the Egyptian gods to whom those tasks had been assigned for centuries.

Of course, not every class is as stimulating as those two. Like History of Life, which is shaping up to be quite a production. Last class, Dr. Dekker opened his lecture by showing us a cartoon of a group of aristocrats fawning over a man clad in his underwear.

"Evolution," he said, "is like 'The Emperor's New Clothes.' What we have in our society is a public school system, media, museums, zoos, the Discovery Channel—all of these avenues built off the 'fact' of evolution [*here, he air-quoted*]. A lot of people have the same opinion, that evolution is all this 'evidence' [*again*], and if I want to be perceived as 'intelligent' [*again*] I need to go along with it. But all it takes is one person to point out the obvious flaws in the 'theory' [*one more time*] and then everyone can see evolution for what it is: a fraud."

So far, I've gleaned a few dominant themes from my classes—a few things Liberty really, really wants us to know:

- Evolution didn't happen. Of course, History of Life is singularly concerned with the topic, but all of my other classes, from Theology to Old Testament to GNED to Evangelism 101, have touched on it as well.

  I've heard several strains of anti-evolution jabs so far. One is when a professor points out that both creationism and evolution are based on faith—faith in God on the one hand, faith that man evolved from pond scum with no divine help on the other. Another is when a professor makes a case for creationism using all of the well-worn scientific canards about gaps in the fossil record and the flaws of carbon dating. The most popular weapon, though, is garden-variety sarcasm. Depending on which Liberty professor you ask, believing that life evolved via natural selection is as plausible as believing that a dynamite stick thrown into a printing factory would produce an exact copy of the Declaration of Independence, believing that a tornado hitting a junkyard would produce a fully functional Boeing 747, or believing that placing all the parts of a wristwatch in a box and shaking it would produce an intact Rolex.

- Abortion is murder. This one also seems to find its way into lessons of every stripe, and it's often thinly veiled, if it's veiled at all. In my New Testament class, for example, we don't simply study the passage in the Gospel of Luke when John the Baptist leaps for joy in his mother's womb at the arrival of the Virgin Mary. We study how John "could listen and think in the womb, which proves that the abortionists are wrong."

- Absolute truth exists. At Liberty, unlike many secular schools, professors teach with the view that there is one right answer to every question, that those right answers are found plainly in the Bible, and that their job is to transfer those right answers from their lecture notes to our minds. It's a subtle difference in ideology, but it makes for big changes in teaching style. Most of my classes use workbooks—thin, self-published transcriptions of the professor's notes with one or two words blanked out per sentence. As the professor teaches, his notes appear on PowerPoint slides, and we fill in the missing words in our workbooks.

A sample filled-in page from my GNED workbook:

GENERAL CHARACTERISTICS
OF A BIBLICAL ETHIC

It is based on God's <u>unchanging nature</u>.
It is dependent upon God's <u>revealed truth</u>. What God says
    must matter to us.
It is authoritative—it is God "breathed" (inspiration).
It is prescriptive—it tells us how we should <u>live</u>.

And from my New Testament workbook:

JESUS COMMISSIONS TWELVE DISCIPLES

1. His <u>preparation.</u> "All night in prayer" (Luke 6:12,
   NKJV).
2. Their <u>job description.</u> ". . . that they might be with Him
   and that He might send them out to preach" (Mark 3:14,
   NKJV).
3. Our application. We must have vision. "When He saw
   the multitudes . . ." (Matthew 9:36, NKJV). We must
   have <u>compassion.</u> "He was moved with compassion"
   (Matthew 9:36, NKJV). We must <u>pray</u>.

I've gotten a lot of questions from my secular friends and family about my Liberty classes. Of course, they want to know what's being taught, and when I tell them, their response is always something like, "Wow. That must be so hard for you." My aunt Teresa, the psychotherapist from Washington, e-mailed me the other week with some practical advice: "Carrying a rock in your pocket from your most comforting geographical location can help ground you," she wrote. "If your mouth is itching to open and say something, just fondle the rock and let it absorb the words and feelings."

My family is right to assume that I have trouble believing a lot of what I'm learning these days. I'm studying Calvinism and Arminianism out of academic interest, not because I think either one describes my personal journey to salvation. Same with creationism. But despite that, I actually haven't been itching to stand up and object during my classes. Maybe I'm compartmentalizing my academic life the same way I'm compartmentalizing my social life, willfully ignoring the offensive things my hallmates say, but answering questions about Liberty's subject material doesn't feel all that different from the other kinds of academic posturing I've done, like when I pretended that I'd read *Ulysses* to impress my Joyce-obsessed high school English teacher.

Plus, I'm not doing well enough in my classes to criticize them. On two of the quizzes I've taken—one in Old Testament, one in GNED—I've scored in the mid-70s. So for now, I think I'll hunker down on my studies and let he who is without Cs cast the first stone.

"'Ey Rooster, lookame go! Rooster! I'm flying!"

Jersey Joey is skateboarding naked, and he wants me to watch. This shtick varies only slightly from night to night. Last night, he created an on-the-spot interpretive dance to a Josh Groban song that involved dry humping a pillow. The night before, he organized a hallwide eighties-rock party, complete with water bottle microphones and tennis racket guitars.

Joey Morone is a freshman from Hoboken, New Jersey, who has assumed a role as the resident rebel of Dorm 22. It's hard to miss Joey, who looks like a young James Dean, speaks with the thick brogue of his home state, and sports a massive amount of highly infectious charisma. One semester after Joey's arrival on campus, Dorm 22 is already starting to sound like a *Goodfellas* casting call. Small-town pastors' kids walk around telling each other, "'Ey, tough guy, you're a friggin' joke, you hear me?"

Jersey Joey isn't a real rebel, of course. At nineteen, he's still a virgin, and he has never tried hard drugs, but he speaks with great pride about making out with girls at home and drinking beer "once in a while." He smokes an occasional cigarette, he lets a curse fly from time to time, and he's gotten fifteen or sixteen reprimands this semester for infractions like "sleeping in convo" and "improper sign-out." This set of accomplishments would qualify him as the cleanest-cut student at many other American colleges, but here, it makes him an unspeakable badass.

Joey lives in room 201 at the end of the hall, with a pastor's kid named Jonah and a brawny, bearded guy named Travis. Because Joey's rebellious friends congregate there every night after curfew, his room has gained a reputation as an enclave of sin. It's a bit of an exaggeration—the most indecent thing that happens in there is an R-rated movie or two—but Joey's friends revel in their renegade personas. A half-dozen room 201 regulars have started a running reprimand tally, taping their violation slips in rows on the wall as they accumulate. Joey has eighteen reprimands so far this year, the most recent of which he received for a decoration he put on his fridge—a ribbon-shaped magnet that read "Support Sluts."

I've been hanging around Joey a lot in the past few weeks, both because his room is two doors away from mine and because he, more than anyone else on the hall, reminds me of my secular friends. He's immature and boisterous, yes, but he's far enough from Liberty's mainstream that I get a certain reversionary comfort from watching him pee in somebody's sink or what have you.

The first time I met Joey, he and his friend Marco were in room 201, reminiscing about the 1990s TV show *Boy Meets World*.

"Dude, Joey, tell me you didn't have the biggest boner when you saw Topanga on that show."

"Nah, man, she's a little thick for my taste."

"Now she is, yeah. But like, in the beginning of the show, she was so hot."

"Of course, but then she went to college and turned into a fatass."

"I bet she would still give a great BJ, though."

The first thing to know about Jersey Joey and his friends is that for a bunch of virgins, they spend a staggering amount of time talking about sex. It's almost pathological. Most nights, the topics of conversation include how hot Jonah's girlfriend is, why Joey should make out with Jonah's girlfriend's younger sister, and how it feels to squeeze a boob.

The amazing thing about Joey and his friends is how they're perceived by the rest of Dorm 22. Far from being outcasts, the room 201 rebels are some of the most popular guys on the hall. Some of Joey's antics—like the naked skateboarding—are greeted with rolled eyes, but for the most part, he's accepted as just another personality. Fox the RA told me that he considers Joey a "pain in the neck," but he added, "I love the guy. He keeps things interesting."

The trick to being a rebel at Liberty, I've learned, is knowing which parts of the Liberty social code are non-negotiable. For example, Joey and his friends listen to vulgarity-filled secular hip-hop, but you'll never catch them defending homosexuality. (On the contrary, Joey's insults of choice are "queer" and "gaywad.") And although they might harass the naïve pastors' kids on the hall by stealing their towels from the shower stalls—leaving them naked, wet, and stranded—they'd be the first people to tell you why Mormonism is a false religion. In other words, Liberty's true social code, the one they don't put in a forty-six-page manual, has everything to do with being a social and religious conservative and not a whole lot to do with acting in any traditionally virtuous way.

But back to room 201. Tonight, after Joey's skateboarding escapades are over, I'm sitting in his room with three or four other guys talking about our classes.

"Rooster, you're a freshman, right?" asks Travis, Joey's roommate.

"Sophomore," I correct.

"Wait, Rooster," says Joey. "You didn't start college this semester? Where'd you transfer from?"

"A school in Rhode Island."

"Which school?"

"Brown."

Joey's eyebrows rocket up his forehead. "You went to Brown? No, you didn't. You're lying."

"No, he's not, dude," says Marco, a freshman from San Diego. "He told me the same thing last week."

Joey looks at me sideways. "Why would you come here from Brown?"

I give him my standard yarn—I wanted to see what Christian college was like—and he sits a little lower in his chair, thinking hard, rubbing his chin.

"That's it?" he says. "No other reason? Your parents didn't make you come here?"

"Nope."

"And we're talking Brown University? Like, Princeton, Harvard, Columbia, Brown?"

"Yeah."

At this point, I'm feeling a little nervous. Unlike the other guys in the room, Joey seems to know enough about secular academia to know that a Brown student transferring to Liberty makes no sense whatsoever, and he's not letting it go. I'm expecting a string of tough questions, followed by a Google search and a background check.

But instead, he asks, "So Rooster, when you were at Brown, did you, uh, party?"

I should mention that until tonight, Jersey Joey and his friends have considered me a bit of a sanctimonious nerd. I think it had something to do with the two or three days after I read that *Taming Your Tongue* book and went around saying "Golly!" and "Gee whiz!" Or maybe it was the time Joey caught me typing my notes into my laptop late on a Saturday night and I told him I was working on a prayer journal. In any case, something I did marked me as less than rebellious in their eyes, and now that Joey's asking me about my old social habits, I figure I should take the opportunity to boost my rep.

"I mean, I partied a little," I say.

"No way," he says. "Like, you drank and everything?"

Joey included, there are now five guys in the room, and they're all staring at me, waiting for my response.

"Yeah," I say. "I drank."

Joey laughs. "Wow, Rooster. I did not see that one coming."

My answer is all it takes to spur a huge drugs-and-booze confessional.

Apparently, before they were forced into sobriety by "The Liberty Way," the men of room 201 were normal, red-blooded high school kids. Joey tells us about the times when he got drunk with his baseball team. Marco tells us about smoking weed back in California. Travis talks about the parties at his high school and how he used to be his local beer pong champion. The next fifteen minutes are a blur of dude-I-was-so-drunk stories and raucous laughter, and just as I'm feeling a little guilty for having set this whole thing in motion, Joey turns to me.

"Look at you coming here from the Ivy League and taking us back to our sinful days. You're a bad kid, Rooster."

Travis smiles. "And we like it."

The next morning, I have my first History of Life exam, a multiple-choice test that draws from our first five lectures, with additional material from our two textbooks, *The Answers Book* and *Refuting Evolution*.

The exam opens with two questions:

- True or False: Evolution can be proven using the scientific method. (Answer: False)
- True or False: Science is the only way to truly know truth about the world. (Answer: False)

Twenty more questions follow, most of which are fairly intuitive. For example, when Dr. Dekker asks if Margaret Sanger (the founder of Planned Parenthood) was a promoter of eugenics (selective breeding, a practice commonly associated with the Nazi Party), you sort of know what he's going for.

What rattled me about this exam wasn't the vague, headache-inducing questions like "science is the only way to truly know truth about the world" or the politicized questions about eugenics. It was the questions that took the dubitable for granted. Like:

- True or False: Noah's Ark was large enough to carry various kinds of dinosaurs.

According to Dr. Dekker, the answer is "True"—since dinosaurs and humans cohabited the earth after the Flood, they would have had to find a way to squeeze onto the Ark. He suggested that they could have been teenage dinosaurs, so as to take up less space.

What's most bizarre about History of Life is that while the scientific propositions Dr. Dekker makes are fairly simple, and while the operating mode of the class is reductive (that is, Dr. Dekker wants us to attribute the origins of life to a supernatural process that took place over six twenty-four-hour days), Dr. Dekker himself seems pretty intelligent. As he told us on the first day of class, he has impressive secular credentials, and he approaches his job with an amount of scientific seriousness. The last few chapters of our History of Life textbook are filled with phrases like "mitochondrial permeability transition pore" and "amino-acyl-tRNA synthetase." In other words, while young-earth creationism could theoretically be taught by pointing to the first chapters of Genesis, Dr. Dekker's class takes the shape of a rigorous scientific examination.

After class today, I spend some time in my room Google-stalking Dr. Dekker to see if he's as legitimate as he claims, and while he's no Stephen Hawking, the man is definitely smart. He got a grant from a federal research agency for his work with Alzheimer's disease, and some of his neuroscience research has been published in reputable, peer-reviewed science journals.

While following Dr. Dekker's web trail, I stumble across a paper he presented at a 2003 creationism conference, about the impact of a young-earth creationism course on the worldviews of the students who took it. The study worked like this: Dr. Dekker gave students in his History of Life classes a survey about their creationist beliefs on the first day of class and repeated the survey on the last day of class. He compared several years' worth of these results, and concluded that "when Christian college students are taught from [a young-earth creationism] perspective, they shift toward stronger beliefs in young-earth creationism."

It's a pretty intuitive conclusion, I guess, but I was surprised that there was any room for beliefs to shift. I assumed that every student coming to Liberty would be a strict creationist already. But according to Dr. Dekker's surveys, apparently not. For example, when faced with questions regarding the age of the earth, the average score of a History of Life student moved up more than 23 points over the semester, from 42.16 to 65.82 (100 being a perfect creationist, and -100 being a perfect evolutionist).

At first, the study seemed heartening. It means that for now, there are probably other students in my History of Life class who haven't fully signed on to young-earth creationism. But I'm not sure that's the right tack to take. After all, it also means that many of those students will have changed their minds by semester's end. It means that even if Dr. Dekker's data is sketchy, his goal—getting Liberty students to accept young-earth creationism—is being met.

Which gets me thinking: if they can change their minds, what about me? I'm probably the least likely person at Liberty to convert to creationism, and I certainly can't imagine it happening in one semester. For one, I'd just have farther to go. My classmates already believe that God answers prayers, miracles are physically possible, the Bible is infallible, and so on. It's a relatively short hop from there to believing in the historicity of the Flood. Whereas for me to become a creationist, I'd have to pass through a hundred intermediate steps of belief. And even then, I don't think I could do it.

But here's the worrisome part: almost a month into my Liberty semester, I'm already starting to feel my beliefs shifting under my feet. Not my belief in evolution—I've stayed put on that—but when it comes to my general intellectual and emotional grounding, I'm feeling a little unmoored.

As I expected, Liberty's church services are starting to feel much more familiar, and consequently, I find myself getting swept up in them from time to time. Instead of being put off when one of Liberty's pastors tells us about man's sinful nature, I feel misty-eyed and reflective. Yeah, I *am* sinful, I think. Maybe I *should* ask God for forgiveness.

I didn't come to Liberty to get a new religion, of course. I came here to spend time with the practitioners of another faith, to learn how they lived. But it was crazy of me to expect that I could situate myself among these people twenty-four hours a day, befriend them, and adopt their mannerisms without also internalizing and grappling with their beliefs.

When I was getting ready to come to Liberty, I read some work by an anthropologist named Susan Harding, who wrote *The Book of Jerry Falwell,* a first-rate examination of the language patterns of fundamentalist Christianity. In that book, Harding wrote about the danger of being converted in a situation like mine, where an outside observer is embedded in a religious community to do research. She wrote: "Anything that makes you more likely to listen, like the work of ethnography, is what actually makes you susceptible [to conversion]." In other words, just by being here, I'm already changing.

I don't like feeling unsettled like this. I'm starting to wish that I had a PhD in anthropology, so I'd be able to contextualize all this new information immediately, shuffling it into categories and translating it to academic jargon. Campus Church would become Inculcation Exercise 6A in my notes. Distance would be built in. But as it stands, I have no defense but the strength of my will. And knowing myself, I don't think I can stay in my state of religious confusion for long. One way or the other, Liberty is going to force me to make up my mind.

Caught Up Together

A pudgy, bald preacher stands on an otherwise empty stage, balancing an open Bible on the palm of his right hand and tapping it urgently with his left index finger.

"Jesus Christ is coming back for his church!" he yells to his audience. "I want you to know, church, that Jesus Christ could come this month! He might come next week! He could even come . . ."

CRRRRRRRRRACK!

White light drowns the room, and a deafening wallop of thunder follows. The preacher's Bible falls to the ground. In an instant, most of the hundred-odd people in the room have vanished, leaving only a few dozen stunned onlookers in their seats. They dart their heads around, glaring open-mouthed at each other, wondering where everyone went. One man in a red polo shirt realizes: this was it—the rapture. The Messiah has returned for his church, and he and the others have been left behind. Grief-stricken, he falls on his knees in the aisle of the church and, taking head in hands, begins to weep.

Dr. Parks turns the classroom lights back on to begin our GNED class.

"Just thought I'd show you that YouTube video before we got started today," he says. "I thought it was sort of neat."

That video (title: "Are You Ready?") was produced by an evangelical church in Texas to warn non-Christians about the second coming of Christ, and despite what Dr. Parks said, it was not just "sort of neat"—it was accurate. The scenario depicted in the clip is within a few hairs of how millions of evangelical Christians expect the rapture to proceed any day now.

In evangelical theology, the rapture refers to the moment when Jesus comes to earth to transport all true born-again Christians to heaven. It comes from the Greek *raeptius*, meaning "caught up," which is found in the book of 1 Thessalonians (the Apostle Paul talks about being "caught up . . . in the clouds to meet the Lord in the air"). The rapture is just the beginning of an entire apocalyptic chain of events, which, if we're getting technical, is called "pretribulationary dispensational premillennialism," or "pretrib."

Evangelical Christians make all kinds of apocalyptic predictions, but the pretrib flavor is far and away the most popular. A few weeks ago at Thomas Road's Sunday evening services, Dr. Ed Hindson, a professor of biblical studies at Liberty, gave a sermon titled "Seven Future Events That Will Shake the World," in which he gave a fleshed-out version of the pretrib storyboard. According to Hindson's telling, it goes something like this:

First, the rapture. At some point in the not-so-distant future, all the Christians on earth will be taken up to heaven. ("For believers, this will be a joyous occasion," Hindson said. "For unbelievers, it will be a terrible time. You think of what Hurricane Katrina did to New Orleans—imagine what millions of people disappearing in a flash will do to the world.") Then, while the believers are in heaven, the Antichrist will rise to power on earth. ("People have asked who the Antichrist is for centuries. Is it Nero? Hitler? Stalin? I had somebody ask me the other day, 'Is it Hillary?' Sadly, it is not. The Antichrist has to be a man.") After a seven-year period of tribulation on earth, the believers will storm down from heaven with Jesus to fight the battle of Armageddon. After conquering the forces of the Antichrist, Jesus will establish a kingdom on earth for a thousand years. At the end of those thousand years, the believers will be whisked away to heaven again, and the nonbelievers will be cast, with Satan, onto a lake of fire for all eternity.

Pretrib rapture theology is a relatively new phenomenon. Most accounts have it appearing in the late nineteenth century as the brainchild of John Nelson Darby, a minor British theologian. But Darby's end-times scenario didn't become widespread until Tim LaHaye, a pastor and educator from Southern California, decided to write a novel based on his pretrib beliefs. LaHaye collaborated with Christian author Jerry B. Jenkins, and what emerged was *Left Behind*, the first in a series of blockbuster books (65 million sold worldwide) that secured LaHaye's place in fundamentalist history.

Tim LaHaye's relationship with Liberty goes back several decades. LaHaye was one of the first prominent members of the Moral Majority, and Dr. Falwell has pulled both Tim and his wife Beverly (a well-known conservative figure herself) in as members of Liberty's Board of Trustees. Accordingly, Liberty has received a sizeable chunk of Tim's *Left Behind* mammon over the years. Among his donations: the $4.5 million LaHaye Student Center, the LaHaye Ice Center, and the LaHaye Lounge. Aside from Dr. Falwell himself, Tim LaHaye has had arguably the largest impact on Liberty, both financially and theologically, of any one person in the school's history. He funded a short-lived School of Prophecy in 2001, and he visits campus frequently to give sermons to the student body. (Incidentally, his grandson lives down the hall from me.)

All semester, I've been trying hard to figure out exactly how seriously Liberty students take the pretrib apocalyptic beliefs of their elders. While most of them believe it in theory, I've only seen the rapture referred to in an oblique, semi-joking way. A girl in my GNED class has a sticker on the back side of her laptop: "In case of Rapture, you can have my computer!" There's a Facebook group called "I hope the rapture comes before my student loans are due."

So do Liberty students really believe the world is ending? It's not easy to tell. If I truly believed the rapture was "imminent," as Liberty's official doctrinal statement says, I think I'd do things a lot differently. I might not buy green bananas, for starters. I certainly wouldn't tell people "See you next week" without some sort of caveat. But nobody here seems to be taking any precautions.

Last night, I started asking guys on my hall what they thought of the rapture. Patrick, a music major from Kentucky, summed up what seems to be the general feeling: "I mean, I think it's coming, but the Bible says we can't know the day or the hour, so I don't spend too much time thinking about it." He added, "You should talk to Adams about this stuff. He's a rapture nut."

Jon Adams is a 22-year-old senior from Kentucky, with fiery carrot-orange hair and thick patches of freckles. He lives a few doors down from me, and tonight, when I ask him about his apocalyptic beliefs, he brings me into his room and sits me down at his desk. He puts on his reading glasses and plucks his Bible from his desk drawer.

"Okay, here we go," he says, rubbing his palms together. Jon opens his Bible and begins laying out his grand theory. It's a bit complex, and it takes him almost twenty minutes to explain, but I'll try to get it down in short form: There's a verse in the Bible that reads, "With the Lord a day is like a thousand years." There's another verse in which God says, "I make known the end from the beginning." Jon interprets these passages as mathematical clues. If a day is equal to a thousand years, and if the end of the world will echo the beginning, then since God created the world in seven days (including a day of rest), he'll destroy it at the end of seven thousand years (including a thousand-year reign of Christ). "In other words, it's going to be seven thousand years from the beginning of the world to the battle of Armageddon," he says. He pecks out a series of numbers on his calculator. ". . . So, by my count, the rapture will come between 2026 and 2030. We'll be about forty years old."

"I could be wrong," he says. "It's just a theory. But then again, I don't think the Bible wastes space. If all those numbers and verses weren't about the end of the world, what were they about?"

Jon is an intelligent guy, and he's obviously spent a good deal of time studying a part of the Bible many Christians gloss over. But I'm confused: if Christians believe that the rapture could happen any minute, why don't people at Liberty take it more seriously?

"I have no idea!" he says exasperatedly. "Some people think it's ridiculous to study the rapture. But if you believe the Bible, you have to believe this stuff. It's our future."

"Do you think about it a lot?" I ask.

"Well, I try not to get obsessed with it," he says. "For me, it's just how I focus myself. Think about it: I have less than twenty years remaining on earth. I have no time to waste. I should do all the good I need to do right now."

It still dismays me to see such an intelligent guy spending his time hashing out Jesus' return like a quadratic equation. But what he said at the end got to me: "I should do all the good I need to do right now." I'm not sure what Jon means by "good"—he might be talking about converting heathens or overturning Roe v. Wade. But giving him the benefit of the doubt, I can think of worse scenarios than having a million more Jons in the world. Do I believe the rapture is imminent? No. If all the Christians who did believe it was imminent went around doing good deeds with frantic urgency, would I object? Of course not.

Problem is, a lot of Christians who believe the world is headed for imminent destruction don't use their eschatology to motivate altruism. Some, in fact, use their belief in the coming apocalypse to justify negligence and destruction. Critics of pretrib theology point out that rapture obsession can make Christians overlook glaring social needs in the present, like genocide, disease, and abject poverty. Not to mention the famously dangerous political situation posed when American evangelicals believe that Israeli Jews have to control the Temple Mount, currently an Islamic holy site, for the apocalypse to be set in motion.

So I'm hoping that my friends at Liberty are taking some of the benefits of a sense of immediacy without taking the screw-it-all recklessness.

Luckily, at the college level, people's concerns seem to have a more pragmatic tilt. I walked into the bathroom today as two guys in adjacent stalls were having a conversation over the barrier:

"Dude, I hope Christ comes back soon."
"Me too. That would be freakin' awesome."

"I hope he doesn't come for, like, thirty years though."

"Why?"

"So I can have a lot of sex with my wife."

Tuesday morning, I get a call from Tina and Teresa, my aunts in Washington. They've been calling a lot recently, but since there's no way to talk privately with them from Liberty's campus, we haven't connected. This time, though, I happen to be buying some shampoo at Target when the phone buzzes against my thigh.

"Kevin!" they yell in unison. "We're so glad to hear your voice!"

Time has done nothing to ease Tina and Teresa's worries about my semester at Liberty. I've gotten this sense from looking at my e-mail inbox, where by now, they've sent a few dozen articles on Christian-led hate crimes and evangelical anti-gay movements in their home state.

"How's your semester going?" Tina asks. I tell her the truth: my classes are hard, but things overall are good. They seem pleased to hear so, or else they're just feigning support for my sake.

"Ooh!" Tina says. "Let Teresa tell you about her high school groups!"

"Oh, Kevin," Teresa sighs. "It has been such a powerful experience."

For the past few months, Teresa has been leading support groups for LGBTQQ (Lesbian, Gay, Bisexual, Transgendered, Queer, or Questioning) students at four different Washington high schools. She teaches her students about the history of alternative sexualities in America, including the Stonewall riots and the Kinsey Reports, and she facilitates discussions about the pressures of being a LGBTQQ adolescent.

"There are just so many teenagers who are so ostracized and hurt because of their sexuality," she says. "And to be able to help a few of them, to give them self-worth and teach them to accept themselves as they are, it's just unbelievable."

I have a conflicted response to phone calls like these. On one hand, I know Tina and Teresa's message is good for me to hear. Sometimes, I get swept up in my day-to-day bustle, and I forget that Liberty is renowned for being the sort of place that makes Teresa's support groups necessary in the first place.

It's hard to keep harping on Liberty's intolerance, though, because just as my aunts are nothing like the demonized stereotypes of gay people that are tossed around at Liberty (they're both psychologically balanced, with stable jobs, healthy family lives, and a long-term, monogamous relationship), the majority of my friends at Liberty aren't the intolerant demagogues Tina and Teresa picture when they think of Liberty students. In Tina's latest e-mail, she mentioned that she and Teresa had run into a group of fundamentalist Christians at an equality rally in Spokane. She described them as "negative and hateful," and reported that they were toting signs with messages like "You deserve Hell" and "God is angry with the wicked every day."

Maybe I'm deluded, but that just doesn't sound like my hallmates. Most of them believe homosexuality is a sin, yes, but they're not going to picket pride parades on the weekend. You'd never catch Jersey Joey or Zipper with a "You deserve Hell" sign.

Near the end of our conversation, Aunt Tina says, "We support you, Kevin. We just want to make sure you're keeping everything in perspective."

"I'm sure many Liberty students are very intolerant people, no matter how nice they are to you," Teresa adds. "And those kinds of attitudes have caused real harm to the gay community for many years."

Tina and Teresa are right. They are. But for the first time this semester, I sort of wish they weren't.

This week is Spiritual Emphasis Week, a time every semester when Liberty gives a jolt to its religious life by bringing in an outside pastor for a series of special sermons. This semester's guest pastor is James MacDonald, a Christian leader from Illinois who hosts a popular Bible-themed radio show called *Walk in the Word*.

MacDonald is a talented orator, and his sermons (there have been two so far, with three more to come) have been frankly riveting. It doesn't hurt that he's a new face on campus, a break from the preachers we see every week. It also doesn't hurt that the praise band MacDonald brought with him from Illinois has a stunning, bright-eyed brunette as the lead vocalist. Whatever the reason, the Spiritual Emphasis Week services have been packed and passionate, a million watts of spiritual energy as opposed to the usual five hundred thousand.

After tonight's service, a bolt of gossip ripples through my hall.

"Did you hear?" a kid named Jonah tells me. "Paul got saved!"

The announcement confused me. Wasn't Paul already saved? Paul told me when we met that his conversion happened during his sophomore year of high school, when his football coach brought him to church. Isn't that a one-time deal? But now, Jonah is telling me that at tonight's service, Paul went down the aisle to confess his sins.

"I guess he thought he was saved," Jonah says. "But, man, there are a lot of people like that here. People who got saved as a kid, but didn't really mean it."

This has been one of the more puzzling observations of my semester so far. Almost all Liberty students profess a personal relationship with Christ (97.4 percent, according to a survey cited in my GNED class). And yet, at every week's Campus Church service, a few dozen students flood down the aisles to be born again. So where do those students come from?

Well, as I'm learning, in the evangelical world, there's saved and there's "saved," and the difference between the two causes 90 percent of the spiritual anxiety on this campus. I was thinking about this topic even before Paul's news, because yesterday, at the dinner table, my hallmate Rodrigo said he wanted to talk to me about something that was worrying him.

"Roose, do you ever doubt your salvation?" he asked, leaning forward over his tray.

I told him, a bit evasively, that I thought a lot of people did.

"Whew," he said. "I'm so glad you said that. It's been keeping me up at night, man. Just thinking back and forth, worrying about myself. Like, what if I'm out there telling all these people about Jesus, and I don't even accept him myself? There are pastors out there who probably aren't saved. Why am I any different?"

He shook his head and continued: "It's scary, Roose. Think about it: you spend your whole life in peace, thinking you're saved, and then, *bam,* you're perishing for eternity. I can't think of anything scarier."

When I first got here, I assumed Liberty students were all ultra-confident in their faith. How could they not be? They're told a thousand times a week that once you're saved, you're always saved—that, to quote a popular worship song, "no pow'r of hell, no scheme of man" can change a believer's status before God. They lead more disciplined lives than all but a handful of modern evangelicals. Surely that must count for something.

Of all the Liberty students I've met, I wouldn't have pegged Rodrigo as a doubter. He's one of the most spiritually mature guys on the hall, constantly quoting scripture and helping younger students grow in their faith. He's a "Servant of the One True God," according to his Facebook profile.

But that's the secret about a place like Liberty: everyone doubts.

Since the news of Paul's re-rebirth, everyone on the hall has been in a good mood. A half-dozen guys took him out for a celebratory dinner after church, and he's been getting backslaps and attaboys all night. Right now, Paul is retelling the story to a group of rapt guys in the hallway.

"I was sure I was saved when I was sixteen," he says, leaning against the wall. "And then during the service, it finally hit me: I'm not living for God. All this sin in my life, all the selfish things I do—it's all distancing me from the Lord."

"How is this going to change things for you?" his roommate asks.

"In a big way, man. I mean, I felt like, all this time, I was pretending to be a Christian. I was going through the motions, but it was all empty inside."

Paul smiles and holds up his Bible.

"Now I just want to live for God, baby."

Wednesday night after curfew, my roommate Eric and I sit at our desks, quizzing each other for our Old Testament exam.

"Who made Israel sin?" he asks, looking absentmindedly at his game of computer solitaire.

"Rehoboam?"

"No, Jeroboam. Close."

"Okay," I say. "My turn: Abimelech."

"Killed sixty-nine of his half-brothers, became king, son of Gideon, blah, blah, blah."

"Who's Gideon?"

He swings around to face me. "Dude, are you serious?"

Of all the problems I thought I'd have this semester, failing my classes wasn't one of them. But midterms are approaching, and unless I turn things around, it's not out of the question. I haven't flunked anything yet, but getting my test scores from Liberty's online grade repository is usually bad for my self-esteem. For example:

Exodus Quiz: Kevin Roose: 60, Class Average: 74.34
Exam #2: Kevin Roose: 61, Class Average: 77.08

I'd feel differently if I were slacking off this semester, but I work twice as hard at Liberty as I ever did at Brown. I make lists. I design charts. For my Theology exam last week, I drew up a set of flash cards and took them everywhere I went. I'm working overtime to catch up, but when it comes to the subjects of my classes—the Bible, Christian doctrine, creationist science—I may be starting from too far behind.

Tonight is a crunch night, because in addition to Friday's Old Testament exam, I have a New Testament exam tomorrow. Dr. Towns told us to be ready to name all twenty-seven books of the New Testament in order, from Matthew to Revelation. So after putting away my Old Testament notes, I pull out my Bible and spend a solid hour trying to commit the New Testament sequence to memory.

I'm not a good memorizer, and twenty-seven is no small number of items. When for the tenth straight time, I put Hebrews before Philemon and forget Titus entirely, I decide I need help. I walk down the hall to consult Jonah, a pastor's kid and one of Dorm 22's resident Bible whizzes.

"This exam is killing me," I say. "I have to name the books of the New Testament in order."

"Really?" he asks. "That's so easy, dude. Just sing the song."

"Song?"

"Yeah, you know . . ." He clears his throat. "Matthew, Mark, Luke and John, Acts and the-letter-to-the-Roooomans . . ." It's a kid's song with a bouncy melody. He rattles it off in less than ten seconds. ". . . First and Second Corinthians, Galatians and Ephesians. Philippians, Colossians, First and Second Thessalonians, First and Second Timothy, Titus and Phileeeemon . . ." [*Pause for breath*] ". . . Hebrews, James, First and Second Peeeeeter, First and Second and Third John, Jude and Revelaaaation."

When I applaud him at the end, he looks confused.

"I thought everyone knew that song. You've never heard it before?"

"Uh, I have," I stammer. "But it's been a while."

Jonah shrugs. "You can sing the Old Testament, too." And he clears his throat again and begins listing the books of the Old Testament to the tune of "Ten Little Indians."

When I get back to my room, I spend some time looking for other Bible mnemonics on the Internet. There are dozens of them, for every piece of Bible trivia you could imagine. There's a song to remember the names of the apostles, a song listing what God made on each day of Genesis, and a song for the twelve sons of Jacob. There are also songs to help you remember the plots of individual Bible stories. ("There was a girl God used for good, and Rahab was her name-o. R-A-H-A-B . . .")

What a great idea. Why didn't I know about these? When I tell a friend from Brown about the Bible songs, he agrees that it's a stroke of genius and suggests some possible adaptations for secular liberal arts students. ("There was an ex-pat lesbian who broke with novelistic convention and Gertrude was her name-o. S-T-E-I-N . . .")

Still, until I learn the Bible songs, I'm at a huge disadvantage. The next morning, I walk into New Testament having studied for three or four hours. When I sit down to take the test, I find myself blanking on the order of the books. Then, I hear the girl on my right humming. The guy on my left starts up, too. Pretty soon, a faint buzz fills the room. *Mhhew, Mrrhk, Mhhhuke, and Mhhohn . . .*

This morning, I got a call from Laura, my evangelical friend from high school, who wanted to know how my semester was going.

"Not bad," I said. "Not bad at all."

Laura laughed, but I wasn't being sarcastic. I've been at Liberty for more than a month now, and while it hasn't always been the smoothest ride, things could certainly be worse. I'm not doing all that well in my classes, true, but my social life is picking up steam, and I haven't cursed in weeks. In fact, at times, I've managed to convince myself that this semester will be a relatively smooth-sailing experience.

Tonight, I am stripped rather violently of my illusions. I'm in my room after dinner, typing up the day's notes while my roommates work at their desks. Suddenly, Eric swivels his chair around.

"Guys, if you hear about any, you know, *homosexuality* in the dorm, let me know. I don't want anyone to get a crush on me, you know?"

I chuckle. Henry does not. He slams his pen down on his desk and looks first at me, then at Eric.

"Don't even talk like that," he barks. "I hate faggots. If something like that happened to me, I would do something about it. I would snap somebody's neck."

"I mean, it must happen," says Eric, not missing a beat. "They're everywhere. Like, my college friends who went to Christian schools, they talk about how guys have . . . tendencies. Like, this one friend saw a guy wearing a Speedo out on the beach . . ."

"I don't want to hear any more," says Henry. "I'm telling you, if a queer touched me, I would do what Samson did to the Philistines. Or what David did to Goliath. I would beat him with a baseball bat."

Eric winces. "Wouldn't it be terrible to be a gay guy's roommate and not know it? Ugh. I'd have to go into therapy after that."

He looks at me for a sympathetic response, but I can't do it. I sit there, trying not to gape, feeling my breath shorten and my toes curl inside my shoes. Unsure how to respond, I stand up and leave the room, mumbling something about being late to a meeting. I walk briskly out of the dorm and into the parking lot, where I sit on a curb, breathing hard, trying to keep it together.

What's sad is that this isn't even the first time this week I've been stunned by overt homophobia in Dorm 22. On Monday, during a conversation with Zipper, my ecstatically happy next-door neighbor, he told me that he respected Dr. Falwell for standing up for the biblical view that "while legally, we cannot throw homosexuals in jail, we shouldn't tolerate them." On instinct, I asked if in an ideal society, homosexuals would be thrown in jail.

"Hmm . . . Well, I do believe in the Old Testament," he said. "And in the Old Testament, they were supposed to be killed. And, I mean, we obviously don't have the same type of system that the Israelites had. But if you look at how God initiated judgment on these people, well, in the ideal society, which is Christ's society, they would be eliminated from the earth."

That time, I managed to shake it off. Zipper doesn't have a malicious bone in his body, and it's possible that he's just too socially insulated to realize the real-world effects of his views. But twice in one week is too much for me. I walk around campus all night trying to decompress.

More than anything, I'm mad at myself. I've been so eager to make my time at Liberty tolerable that I've been sweeping all kinds of dirt under the rug. Homophobia? Nah, they're just a little behind the times. Using religion to justify violence? Nope, not since the Crusades. But tonight, sitting there at my desk as my roommates reenacted *The Laramie Project*, I realized how naïve I was. My aunt Tina was right: this stuff does exist, and it does hurt people, and although there are lots of people at Liberty who condemn violence against gays—including Dr. Falwell himself—the number of students who want to give them the Goliath treatment isn't zero. In fact, the number who live in my room isn't zero.

All semester, I've struggled to balance the dominant personality traits of the Liberty students I've met. On one hand, there are scads of compassionate, gentle-spirited people to be found here—the kind you wouldn't think twice about hiring as a babysitter or a camp counselor. On the other hand, these same people can turn around and floor me with their socio-political views.

Here's what worries me the most: I came to Liberty to humanize people. Because humanizing people is good, right? But what about people with reprehensible views? Do they deserve to be humanized? By giving Jerry Falwell's moral universe a fair look, am I putting myself in his shoes? Or am I really just validating his worldview? What's the difference between what I'm doing and certain Iranian presidents who want to "do more research" into the Holocaust? Where's the limit to open-mindedness?

I ask myself these questions and more for hours, and when I calm down, I reach this conclusion: humanizing is not the same as sympathizing. You can peel a stereotype off a person and not see a beautiful human being underneath. In fact, humanity can be very ugly.

In my case, I don't know if I can act toward Eric and Henry as if I agree with what went down tonight. And now, for the first time all semester, I'm worried about what happens if they find out who I am. I've been assuming that it would just be a matter of awkwardness, but maybe I should be afraid for my safety.

Two days later, I'm still in a funk about my roommates' gay-bashing. I can't pay attention in my classes. Whatever spiritual momentum I built up over the past few weeks has gone down the drain. I haven't been able to look Henry or Eric in the eye. I feel like I did during orientation week—anxious, out of place, aloof.

To cheer myself up, I call Anna, the girl from Bible study. Anna and I have gone out four or five times since our first date, and we've become a semiofficial item. We haven't had the conversation that, in Christian circles, is called the DTR, for "Defining the Relationship," but it's pretty clear where we stand. We've stuck mainly to the half-dozen coffee shops in the greater Lynchburg area, and we haven't so much as held hands, but we do spend a fair amount of time flirting. Last time we were out, when I spilled coffee all over the table, she laughed and called me a retard, then corrected herself. "I mean, a cute retard."

This week, I've started to get myself into trouble with Anna. Here's the problem: I really like her. I can't help it. She's bright and witty, a rare practitioner of the kind of humor that's used not to hide personal insecurities but to bring joy to the people around her. She has this other side, too—the deeply spiritual, insatiably curious side—and when she gets into that mood, her eyes fill with a childlike wonder that makes me wish I saw the world the way she does. She's the kind of girl who zones out during your conversation at Starbucks and interrupts you five minutes later, during one of your funniest and best-rehearsed stories, to say, with a huge smile on her face, "You know, I really like the shape of the lights here."

Anna's not a rebel, but she's not ultra-pious either, and when I'm around her, it feels natural to let my guard down. So tonight, when we're sitting in the Drowsy Poet Café drinking milk shakes and she asks me what I plan to do after college, I tell her reflexively that I want to be a writer.

"What kind of writer?" she asks. "Like a journalist?"

"Yeah."

I wasn't supposed to tell Anna anything about writing, of course. I was supposed to say that I wasn't sure what I wanted to do, or that I was studying religion with an eye toward grad school. That's what I've been telling everyone else. But I was so comfortable, it just slipped out.

"You know," she says, "when we first went out, I thought you were writing a story about me."

My eyes widen, and a string of unbiblical language rockets through my brain. Jesus. Am I really this transparent?

"Why . . . did you think that?" I ask.

"You asked all these weird questions! How were my parents' rules growing up? How did it feel to go from a small Christian high school to a huge Christian university? I was like, is he recording this?"

Eventually, I manage to laugh it off and veer into another topic, but Anna's words haunt me all night. I drop her off at her dorm, park my car in the lot in front of Dorm 22, and head back inside. On the way across the parking lot, my heart sinks, my head drops, my steps get slow and heavy, and I feel my eyes start to tear up.

When I came to Liberty, I thought my biggest moral quandaries were going to revolve around people who rubbed me the wrong way. I never expected to find Liberty students I liked *too* much. But I'm starting to care about some of the people I've met here, and it's taking a toll on my conscience. Hiding a huge part of my life from my roommate Henry is no skin off my back, but with my favorite Liberty students—Anna, Paul, Jersey Joey—I'm finding it hard to keep secrets.

Graham Greene, the great Catholic novelist, talked about a "sliver of ice" that sits in every writer's heart, allowing him to stay emotionally detached from the subjects of his work. And maybe it means I shouldn't have taken up this project in the first place, but I don't know if I can find that ice. Every time I go out with Anna, I ask myself: Do I really want to get closer to her? Isn't that just going to make things worse when I leave? Last night, when I sat down to write a few paragraphs about Jersey Joey, I heard him in my head, saying to me at the end of all this, "Rooster, you were lying to us?"

The idea that undergirds my whole semester at Liberty has always been the possibility that I could belong to two worlds at once. But tonight, I don't feel like I belong to either. I can't be completely open with the people I meet here, no matter how well we get along. And the next time I call home, I certainly can't tell my parents that I'm falling for an evangelical girl. Each world is getting a partial story.

Later tonight, Anna calls me, presumably to set up another coffee date. But I can't bring myself to pick up. I let it ring until it goes to voicemail, and then I climb into my bed, pull the sheets up to my neck, and stare at two leftover dots of sticky tack on my ceiling for an hour and a half until, finally, I fall asleep.

Troubled on Every Side, Yet Not Distressed

It's the beginning of March, and Liberty University is at war.

The enemy is a Philadelphia-based group of atheists called the Rational Response Squad. A few months ago, the RRS issued a rallying cry to young secular humanists around the world: videotape yourself denying the existence of God, and post the video on YouTube. They called this the Blasphemy Challenge. The first 1,001 people who answered the challenge, they said, would receive a free DVD of an atheist documentary, and the rest would get the satisfaction of having spoken out against the tyranny of theism. It proved a tempting offer. Over eight hundred atheists, many of them college age or younger, have uploaded their antitestimonies so far. The Rational Response Squad's mass blasphemy efforts have captured the attention of the mainstream press, the nation's religious leaders, and most recently, the student body here at Liberty.

This isn't the first time organized atheism has punctured the Liberty bubble. Last fall, the Oxford biologist Richard Dawkins, author of *The God Delusion* and agitator in chief of the New Atheism movement, lambasted Liberty's science program on C-SPAN for teaching young-earth creationism, calling it "an educational disgrace" and urging Liberty students to "leave and go to a proper university."

That was bad enough, but now, the Blasphemy Challenge is taking the anti-God struggle to the grassroots. All over Liberty's campus, ideological panic is breaking out. Facebook groups are popping up: "Christians Against the Blasphemy Challenge," "Challenge Blasphemy," "The Holy Spirit is using my soul, therefore I cannot take the Challenge." Students are asking each other, *What do we do? How do we respond?*

Enter Dr. Ergun Caner. Dr. Caner, one of Liberty's star preacher-professors, is a thirty-nine-year-old Turkish man with the barrel-chested frame, shaved head, and long pointed goatee of a professional wrestler. He preaches at the Wednesday night Campus Church services, and his edgy, humor-laden sermons have made him a beloved campus figure. Earlier this semester, some of Dr. Caner's students began e-mailing him articles about the Blasphemy Challenge. When he investigated, he became concerned—not because atheists were coming out of the woodwork, but because Liberty students were responding to those atheists in the worst possible way: by posting emotional counterarguments on YouTube and shouting down nonbelievers on Internet message boards.

At last Wednesday night's Campus Church, Dr. Caner explained his frustration with Christian reactionaries.

"We're not doing any good by just saying *that* we believe," he said. "We need to explain *why* we believe! Why we can prove God existed, that Jesus Christ was a real man and the son of God, why he died and was resurrected. We can prove all of this, but we're not doing it."

Dr. Caner took matters into his own hands, challenging the Rational Response Squad's top apologists to a debate about the existence of God. Proving Christianity's truth claims is the best way to subdue the spread of atheism, he said, not yelling and arguing.

"A guy a long time ago named Kierkegaard said that we just can't know about things of faith, we have to take a leap. But Christianity is not a leap. According to the Bible, our faith is hooked to the rational coherence and the veracity of the one named Jesus, who was who he said he was, did what he said he did, lived a virgin-born, sinless life with miraculous works, had a literal, vicarious death, a literal burial, and a literal, bodily, visceral resurrection.

"You, who are believers in Jesus Christ, do you want to know what the secular world believes about you? They think what you believe is great! But you can't prove it! When the secular mind doesn't believe you, it's because they've made a gap between faith and knowledge, faith and reason, faith and logic. And it is a gap that we're about to bridge."

Word came back quickly from the Rational Response Squad—they accepted Dr. Caner's challenge. Next week, Dr. Caner will debate three members of the squad on their weekly radio show. Immediately after the announcement, I got a barrage of mass e-mails like this one: "We're gathering together outside of the bookstore to pray for Dr. Caner's success in the atheist debate. Please join us!"

Tonight, a group of my hallmates are discussing the debate over dinner.

"This is so exciting, man," says Marco. "Think about it. What other school would challenge a bunch of atheists?"

"I don't know," says Luke, a tall, good-looking biology major who lives down the hall. "Do you think we need to be out there proving Christianity?"

"Why not?" Marco asks. "You heard what Caner said. It's about loving God with your mind."

"Yeah, but people don't come to faith in Christ because of logic. They come because they have an open heart. To me, debating atheists kind of feels fruitless. Like, if their hearts are that hardened, it might take more than rational proof to convince them."

I don't really know what to think about the atheism debate. On one level, I guess it will be exciting to watch an explosive Christian apologist go mano a mano with a group of mockers and scorners. But I'm skeptical about Dr. Caner's ability to win this one, mostly because, well, isn't this sort of an old battle? In Theology class, we've been reading about theologians going all the way back to Thomas Aquinas who have agreed with Kierkegaard in saying that while logic can get you most of the way to faith in God, it can't cross the bridge completely. Charles Spurgeon, the legendary nineteenth-century Prince of Preachers and a man whose work Dr. Caner quotes regularly, warned Christians against "perpetually demanding arguments and logical demonstrations" for their faith. Even C. S. Lewis separated faith into two steps, Faith A and Faith B— Faith A being a general intellectual assent to the existence of a higher being and Faith B being an orthodox belief in the specific God of the Bible. Faith A, Lewis said, can be proven logically, but Faith B requires a leap.

All this is to say: I'm not sure Dr. Caner has much help from history. But who knows? Maybe trying to prove the Christian faith isn't an intellectual suicide mission.

A few hours after dinner, I sit down with Marco in his room. He's eating a bowl of Easy Mac while browsing rationalresponders.com, looking through some of the squad's articles, with titles like "The Irrationality of Theism" and "God: The Failed Hypothesis."

"I think this is the weakest part of my Christianity," he says, looking up at me with a spoonful of orange sludge in hand. "I honestly wouldn't know how to respond to an atheist with anything rational. But I really like the fact that Caner is debating them."

His eyes wander back down to the screen.

"I'm just glad it's not me in there," he says. "That's all I can say."

Later that night, I head to room 201 to hang out with Jersey Joey and his gang of rebels. Three of them—Travis, Alex, and Joey—are huddled around Joey's laptop, browsing the Facebook photos of the girls they know.

"Ooh, Sandra has a booty," says Alex. "Look at it! You could use that thing as a table!"

"Yeah, but she's got no boobs," says Travis.

"True," says Joey. "She's on the itty-bitty titty committee."

They click through a dozen-odd photos, subjecting each of the girls to a brutally honest critique:

"Emily has a fish face. She looks like a grouper."

"Leslie is so pretty it's not even funny. That's wifey material right there."

"Ooh, she looks like Sofia Coppola, but sort of retarded."

"This girl's got a pretty nice rack."

I've been spending a lot of time in room 201 this week, and I'm finding that it's a great place to be. For one, when I'm hanging out with Joey and his friends, I can jettison my ultra-pious Christian persona. I don't have to pepper my conversations with phrases like "Lord willing" or "Praise be to God." I can let loose with a "damn" or a "hell" once in a while, and no one blinks. In fact, a bit of cursing is probably good for my rebel image.

But the bigger reason for spending time in room 201 is that by hanging out with Dorm 22's outliers, I'm seeing sides of Liberty I never would have seen otherwise.

For example, I've learned that Jersey Joey is a Democrat. Over the past few weeks, Joey and I have had some long, involved discussions—mostly late at night, mostly while playing video games—and in these talks, he's told me that his mom and dad, a nurse and a union electrician respectively, raised him as a political moderate. They're churchgoing Christians, and Joey went to a small Christian academy for high school, but he never bought into the extreme right-wing politics. Joey's time at Liberty has made him slightly more conservative—he's now convinced that abortion is wrong—but he refers to *The 700 Club*'s Pat Robertson as a "first-class nut job," and although he's still a virgin, he doesn't think premarital sex is necessarily sinful. He's also lukewarm on Dr. Falwell—"I mean, I can appreciate what the guy has done," he says, "but I don't agree with most of the things he says."

Joey's ideological rebellion surprised me, but not nearly as much as what I learned about his roommate Travis, a lumberjack-looking guy with freckles and red hair who hails from nearby Manassas. Namely, Travis isn't even an evangelical Christian.

I first learned this on Tuesday, when Joey offhandedly mentioned that his prayer group had spent ten minutes praying for Travis.

"Why?" I asked. "Is something wrong with him?"

Joey looked at me in astonishment. "You don't know about Travis?"

"No," I said. "What happened?"

"He's not saved."

"What?"

"Yeah, dude. Travis is unsaved. I can't believe you didn't know."

Joey proceeded to tell me that there are several tiny pockets of non-Christians at Liberty (and by "non-Christians," of course, he means "non-evangelicals"). One is composed of varsity athletes who came to Liberty on sports scholarships, either not realizing or not caring that Liberty was an evangelical school. Another is a group of international students, predominantly Buddhists from Asia, whose parents wanted them in a school with conservative social rules and were willing to ignore the religious discrepancy. Then there are people who came to Liberty because it was a decent, affordable school close to home. Travis originally came to Liberty for reasons one and three—he wanted to play football, and he lives an hour or so from campus. He got cut from the team during his freshman year, but he decided to stay at Liberty, even though his beliefs didn't match up with the school's doctrinal statement.

Later that night, when Travis walked into his room, I asked him about his lack of faith.

"I didn't know you weren't a Christian," I said.

Travis smiled. "Most people don't figure it out for a while. If you're a Liberty student, people just sort of assume you are."

He explained that although he believes in God, he hasn't felt the need to accept Christ as his savior, in part because his rebel friends, who are all Christians, don't act any differently because of their faith. "If I become a Christian, I'm going to change," he says. "I'm going to stop cursing, stop drinking on the weekends, stop looking at girls the way I do. And I'm not ready for that yet. Maybe somewhere down the road, but not now."

When I ask Travis if he ever gets harassed for being a non-evangelical, he said, "When I first got here, it would come up, and people would be like, 'Oh my gosh!' It was a big deal. But now that I've been here, and people know me, I think they just feel bad. They always try to get me to accept Jesus, and when I don't, they feel like they've failed."

Surprisingly, even though Travis doesn't consider himself a believer, he likes being a Liberty student. In fact, that's the amazing thing about the entire room 201 gang: they love Liberty. None of them were forced to come by their parents, and none are itching to leave. They all chose Liberty over less-strict schools, in part because of the structure it gives them.

"Other than the curfew and the rules about girls, Liberty is perfect for me," said Joey. "It's nice and stable, and you don't have to worry about anything."

Even Marco, who almost left Liberty after his first semester, was enticed to stay. "Once you leave," he said, "you get a little bit of freedom, and then you realize that you want to come back. You want that focus."

Another interesting thing about Joey and his friends is that they seem to have a sort of rebel radar—that is, they're good at sniffing out other Liberty students who don't quite fit the mainstream. I think this is why they've let me hang out with them. When I'm in Room 201, I act like the old-model Kevin, and even though I haven't told them everything about my past, I think they sense that something is different about me, that I'm somehow struggling with Liberty's orthodoxy.

Tonight, before we go to bed, Joey turns to me.

"Rooster, leave the room for a minute."

"Why?"

"Just leave the room. We need to talk about something."

What's going on? Did I do something wrong? Am I being exiled?

I walk outside and close the door, pressing my ear against the keyhole to hear what's going on inside. From behind the door comes quiet, mischievous giggling. Then, Joey yells, "Okay, come in!"

Slowly, warily, I open the door.

"Rooooooose!" They're all screaming my name, and they rush over to me. Joey grabs my arm, drags me over to his bed, and wrestles me down. I try to resist, but it's no use. When my shoulders are pinned to the ground, I open my eyes and see three guys staring at me, smiling nefariously.

"Rooster, welcome to room 201," says Joey. "We're making you an official member."

"Yeah," says Alex. "But first, you gotta get dry humped."

And so, for the next thirty seconds, the rebels of Dorm 22 give me a dry-humping initiation, their version of a peace pipe. They're really thrusting, frankly, and it would be sort of painful if everyone weren't laughing so hard. When they've had enough, they roll off of me, wiping the tears from their eyes.

"You're cool with us, Rooster," says Joey. "Ya big queer."

*   *   *

A few minutes after curfew on Thursday night, Paul Maddox storms into my room.

"Man, this pisses me off. He can't go two days without saying something."

"Who?" I ask.

"Malone."

"What'd he say this time?"

"Some crap about my girlfriend."

The past few weeks have been filled with ups and downs for Paul. First came Spiritual Emphasis Week, when he got saved. That kept him on cloud nine until the following week, when he attended football tryouts and narrowly missed making the squad. He spent three or four days moping around the hall, talking about how badly he'd been robbed. Then, forty-eight hours later, during Liberty's prefrosh recruitment weekend, a seventeen-year-old high school senior named Lauren approached Paul to ask him for directions to the student center. He walked her there, they spent the rest of the day together, and by the end of the weekend, they had fallen in love. Lauren lives in Florida, but they decided to try a long-distance relationship until she arrives at Liberty in the fall.

Now, there's another problem. A few days ago, Ryan Malone, one of our hallmates, began criticizing Paul's new relationship. The issue, he said, is that Lauren is white, and Paul is black, and Ryan is . . . well, how can I put this? Here, I'll let him introduce himself.

"My name is Ryan, and I am a good ol' boy," he told me over our first handshake. "I try to make that very plain. No use hidin' what you are."

Ryan, a born and bred Georgian, comes from the Larry the Cable Guy school of southern heritage. Which is to say, he embraces all of the sub-Mason-Dixon stereotypes unabashedly—wears red flannel shirts, has the *Dukes of Hazzard* theme song as his cell phone ring tone, and intones things in his sleepy southern drawl like, "Wee-oo, now that lil' lady right there has a big ol' hitch in her giddy-up." He has thick silver braces, which, combined with his accent, make him nearly unintelligible. For the first week of school, I honestly thought his name was Ron.

I liked Ryan/Ron when I met him—he's a charming guy, and he calls me Yankee Doodle on account of my northern heritage. But last week, when we drove off campus for lunch, I got my first glimpse of a less charming part of his personality. On the way to the restaurant, we passed a black man and a white woman holding hands, waiting to cross the street.

"Did you ever notice that when you see a couple . . . like that . . . it's always a black guy and a white girl?" he asked.

"What do you mean?" I asked.

"You know, a couple *like that*."

"An interracial couple?"

"Yeah. I don't like to see that in public."

He tapped the steering wheel. "You know, that's how wrestling started—bunch of colored guys fighting each other over white girls."

I looked at him for a facial read, expecting to find him smiling. But no, he was drumming away on the steering wheel, whistling along nonchalantly to Huey Lewis.

"So . . . hold on," I asked. "You really don't like to see interracial couples?"

"Not if I can help it."

Ryan looked over, saw my face, and continued: "You have to admit, dude, there are differences between blacks and whites. I don't care if you think it's stereotyping. It exists. They're normally raised in a . . . poor lifestyle, I guess. It's not *because* their skin is black, but it happens that way."

Without prompting, he added, "They think we owe them something—reparations or whatever. I don't regret slavery, because if it weren't for slavery, this country wouldn't be what it is today."

When I was preparing to come to Liberty this semester, I got a lot of questions from my friends and family about the school's racial heritage. The link between right-wing Christianity and the African American community has been historically tense, and people wanted to know: Are there black people at Liberty? Don't they have a ban on interracial dating?

I hoped to send back a happy report. After all, Liberty's website and brochures feature lots of photographs of contented-looking students of all races. I read that Liberty's racial breakdown (roughly: 80 percent white, 10 percent black, 10 percent other) is fairly average among American universities. There are at least a dozen nonwhite guys on my hall, and I hadn't noticed any signs that they were being treated differently than anyone else. But given the amount of buzz surrounding Paul's new girlfriend, I can't dodge the issue.

Earlier this week, after one of Paul's friends told him that Ryan objected to his new relationship, Paul decided to take him to task. What followed was an hour-long shouting match involving, at some points, more than a dozen people. I got to Ryan's room just in time to catch the tail end.

"I am not a racist!" said Ryan.

"Hold on," said Paul, his eyebrows at full mast. "You wouldn't let your daughters date black guys, but you're not a racist?"

"It's just too big a difference," said Ryan. "It's just the way I've been raised. You want to be bringing home a certain kind of people to your family."

"What do you mean 'a certain kind of people?'" asked Marco, a friend of Paul's.

"He means white people!" Paul said.

"Leave Ryan alone, man," added Judd, a stocky, linebacker-looking guy from Virginia. "You guys just don't understand what it's like."

I should say, first, that Dorm 22 is not at all evenly split on the issue of interracial dating. Only two or three guys, Judd included, have come to Ryan's defense. The night after the Paul/Ryan standoff, Stubbs the RA addressed the conflict at the weekly hall meeting.

"Guys, I understand there have been some comments about race on the hall. As a friend, and also as your brother, I'm asking you all to guard your speech so it will be pleasing to each other, as the Bible says. But also as your RA, I'll remind you that any racially insensitive comments are punishable with eighteen reprimands and a $250 fine."

It was heartening to hear nearly everyone on my hall condemning Ryan for his harsh words and good to learn that Liberty has a rule on its books about racial harassment. But tonight, out of curiosity, I started to do some research on Liberty's institutional past with respect to race. What I found was illuminating.

Liberty's racial past, it turns out, is somewhat murky. When Dr. Falwell was planning his Christian school in the early 1970s, one of his primary models was Bob Jones University. Bob Jones, of course, is the fundamentalist college in Greenville, South Carolina that became nationally known for its ban on interracial dating, which remained in place until the year 2000. There's no evidence that Liberty has ever banned interracial dating, but some have suggested that Liberty and its feeder school, the K-12 Lynchburg Christian Academy (now Liberty Christian Academy), were founded as all-white schools in response to mandatory integration. Dr. Falwell denies any link, but Lynchburg Christian Academy was founded along with a wave of "seg academics" that swept the South in the aftermath of the Supreme Court's decision in *Brown v. Board of Education*, and in 1966, the *Lynchburg News* called Lynchburg Christian Academy "a private school for white students."

Dr. Falwell's personal history is considerably less murky. In the early years of his preaching career, he was an outspoken segregationist. He lobbied against the Civil Rights Act (which he called the "Civil Wrongs Act"), and in 1958, he denounced the Supreme Court's decision in *Brown v. Board of Education,* saying, "When God has drawn the line of distinction, we should not attempt to cross that line." In the irony-in-hindsight department, Dr. Falwell also chided Martin Luther King, Jr. in 1965 for getting involved in public advocacy, saying "preachers are not called to be politicians but soul-winners."

Today, Dr. Falwell has publicly repented for his racism, and racist attitudes at Liberty are only present by vague association, like the fact that the School of Government is named for Jesse Helms, the late Republican senator from North Carolina who famously launched a Senate filibuster against making Martin Luther King, Jr.'s birthday a national holiday. Largely as a result of minority recruitment efforts Dr. Falwell began after his race conversion, both Liberty Christian Academy and Liberty University now have sizeable minority enrollments, and the GNED curriculum includes a lesson on using the Bible to combat racism.

Still, after seeing racial tension firsthand on my hall, I've realized that despite making some progress over the past thirty years, Liberty hasn't completely healed the divisions in its past. Tonight, I stop by Paul's room after dinner to check on him. He's sitting on his bed with Marco, looking noticeably down in the mouth.

"Roose, you seem pretty cool," he says when I walk in. "Can I tell you guys something? Since I've been here, I can't stop worrying about what people think of me because I'm black. I walk around campus all nervous—it's all I think about. Girls put their heads down when they pass me. And my football coach in high school told me to say hi and smile at everyone. So I try. But it's hard, man."

It's probably good that I've been forced to talk about Liberty's racial culture, because it will allow me to bring up something I've been considering a lot lately, sort of a caveat for my entire semester. Namely, it's becoming clear that I'm in the best possible position to enjoy Liberty. As a white, Protestant, heterosexual male, it's relatively easy for me to come here and find things to like about it. If even one of my demographic categories were changed, I'd be having a much different time, potentially filled with much more hostility and much less desire for reconciliation. If I were black, I'd be facing some of the same issues as Paul. If I were a woman, I'd be seeing a much different side of Liberty's gender dynamics. And if I were a Muslim or a gay man, there's no way I'd be here at all. I have to keep that in mind.

After a few seconds of silence, Paul shakes his head, and puts his head in his hands.

"Man, I just thought everything would be better here," he says. "We're all Christians, yeah, but I guess that's not everything."

During a break in my Wednesday classes, I pick up *Left Behind*, the famous apocalyptic novel written by Liberty benefactor Tim LaHaye and his cowriter Jerry B. Jenkins. *Left Behind* has been sitting on my shelf the entire semester, but it took the conversations with my hallmates about the rapture to convince me I needed to read it.

The first thing I noticed about *Left Behind* is that one of its protagonists, a guy named Buck Williams, bears a slight resemblance to me.

Buck is a young reporter who works for a secular publication called the *Global Weekly* and who is unfailingly described as an Ivy League gradu- ate. Buck believes in God, but not in Jesus—he isn't "prepared to go that far"—and after the rapture takes place, he decides to investigate the mass disappearance. He spends time with people who were left behind in the rapture, but who converted to Christianity shortly there- after, and the more time Buck spends with them, the more he begins to believe in it himself.

I don't know if Buck undergoes a religious conversion—I haven't gotten that far yet—but from the way the narrator is describing his inner thoughts, it's looking pretty likely. Consider this passage: "[Buck] was Ivy League educated. . . . He had built his life around achieve- ment, excitement, and—he couldn't deny it—attention. . . . And yet there was a certain loneliness in his existence."

Seeing *Left Behind*'s secular reporter character struggling with Chris- tianity, and with Paul's conversion still on my mind, I couldn't help but compare his fate to mine. And when I did, I realized that unlike the two of them, I don't think I'm drawing near to a conversion experience.

It's not that I'm not finding things to like about Liberty's religious life. I am. As I said, I'm already feeling my views challenged and aug- mented by the people around me. I love the way my hallmates pray for each other. I love hearing my next-door neighbor Zipper talk about his prayer walks. I love singing in the Thomas Road choir on Sundays. But I haven't had any serious conversion thoughts yet.

One problem, I guess, is that I haven't been convinced that Liberty's way is the only way. In my Theology class, we're learning about all the historical movements that preceded and shaped modern-day Christian- ity, and I can't help believing that Liberty's conservative evangelical- ism is just one of many possible outcomes of a centuries-long process of religious evolution. If Jonathan Edwards had decided to become a blacksmith or a pastry chef instead of leading the Great Awakening, would evangelical Christianity still have become America's dominant religion? I have a hard time thinking so. When you take the histori- cal view, it seems just as likely that Quakerism would have taken over the country's religious landscape, and instead of Thomas Road Baptist

Church, we'd have Quaker megameetings with TV cameras showing twenty thousand people worshipping in silence.

Speaking of Quakers, there's also the problem of my family. I'm still hesitant to accept too much of Liberty's spiritual outlook because I worry what they'd think of me. It was bad enough when I joked about Jerry Falwell being a moderate. How would they react if I said that I had gotten saved at Thomas Road Baptist Church?

And yes, I know that Jesus said, "I have come to turn a man against his father, a daughter against her mother" (Matthew 10:35). I know Jesus also said that a true disciple must "hate his father and mother" (Luke 14:26). But those are incredibly hard verses to put into practice. I hope Jesus would understand my dilemma.

Thursday afternoon, I'm having lunch in the dining hall when a girl from the sister dorm comes to sit next to me.

"So," she says, prodding me with her elbow. "I hear you're talking to my friend Anna."

In the secular world, the relationship phase between casual friendship and full-on dating was called "hooking up," but in the no-touch evangelical world, I guess you "talk" instead.

"When are you going to ask her out?" the girl asks.

This week, I've spent about 80 percent of my mental energy trying to figure out what to do about Anna. After our date last week, I briefly considered telling her everything about myself, including the fact that I was a writer. Then I realized how badly that could go. Asking her to keep my secrets safe wouldn't be fair to her, and if she told her friends, it would be a matter of time before everyone on campus knew. So without that option, I had to make a choice: to date or not to date? I flipped coins. I prayed. I asked friends at Brown for advice, but they mostly seem interested in how far I've gotten with the virginal evangelical girl. (They send notes like, "I hope you go all the way, aka hair tussling.")

The situation with Anna points to the biggest ethical dilemma of my semester. Namely, if I were a normal Liberty student, I would have no qualms about making friends, dating girls, and following all my social impulses. But I'm not a normal Liberty student, and as I'm learning,

I'm not immune to guilt. At some point, these relationships begin to get a little too close for comfort, and I feel compelled to pull back, distance myself, lessen the eventual blow.

It kills me, but in Anna's case, I think I have to stop seeing her. She's too savvy, too likely to realize that I'm being cagey. Plus, I don't want to hurt her when she finds out that I'm not an evangelical. Going on a few dates is one thing. Getting romantically attached is another.

So tonight, I call her.

"Starbucks tomorrow?" she asks.

"I can't," I say. "Sorry."

"All right then. The day after?"

"Not then, either," I say. "Actually, my whole week is sort of crazy."

The line goes silent. Ugh. This is awful. I'm holding the phone a few inches from my ear, cringing as I form my words.

"Oh . . . okay," she says.

"I'm really sorry, Anna."

"It's okay. Just let me know when you want to hang out."

"I will," I say. "I definitely will."

I hang up the phone, stand up, make a loop around the perimeter of my room, and sit back down at my desk. I start in on my Theology homework, but it's no use. I'm too distracted. Every bone in my body wants to pick up my phone, redial Anna's number, and tell her that I'm horribly attracted to her, that I would date her in a second if it weren't for this project. But instead, I sit at my desk, chewing on my pen, thinking: *sliver of ice, sliver of ice, sliver of ice.*

This is a big week at the Thomas Road Baptist Church. Earlier in the week, as he sometimes does in the days leading up to landmark events, Dr. Falwell sent an e-mail to his Falwell Confidential listserv.

"This Sunday," he wrote, "I will preach a very unusual sermon. My topic: global warming."

I've been attending services at Thomas Road for about a month now, and most of the time I'm there, I forget that it's such a controversial place. A lot of what goes on inside the walls is pretty standard fare—Vacation Bible Schools, yard sales, church dinners. Even the sermons are relatively benign, with titles like "Fire on the Mountain and Fire in the Heart" and "Continuing to Climb the Ladder." In fact, for a while, I wondered whether Dr. Falwell had mellowed with age.

Given this week's sermon preview, it doesn't seem likely. In another e-mail, he promised to "reveal why Al Gore and others are promoting the 'earthism' movement and why this clandestine effort will eventually do great damage to America, unless it is unveiled, opposed and stopped." (Side note: I'm not sure how a movement that has been the subject of everything from Thomas Friedman books to entire issues of *Vanity Fair* qualifies as "clandestine," but it's a nice touch.)

On an average Sunday, three or four thousand parishioners turn out for Thomas Road's eleven o'clock service, but the promise of an anti-environmental tirade has attracted a standing-room-only crowd nearly twice that size. Folding chairs are being set up in the aisles, and the ushers have run out of church bulletins. After we sing some worship songs—"How Great Is Our God" and "How Great Thou Art"—Dr. Falwell walks to the pulpit, smiling as he surveys the crowd.

"The myth of global warming," he says. "That statement alone will provoke five hundred letters to the editor by the tree huggers and the liberals and anyone who gets upset at any challenge to the alarmism and the hysteria that's going on. There's a claim out there that man-made global warming will bring an end to spring and summer and fall and winter, and the sea will rise to horrific levels, and the heat will melt Antarctica, and the North Pole will melt, and we will find ourselves in a global tsunami, unless the United States—no one else, of course!—does something about it. The fact is, it's all phony baloney!"

The old man who sits next to me in choir wrings his hands, waiting for the fireworks to begin.

"The promoters of this alarmism are to be expected," says Dr. Falwell. "The United Nations—no friend of the U.S.—liberal politicians, radical environmentalists, and of course, liberal clergy, Hollywood, and pseudoscientists." He points us to Thomas Road's website, where we can download "A Skeptic's Guide to Debunking Global Warming Alarmism," the production of a small group of religious scientists and conservative politicians who call themselves the Interfaith Stewardship

Alliance. "To rebut those other green—and maybe *red*—scientists," he says, "a group of evangelicals is seeking an *effective* and *sensible* approach using *established* norms of economics and science."

He continued like this for half an hour, attacking "global warming alarmists" like the Weather Channel—whose crime, in Dr. Falwell's eyes, was airing a series on climate change called *The Climate Code*. He fired off on the Kyoto Protocol ("abominable"), the European Union ("would love to see America deflated to a second-rate power") and the political left ("wants to change the subject concerning the world's moral bankruptcy"), and linked the roots of the environmental movement to the Devil himself, saying, "This is Satan's attempt to redirect the church's primary focus." He quoted exactly two Bible passages in support of his position: Psalm 24:1 and Genesis 8:22 (KJV), which ostensibly prove that "the earth is the Lord's" and that normal weather patterns will continue "while the earth remaineth."

"Now, how long will the earth remain?" he asked. "It will remain until the new heavens and the new earth come. And that won't happen until, well, over in the last two chapters of the Bible—after the tribulation, after the thousand-year reign of Christ, then the new heavens and new earth. Why? Because the former things are passed away. The earth will go up in dissolution from severe heat. The environmentalists will be really shook up then, because God is going to blow it all away."

You've got to hand it to Dr. Falwell. After fifty years of attack preaching, the man knows how to craft a rant, and today he was in fine form. Not only did he manage to go after environmentalists, communists, Hollywood liberals, and Al Gore (whose Oscar-winning documentary *An Inconvenient Truth* he rechristened "A Convenient Untruth") in one fifty-minute sermon, but he managed to come off as forceful and commanding while doing it. A lesser demagogue might have foamed and snarled his way through a sermon like "The Myth of Global Warming," but the way Dr. Falwell did it, it was jocular, almost playful in tone. He smiled when he talked about God blowing the earth away, not in the creepy, I-am-eagerly-anticipating-Armageddon way, but in the way that says, "Wait till MoveOn.org gets a load of *this*." I disagree with everything he said, and yet, I couldn't look away. It was a masterful, dexterous, transfixing tongue-lashing, and watching it was like seeing Baryshnikov dance.

That said, at some point during today's sermon, I started feeling a little bad for Dr. Falwell. I thought back to the exhibits I saw at the Jerry Falwell Museum the other week, the relics of an era when Dr. Falwell and his Moral Majority set the agenda for millions upon millions of evangelicals. Today, America's evangelicals have largely moved on. No more than a few handfuls of evangelical leaders are still speaking out against environmentalism, and in fact, many have embraced environmentalism under the banner of "Creation Care." Rick Warren, pastor of Saddleback Church and author of *The Purpose-Driven Life*, has supported an initiative to fight global warming. Even Pat Robertson, Dr. Falwell's longtime co-belligerent, has acknowledged the threat climate change poses.

Many observers of Christian culture have noticed that there's a generation gap within the evangelical church. At Liberty, the gap is reaffirmed every Sunday morning. Thomas Road Baptist Church operates on the model of the twentieth-century megachurch, whereas down the street at Liberty's student only Campus Church services, a new, slightly different kind of evangelicalism is being practiced. Services at Thomas Road are often angry and hyper-political, whereas the Campus Church services I've seen have been focused on issues like prayer and spiritual growth, not abortion, gay marriage, and global warming.

A few days ago, after Dr. Falwell spoke in convocation, I heard one of my hallmates, a red-haired Californian named Chad McCourt, call Dr. Falwell "a crazy old coot." It was one of the first times I'd heard a Liberty student say anything critical about the chancellor, so I asked Chad what he meant. He laughed, and explained that while he liked Dr. Falwell, he wasn't a full-fledged supporter.

"Like, you know that crazy uncle everyone has, who shows up drunk to the family reunions sometimes and embarrasses himself? And you still love him because he's your uncle, but you sort of wish he would stop drinking? Well, that's sort of how I feel about Dr. Falwell. Most of the time, he's great. Inspiring, godly, all of that. But once in a while, like when he made those comments about September 11 . . . not so great."

I'm pretty sure Chad McCourt is an anomaly. From the laughs and the applause and the "Amens" Dr. Falwell got this morning, it's clear that a lot of Thomas Roaders do take his views to heart. I have no doubt that a huge majority of the people I've met at Liberty believe global warming is a hoax, and I know that almost all of them are every bit as anti-gay and anti-abortion as the chancellor himself. But I'm hoping that there are at least a few who think like Chad, who appreciate Dr. Falwell as an entertainer without subscribing to his wackier sociopolitical views. Wishful thinking? Probably. But it's more a pleasant scenario than the alternative.

Whether Ye Be in the Faith

On Monday night, the radio debate between Dr. Caner and the Rational Response Squad finally comes to pass.

I listened to the debate—all three hours and forty minutes of it—and it was time well spent. The Rational Response Squad members, two men and a woman, were just like you'd expect professional atheists to be: exact, articulate, and a little prickly. And Dr. Caner . . . well, to everyone's surprise, he didn't play the part of the angry fundamentalist. In fact, he seemed somehow *too* polite, almost wishy-washy. He said things like:

"I like doubt. I think doubt is healthy."
"I wouldn't expect you guys to bow on your knees and accept Jesus."
"There are times when what we call Christianity is unhealthy."

Dr. Caner got a few good points in. He put forth a fairly convincing version of the argument from design (the world is so beautiful and so orderly that it must have been designed by a creator). But ultimately, he was outmatched. The atheists anticipated his arguments and had counterarguments in hand. They knew the Bible inside and out and confronted him with hard-to-spin textual contradictions, like the fact that the account of creation in the first chapter of Genesis differs pretty widely from the account in the second chapter. And although Dr. Caner came up with explanations for the discrepancies, they were hardly rock solid.

Ten minutes after the debate, Brad Miller comes into my room. At twenty-five, Brad is one of the older guys on the hall. He took three years off between high school and college to travel with his Christian music group, but decided to come to Liberty to train for the ministry. He looks a bit like Weezer front man Rivers Cuomo, with a spike haircut and a pair of black-framed hipster glasses. His role on the hall is the advice giver, the wise sensei who tutors the younger guys, the giver of stirring theological lessons. But tonight, Brad's steps are plodding and his aura sags.

"Did you listen?" he asks.

I nod.

"The atheists definitely knew what they were talking about," he says. "I almost don't want to say it, but . . . they beat him."

"You think so?"

"Yeah, man. If that was a boxing match, I think they won 9–1 or so."

He digs the toe of his Converse All Star into the ground.

"Man, that scared me. I'm going to talk to my professors about some of the arguments they made. I don't know what to think right now. That was weird."

He's right. It was weird. In fact, the debate was one of the most bizarre reversals of type I've ever seen. By the end, Dr. Caner had given up so much territory that the atheists were singing his praises. One said, "I'm not a big fan of Liberty University, but in my limited knowledge of it, you're the best thing to ever happen to it." Another said, "You're going to bring down Christianity, so God bless you."

In my mind, the oddest thing about the debate is that it happened at all. An organized debate between a Liberty professor and a group of atheists would never have happened twenty years ago, in large part because Dr. Falwell would never have allowed it. He comes from the old school of hard-line fundamentalism, with a larger-than-life certainty

that triumphs by brute force. In that world, what-iffing and problema-
tizing are for pantywaist preachers and theo-babbling ecumenicists. So
why the switch? Why did Dr. Falwell, who rules his faculty with an
iron fist, condone Dr. Caner's debate? And why did he hire a professor
in the first place who believes that "doubt is healthy" and that Christianity can be "unhealthy"?

In recent years, Dr. Falwell has become comfortable bending Liberty's practices to increase enrollment. When he realized that Liberty's strict dress code was pushing prospective Liberty students to less
conservative colleges, he loosened it. When Liberty lost students to
neighboring schools because it didn't have an engineering department,
he commissioned one. And maybe hiring an articulate, edgy, TV-ready
theologian like Dr. Caner was another way to beef up Liberty's public
profile and bring in more students.

Of course, allowing a debate with atheists about God's existence is
fundamentally different from changing dress code or adding new programs. Long hair and untucked shirts aren't going to change the way
anyone believes in God. Tacking on an engineering school isn't going
to do anything except make Liberty the only school in America where
the engineering majors and the football players have exactly the same
amount of sex. But what if Dr. Caner's assertion that "doubt is healthy"
works its way into History of Life courses? What if Liberty students,
prodded to question their beliefs, start attending synagogue on Satur-
days just to see what's out there?

For more than thirty years, Liberty's operating mode has been
primarily dogmatic. Here, knowledge is passed down from professor to pupil, variations in worldview are systematically stripped
away, and faith is explained and reinforced, never questioned. So
maybe this debate will be a watershed moment in the history of this
school, the dawn of an age in which Liberty students will be en-
couraged to test their beliefs, weigh alternatives, and engage their
critical-thinking skills.

Introducing a little doubt at Liberty wouldn't be a bad thing, but
somehow, I'm not sure it's what Dr. Falwell intended.

*　　*　　*

The next night, I go out in search of fun with my next-door neighbor Zipper. Finding enjoyable nighttime activities in Lynchburg isn't the easiest task, but I figure taking along the human equivalent of a sunny day can't hurt my chances.

Zipper is cheerier than usual today, mostly on account of his "media fast," a spiritual exercise he learned from a Christian devotional book. A media fast, he explains, is a sort of spiritual detox period during which you cut yourself off from all forms of secular entertainment and devote that time instead to Christian activities like prayer and Bible study. Zipper liked the idea of jump-starting his faith, so he decided to try it out. For the next three weeks, he's swearing off TV, secular music, video games, and time-draining websites like YouTube and Facebook. Instant messaging is allowed, he decided, but only for spiritual communication—sending prayer requests to his Christian friends back home, for example.

"It's an awesome exercise," he says. "It's really changing my life. I'm only on day four, but I already feel the world slipping away and the Lord coming into focus."

If you were a conservative evangelical parent, Zipper is exactly the son you'd want. He wants to be a youth pastor when he grows up, and his personal hero, "after Christ, of course," is his grandfather, who has read the Bible cover to cover more than fifty times in his life. He's proudly inexperienced with girls and has decided to save his first kiss until his wedding day. ("I just want to make sure it's the best kiss of my life!" he says.)

For the first few weeks of school, Zipper's eternally upbeat personality was novel and refreshing. Whenever he'd come into my room to tell me about the great things God was doing in his life, I felt William James's "better moral air" washing over me. But now, after this week filled with debates and doubt, his unflinching piety seems a little unrealistic. I keep wondering: What's he hiding? Can any nineteen-year-old male really be this squeaky-clean?

Later in the drive, I decide to press him for signs of moral weakness.

"Here's a question for you," I say. "Do you ever get the itch to be at a secular school, where life would be a little less restricted?"

He looks at me sideways.

"You wouldn't have to drink or anything," I add.

Zipper does some calculations, cross-checking this new information with the rule book in his head. "Umm . . . let's see . . . secular school . . . not drinking . . ."

"You like to dance, right?" I interject.

"Yeah, I like to dance," he replies, still squinting in deep thought. "Well, depends on what type of dancing. I'm not a big fan of the humpin'-and-grindin' junk."

He opens his eyes and gives his verdict: "Yeah, I guess being at a less restricted school would be okay. I mean, in high school, I never really did a whole lot in the party realm. Me and my friends, we'd just find random hilarious stuff to do, and we'd go do it. We'd run through McDonald's wearing different costumes, stealing food from each other in the car, stuff like that."

"Yeah, but do you ever feel like Liberty is too legalistic?" I ask.

He thinks for a while, rubbing his index finger along his upper lip.

"I mean, I know Jesus was down on the Pharisees for legalism. But I don't really know about all that. I guess the best thing to do is go back to the Bible and see what it says. I think once you start going too deep, is this too legalistic, is it too this or too that, then you start getting distracted from the real message of Christ. That's what my pastor tells me."

Forget it. If Zipper has a wild side, it's buried beneath a hundred layers of austere Christian piety. And now, I feel like a jerk for digging.

After a little more driving, we find our entertainment: a mini-golf course that will be open for another twenty minutes. We've got time for nine holes if we play quickly, the manager says.

As we step out of the car, I say, "Zipper, you are a great man."

He puts his hand on my shoulder.

"Kevin Roose, I serve a great God."

Unlike every other time I've hung out with Zipper, this time I come away feeling slightly depressed. Hearing about his relationship with God reminds me that although we live in adjacent rooms, we're still miles apart in the belief department. I've never felt the kind of intense divine presence Zipper seems to feel every time he wakes up, and I'm not sure I ever will. In fact, my spiritual life hasn't budged in several weeks.

I think part of the problem is that, while I'm getting a lot of impromptu spiritual tutoring from my hallmates, I have no regular sources of wisdom, no adult mentors. It seems like every time I talk to Zipper, he tells me something his pastor said or something his youth group leader gave him to work on. His spiritual life has a support staff.

The next day, I decide to get some help. I ask James Powell, my hall's Spiritual Life Director, how I could get a regular mentoring session going with a pastor on campus.

"Prayer group not doing it for you?" he asks.

In truth, it's not. We mostly sit around and talk about our March Madness brackets and our love interests. I tell James I'm just looking for an adult mentor, someone who can give me answers with experience behind them.

"Yeah, I understand," he says. "You should e-mail Pastor Seth."

Liberty's Campus Pastors Office is a vast, multifaceted operation with a half-dozen ministers assigned to various aspects of the school's spiritual life. Pastor Seth Holland is the discipleship coordinator, the guy who trains Liberty's SLDs and mentors students on the side. I e-mail him, asking if he would be willing to meet with me. He writes back a few hours later: "Kevin, I really enjoy talking with guys and discipling others." He agrees to mentor me and tells me to come by his office for a preliminary meeting. He signs his e-mail "Steadfast in His Service, Seth."

I go to Pastor Seth's office the next day for our appointment. He's a young guy, midtwenties, with short brown hair, a too-big black suit, and a cell phone clipped to his belt. He's also a big C. S. Lewis fan, judging from the Aslan posters adorning his walls and the Narnia figurines arranged in battle formation on his bookshelf, next to the stack of Dr. Falwell's books.

Pastor Seth sits down facing me.

"So tell me about yourself," he says.

"Well, my name is Kevin, and I . . ."

"Wait, I know," he says. "Have you ever heard of the naked method of getting to know someone? Like, getting naked?"

Hold the goddamned phone. Did he say getting naked? Am I locked in?

"*Ha!*" he says, laughing and slapping his thigh. "Don't worry. It's an acronym. You ask a person in order: name, address, kin, experiences, dreams. The N.A.K.E.D. method. I use it all the time."

The color returns to my face, and I remove my fingernails from my knee. Wow. What an awful name for an icebreaker. No, that's not even an icebreaker. That's an ice maker.

After we go through the N.A.K.E.D. method, Pastor Seth asks me a few more questions about myself, then shows me a goal sheet he made before today's meeting.

Purpose:

- To assist and give guidance to Kevin in his personal walk with the Lord, his understanding of God's Word, and to hold him accountable in any ways he asks.
- To work with Kevin on developing a committed, serious prayer life.
- To help Kevin understand what it means to be an authentic man of God.

As Seth talks to me about his intentions to help me with my spiritual life, I start to warm up to him. "I want you to know that I am an open book," he says. "I may not have all the answers, but God has given me a lot of experience helping people, so as we talk through things, feel free to ask me anything. No question is too small or too big for us to work through."

Before I leave, Pastor Seth gives me a Bible assignment. Before the next time we meet, he wants me to read the books of James, Ephesians, and Galatians and take notes on anything that jumps out at me as particularly wise or challenging. "And don't skim," he says. "I'll know if you skimmed."

I'm actually sort of excited about being Pastor Seth's disciple. Despite the fact that I'm not quite an "authentic man of God," as he puts it, I really enjoy talking about theology and belief, and I'm really trying to wring some spiritual truth out of this semester. If anyone is qualified to answer my questions, it's a pastor on Liberty's payroll. So I pledge to use my sessions with Pastor Seth wisely. I'm going to do all my assignments, and I'm going to use him as a sounding board for all of my spiritual struggles.

"I barely know Kevin, God, but I'm excited to get to know him," he prays. "I pray that you'll use me in his life to grow him to be more confident. I pray that you'll bless the next few months of our time together, that you'll have it be very fruitful to both of us, God."

Later that night, while Eric and I are working on our homework, Henry—our twenty-nine-year-old roommate—barges into the room with something to say.

"You know who I can't stand?"

Eric rolls his eyes. "Who, Henry?"

"Sharpton."

"Sharpton? You mean Al Sharpton?"

"Yeah, that guy. He has corrupted the name of the Lord. You can't be a Christian minister and preach the stuff he preaches. Alternative lifestyles, polygamy, homosexuality, and all that. Sharpton supports that kind of junk. He's a charlatan."

"Oooo-kay," says Eric. "Gotcha."

In the past few weeks, my domestic situation has gotten a little dicey. After his bizarre rant about homosexuality, Henry's angry streak has only gotten more intense. Every few nights, he pops out from behind his desk to make a new comment about the socio-political ill occupying his mind. I'd compare him to an amateur Rush Limbaugh, but I think even the dittoheads would blanch at the things that come out of Henry's mouth. So far this week, he has sounded off on Paris Hilton ("She's a whore, and I can say that because it's a word in the Bible"), girls with short hair ("If my wife ever cuts her hair, I'm going to teach her about female submission to her husband"), and Andy Hillman, our Evangelism 101 professor ("that guy is a faggot").

Eric, for one, is getting sick of it. He agrees with Henry that homosexuality is sinful, of course, but he seems just as put off by his pathological rage as I am. In one of his GNED essays, Eric used Henry's aggressive homophobia as an example of poor Christian behavior, comparing it with a secular person who has a phobia of Liberty students without ever having met them.

Partly to avoid the growing enmity between Eric and Henry, I've been spending a lot of time outside the room, wandering Dorm 22 in search of late-night theological discussions.

They aren't hard to find. You'd think that after a full day of sermons, Bible lessons, and prayer groups, the guys on my hall would be sick of talking about religion, but most nights after curfew, you can find dozens of conversations about every theological issue under the sun. In the past few nights, I've heard guys hashing out theories of salvation, discussing the book of Revelation, and debating the biblical stances on everything from alcohol use to capital punishment. Once in a while, I'll hear someone talking about the ACLU or abortion, but that's about as partisan as it gets. Other than my roommate Henry, no one in Dorm 22 is having any truly crazy discussions.

In the wake of the Rational Response Squad debate, and the near-universal acceptance of the fact that Dr. Caner got beat pretty badly by the professional atheists, I wondered whether there would be mass spiritual panic among my friends. But that hasn't happened. Church attendance is still high. Guys are still praying and reading the Bible as often as they always have. The day after the debate, the SLD James Powell taped an index card to his wall with a quote from a Christian author named Elisabeth Elliot: "Don't dig up in doubt what you planted in faith." But even Powell told me the other day that his relationship with God is "really, really strong right now."

The reason Dr. Caner's flameout didn't make a bigger dent in this school's spiritual life, I think, is that Liberty students have much more pressing things to do than contemplate the existence of God. There are papers to write, grad school applications to complete, girls to ask out. Even if you were convinced by the Rational Response Squad, entertaining a crisis of faith would mean reevaluating every aspect of your life, from the friends you hang out with to the classes you take to, really, whether you should be at Liberty at all. In a faith system as rigorous and all-encompassing as this, severe doubt is paralyzing. Better just to keep believing, keep living life, and take up the big questions later, when not so much is at stake.

Tonight, I spend some time in Brad Miller's room. Brad, the guy who seemed most worried after the Rational Response Squad debate, has been too busy planning his wedding to become an atheist. He and his fiancée Lydia are getting married in July, six weeks after school lets out. Brad and Lydia are the archetypal twenty-first-century evangelical couple—he with his hipster-next-door vibe, she with her flowing blond locks and impossibly peppy mien. Their engagement photos, thumbtacked all around Brad's room, show the lovers cavorting on the beach, hair blowing in the wind, both chiseled faces looking reverential and pure, the whole thing looking very much like the photos that come inside new picture frames.

With the wedding coming up so soon, a lot of the late-night talks in Brad's room have centered on topics like love, family, and parenthood. Tonight, Brad, his roommate James, and Jake, one of the hall's Spiritual Life Directors, have spent nearly an hour talking about something called the Quiverfull movement.

The Quiverfull movement, I learn, is a small, highly controversial subgroup of evangelical Christianity whose members attempt to have as many children as is biologically possible. Quiverfull couples (the movement takes its name from a Bible verse that praises a man "whose quiver is full" of children) swear off all forms of contraception—including sterilization and the rhythm method—and attempt to produce as many offspring as they can, as fast as they can. The logic goes like this: a Christian couple wouldn't turn down perfect health or massive amounts of money, so why would they turn down children, the biggest blessing of all? Some Quiverfull couples top out naturally at two or three kids, but more often, the number climbs to twelve, thirteen, fourteen, or higher before menopause hits.

Brad, James, and Jake are all tentatively committed to having Quiverfull families. Brad is being forced to make a decision soon, as his wedding is less than four months away. If he decides to go the Quiver-full route, by my calculation, Lydia will likely be in her third trimester this time next year.

"So wait," I say. "You guys all want to have as many kids as possible?"

"Yeah," says James. "Why wouldn't you, Roose? God commands us to be fruitful and multiply."

"I can't wait to have a whole bunch of kids," adds Jake.

"But what about money?" I ask. "What if you have more kids than you can afford?"

"Then your priorities are wrong," says Brad.

"Yeah," says Jake. "Plus, God knows how much money I've got. If he knows that one more kid will bankrupt me, he'll close my wife's womb until my financial situation improves."

"Totally," says Brad. "God is the only contraception that works a hundred percent of the time."

Okay, okay, I take it back. *Some* people are having crazy discussions.

Well, it's almost the halfway point of my semester—two days until Spring Break—and I feel great. In nearly two months of booze-free Christian living and twice-a-week jogging, I've lost fifteen pounds without trying, and I forget what a hangover feels like. Every morning, I jump out of bed and greet myself in the mirror, like a character from a Rodgers and Hammerstein musical. All college students should do a semester at Liberty for the health benefits alone.

Also, maybe it's the exercise endorphins at work, but my mood has improved tenfold from this time last week. This morning, I tried to come up with possible explanations for my mental turnaround, and I thought of a bunch:

- First, I'm busy. Frighteningly busy. These days, I'm taking six classes, singing in the Thomas Road church choir, playing on an intramural softball team with my hallmates (team name: the Billy Goats), running around to every extracurricular meeting I can find, and trying to spend a few hours a day taking notes. It's exhausting, but I've always been happier when I'm constantly on the move. It's my natural pace. No time to mope.

- Second, I've been spending a lot of time with Jersey Joey and his band of Christian rebels. It's not exactly spiritual time—lots of video games, lots of raunchy sex talk—but getting to know those guys has freed me up to be more honest at Liberty, since I know that I can be different and still be accepted. Now, inspired by Joey and Co., I joke around with the guys on my hall, and I tell them stories from my time at Brown. I even told Joey the other night that I had once dated a Jewish girl. (His response: "Rooster, let's be realistic here. We both know you only date dudes.")

- Finally, I'm starting to appreciate the rigid behavioral structure of Bible Boot Camp. This week, I've been reading a devotional book called *Every Young Man, God's Man*. The book devotes a fair chunk of text to devil avoidance. The author says that Satan can cause you to sin by tempting you to give up your moral self-control, a process he calls "yielding." He lists several examples:

  "Chris keeps copies of Maxim in his apartment bathroom. *Yielding*."

  "Tim says that oral sex with his girlfriend is, technically, not having sex. *Yielding*."

  "Sean totally plagiarized major sections of his sociology paper so that his sociology teacher would give him an A. *Yielding*."

I'm a long way from believing in a personal Satan who goes around tempting innocent Christian kids, but I am starting to understand how when your life is a constant battle against "yielding" and "falling," the resulting feelings of restraint can be triumphant.

Think about it this way: one day as a Liberty student is filled with a hundred chances to sin, and at the end of that day, if you've kept all hundred at bay, you lay your head on the pillow feeling like you've just reached the end of a moral marathon. You think: *I could have skipped church today, but I didn't. I could have looked at the girl in the short skirt, but I averted my eyes.* It's what Plato called "suppressing the appetites."

The other day, I read some research by a sociologist named Margarita Mooney. Mooney studied both religious and non-religious college students and demonstrated that students who attended religious services weekly or more were both happier and more successful in school than their non-religious counterparts. As she put it, "religious observance increases students' satisfaction with academic life, social life, and the college experience in general." And while I'm not sure that the strictness of Liberty's rules has a direct correlation to happiness, there does seem to be an overall personality trend at this school. Liberty students seem less cynical than the secular students I've known. They seem more optimistic, more emotionally fulfilled. And after two months of living with them, sharing in their moral victories, I think that optimism and fulfillment may be rubbing off on me.

I still don't feel like I fit in here, for reasons too numerous and obvious to list. But, against all odds, I'm starting to have a good time. I suppose I'm just going through the same process as anyone touching down in a foreign land would—acclimating, coping, making lemonade out of lemons. This might not be true happiness I'm feeling. But for now, it's enough.

The Workers Are Few

Scott shouts to be heard over the crowd.

"*FATHER GOD*, standing here, we know how you must have felt watching *SODOM AND GOMORRAH*. We know how your *APOSTLE PAUL* must have felt watching the *DEPRAVITY AT CORINTH*. Heavenly father, help us drive *SATAN FROM THIS PLACE!*"

We unbow our heads and our mouths hang open as the twin sights of Spring Break: Daytona Beach come into view.

On the right, it's a sea of leather. This is the tail end of Daytona Bike Week, and over the last six days, half a million motorcycle enthusiasts have made the pilgrimage to these beaches, bringing with them an insatiable thirst for domestic beer and a staggering quantity of Hulk Hogan mustaches. Their T-shirts say things like, "You can ride my bike if I can ride your bitch!" and "Welcome to America. Now speak English or get out!"

On the left, a more traditional spring break scene unfolds. Hundreds of rowdy coeds are packed into Froggy's Saloon, where a waifish, nubile blonde gyrates seductively on top of the bar, her belly button ring shimmering like a bass jig in the sun. Mötley Crüe's "Girls, Girls, Girls" plays to wild cheers as the blonde fishes bills out of the empty beer pitcher marked "Tips for Tits."

When the blonde—who is *maybe* eighteen—removes her tube top to reveal a pair of star-shaped nipple shields, Brandon, a short, demure Liberty sophomore from New Hampshire, holds his beach towel over his eyes. On his wrist sits a white "LivePure" bracelet. Scott, our group leader, rubs Brandon's back. "Satan is strong here," he says. "But remember: every person is a person for whom Christ died, whether they're wearing a lot of clothes or no clothes at all."

I guess I should explain myself. Back in February, on a lark, I attended the Mission Fair, a large meeting for Liberty students interested in going on evangelism trips around the world. Missionary evangelism, the act of proselytizing in non-Christian communities, is an integral part of the Liberty experience. Some Liberty students will become full-time missionaries after graduation, but many more will dabble in missions, going on one or two short-term trips during their four years of college. This year, teams from Liberty are slated to go to Haiti, China, and Indonesia, among others.

During the Mission Fair, I heard a pitch for Daytona Beach, the only domestic mission trip Liberty offers. I was confused. Evangelizing to secular spring breakers in Florida struck me as an enormous waste of time. Why not go somewhere where Jesus would be an easier sell? Like Islamabad? Or a Christopher Hitchens dinner party?

I understood better when the Liberty mission coordinator explained that Daytona's bacchanalian atmosphere is part of the allure—it's what's called "battleground evangelism."

"If you want to go to Florida," he said, "be warned: This is going to be 24/7 spiritual warfare. We're talking about Satan's home turf here."

As he spoke, I felt that familiar intrigue, the one that brought me to Liberty in the first place. I knew I had to go. After all, one of the things I haven't seen yet is Liberty students outside their insular safe space, in real-world settings where they have to interact with people like, well, me. Or at least the old me. So a short application, two weeks, and a $600 trip fee later, I was in a white Ford panel van, making my way down I-95 with fourteen Liberty students and two group leaders.

Scott, a sprightly fifty-eight-year-old with a high-pitched Carolina twang and a full head of silver hair, is by all appearances the LeBron James of evangelism. Twenty minutes after our van pulled out of campus, he stopped at a gas station to fuel up and spent five minutes telling the cashiers about Jesus with amphetaminic enthusiasm. Later in the ride, he proselytized two waitresses, a parking lot attendant, and a Georgia tollbooth worker.

On the twelve-hour van ride to Daytona, I had a chance to meet the other members of the team. There's James, a Baltimorean with a soul patch; Aaron, a quiet black guy who speaks in a low rumble; Valentina, an Italian girl from New York City with lips on loan from Angelina Jolie; and a gaggle of vaguely attractive all-American girls, none of whose names I remembered five minutes after our introduction.

After our first traumatic stroll on the beach, we climb back into our white panel van (which Scott has dubbed "the Jesusmobile") and head to the First Baptist Church of Daytona Beach, our Daytona headquarters. By special dispensation of the FBCDB staff, we'll be eating meals and sleeping on air mattresses in the church's Sunday school wing for the next eight days.

Scott and his wife Martina, a friendly Jamie Lee Curtis–looking woman who came along as the trip's coleader, guide us through an all-morning training session on the whys and hows of evangelism. We sit on folding chairs in the Sunday school room and eat snack-size bags of pretzels while Scott recites the "Great Commission," the verse that serves as the theological frame for all missionary work. It's found in Matthew 28:19, when Jesus says to his disciples, "Go and make disciples of all nations, baptizing them in the name of the Father and of the Son and of the Holy Spirit."

"The first thing you should think when you meet anyone," Scott says, "is 'Are they saved?'" It's safe to assume that almost everyone coming to Daytona for spring break is unsaved, he says, adding, "It's a very dark place out there."

Before we take our evangelical Delta Force to the beach, though, we need to learn how to witness.

First, a few words on lingo. There are several words for what exactly will be transpiring here. "Spreading the gospel," "sharing the faith," and "evangelizing" are all common terms for the act of attempting to convert nonbelievers, but "witnessing" seems to be the most all-purpose. From what I understand, you can "be a witness," you can "witness to" someone, or you can "witness" generally, like on a street corner. "Fishing," a more insidery term, refers to Jesus' claim that he would make his disciples "fishers of men." (When we arrived at our host church, the pastor thanked us for coming to fish in his pond.)

I should also say that what we're doing would strike many Christians as odd. Proselytizing to strangers, which one Christian I know calls "cold turkey evangelism," is a dying art, and many evangelicals prefer less confrontational methods. There's friendship evangelism, which means spending time with a nonbeliever, establishing rapport for months or even years before you bring up the subject of God. There's lifestyle evangelism, in which you do Jesus-like good deeds in the hope that nonbelievers will be so impressed that they'll begin to link moral goodness with Christianity. There are doubtless others, but on this trip, we'll only be using the cold turkey method. All strangers, all confrontation, all day.

The best witnessing tactic, Scott says, is beginning conversations subtly, so strangers don't grasp your intent immediately. He suggests opening with "Hi, I'm taking opinions today. Would you be willing to help me out?" Then, he suggests following up with a weed-out question, like "Who's the greatest person you know?" or "What's the greatest thing that has ever happened to you?"

Unless the person answers "Jesus Christ" or "Getting saved," Scott says, you can be fairly sure you're talking to a non-evangelical. Then, you transition to a more direct question:

"Do you ever think about spiritual things, like heaven and hell?"
"What do you think happens to us when we die?"
"Would you consider yourself a good person?"

This last one—"Would you consider yourself a good person?"—is the first step in the Way of the Master evangelism program, Scott's favorite technique. The Way of the Master, which was formulated by a New Zealand pastor named Ray Comfort and marketed by *Growing Pains* actor and evangelical pitchman Kirk Cameron, is based on a four-question sequence designed to demonstrate systematically to a nonbeliever that he or she is not, in fact, a good person—that all have sinned and fall short of the glory of God.

The four questions, Scott says, can be remembered with the mnemonic WDJD. ("What *Did* Jesus Do?")

W—"Would you consider yourself to be a good person?"

Usually, Scott says, a nonbeliever will say "yes" or "generally," at which point you move on to:

D—"Do you think you've kept the Ten Commandments?"

Again, a nonbeliever will typically say "for the most part" or "usually." If so, Scott says, we should lead the nonbeliever through some of the commandments. ("Have you ever disobeyed your parents? Taken the Lord's name in vain? Stolen?") Any honest person will agree that he or she has broken some or all. "The commandments act as a mirror for our sins," he says.

J (Judgment)—"If God judged you by the Ten Commandments, would you be innocent or guilty?"

Most people who have stuck around this long will answer "guilty," Scott says. Then, you hit them with the kicker:

D (Destiny)—"If you're guilty, where do you think you will spend eternity—heaven or hell?"

"This step is where people realize they're hell-bound, and they make decisions for Christ to save themselves," he says.

A sophomore named Samantha raises her hand and asks the question we've all been considering.

"But what if they don't?"

"Good point," Scott says. "These people may not be ready to accept Christ, but we can plead with them to consider it, because hell is a real place. So just ask them two or three times: Why would you *not* consider this? Why would you think it *doesn't* matter?" As Scott says this, fourteen skeptical faces stare back at him. Team Daytona seems to have realized en masse that these conversations will only remain *hypothetically* awkward for a few more minutes.

"Never forget, guys," he says, "What we're doing is kind! Many Christians don't share Christ because they feel like they're bothering people. But we're sharing the information that will help them avoid God's wrath and go to heaven! We're doing something better than the best Christmas present they'll ever get!"

Before we go, we pray.

"Lord, prepare the hearts of the spring breakers," says Scott. "Make the issues at stake clear to people, Lord, and draw them to yourself. Let us turn them from their ways."

Five minutes later, as Scott steers the Jesusmobile to the beach, he swivels to face us.

"Oh, and don't forget, guys: keep a journal of your witnessing experiences, so you can remember who you talked to."

Yes, sir.

1300h: Reece

Today, we will be doing our beach evangelism in pairs. The fortunate part of this arrangement is that I'll be able to see other members of my group in action. The unfortunate part: I'll probably be expected to participate. Luckily, my first partner, a sophomore named Claire, is what the cognoscenti call a "bold witness." Claire, a brown-haired bombshell who wears those trendy drink-coaster-size sunglasses, agrees to let me watch the first few times, since I hinted when we started that I was new at this.

Here's what they don't tell you in evangelism training: being a bold witness doesn't matter if no one is listening. Claire approaches two dozen people in five minutes, none of whom stay with her past the first question. Spring breakers don't like to be interrupted, and when she tries a more direct approach, saying, "Excuse me, I'd like to talk to you about God," it's not pretty. Sorority girls laugh in her face. Bikers stare at her chest, then laugh in her face.

When Claire finally gets someone to hear her out, it's a Rastafarian-looking guy sitting on a bench, wearing parachute pants and a green and yellow basketball jersey. He introduces himself as Reece.

"Reece, would you consider yourself a good person?" she asks.

"Yeah, I guess."

Reece answers the WDJD questions nonchalantly. "Yeah, I've stolen. Yeah, I've disobeyed my parents. Yeah, I'm probably guilty." When Claire gets to D, the one about heaven and hell, Reece rubs his eye with the back of his hand.

"I'm gonna live forever," he says. "Heaven is a state of mind, you know? You ever watch the *Matrix*? When Neo went to the Oracle, and he's like 'Am I the one?' and she's like 'No you're not, because you don't know.' It's like that. You gotta know, you know?"

"No, I don't know," Claire says.

Reece tells us he's sorry, but he has to go meet some friends at a different part of the beach. Claire prays for him quickly, and Reece goes on his way. As we continue down the boardwalk, Claire turns to me.

"I think that man was on drugs."

1315h: *Janice*

Two failed approaches later—an old lady who shooed us away and a biker who was "rushing to meet some buddies"—Claire tells me it's my turn.

When Scott started schooling us on the Way of the Master method, it became clear that over the course of the week, I'd be expected to push Christianity to strangers. This made my conscience's usual swampy morass a little swampier. At Liberty, see, no one asks me about my faith anymore, so to blend in, I rarely have to do anything more active than keep up my Christian signifiers—going to Bible study, praying before meals, being on time to church. This is what passes for ethical conduct in my world. It probably wouldn't fly in front of the Senate Judiciary Committee, but it's how I sleep at night.

Evangelism to strangers, though—that doesn't sit nearly as well with me. So while Scott was talking, I set some guidelines for my Daytona mission that made me a little more comfortable. First, I would distance myself reasonably from evangelical theology. If I told someone about Jesus, I'd begin, "Well, according to *one* reading of the Bible . . ." or "*Some* Christians think . . ." Second, I wouldn't condemn anyone. And third, if things ever got to a point where I was doing *too* well, where someone was on the verge of converting, I'd find a way to get out of the conversation quickly, no matter how out of character it was.

I may never have to put these rules into effect, though, because I'm too scared to make my first approach. I wander the sand with Claire for five or ten minutes looking for a suitable target. The two middle-aged men checking their BlackBerries? The preteen boys stomping on a sand castle? No, won't do. I almost approach a pack of hot, bikini-clad girls, but I stop short due to my recurring fear that all hot, bikini-clad girls are linked by some sort of high-tech underground network, and blowing it with one group of them will permanently ink my name on the blacklist.

Claire points to a guy in a beach chair. "How about him?"

"It looks like he's about to leave. Doesn't it?"

"Okay, the guy next to him."

"He's tanning. We probably shouldn't disrupt him."

After a dozen of these, Claire looks a little irritated. "You know, you shouldn't be afraid," she says. "You have Holy Spirit boldness inside you."

Finally, I see a thirty-something brunette sitting on the flatbed of her pickup truck, legs dangling over the end. I look at Claire, who nods. She'll do. I steel myself and walk toward her, feeling my palms moisten.

"Hello there."

"Uh, hi." She's a Hispanic woman wearing a pink bikini, drinking Rolling Rock with a foam koozie. I introduce myself, and she tells me her name is Janice.

"Janice, I was, uh, wondering if I could ask you a question."

"Sure, go ahead."

"Would you consider yourself a good person?"

She pulls off her sunglasses and looks at me queerly. "Yeah, I guess I'm good."

"Do you think you've kept the Ten Commandments?"

"Probably not."

"Have you ever told a lie?"

"Of course. I've committed a whole bunch of sins."

"So where do you think you'd . . ." I realize I'm about to ask the questions out of order—D instead of J—so I self-correct. ". . . Uh, I mean . . . if God judged you by the Ten Commandments, do you think you'd be innocent or guilty?"

She leans forward. "Are you trying to convert me?"

I look back at Claire, who nods. "Well, yeah, but . . ."

"Listen," she snaps, "this is pretty rude of you. I'm out here trying to enjoy my day at the beach, and you're coming over here telling me that I need Jesus. Or are you with the Mormons?"

I squeak out, "No, ma'am, not with the Mormons."

She smiles snidely, puts her sunglasses back on.

"Well, I don't want to hear it, thanks very much. Man, the Bible-thumpers are the ones you gotta watch out for. They're some sick ass-holes—no offense."

As we turn and walk away, Claire sighs. "Well, I think her soul is hardened, but at least we got to tell her about hell. That's a start, right?"

Even before this trip, I hated confronting strangers. I had a summer job once at a Manhattan juice bar. Every day, my boss would stick me on a SoHo street corner handing out coupons for raspberry smoothies. It was miserable. I'd spend five hours a day waving coupons at pass-ersby, and when they didn't completely ignore me, they'd look at me like I was trying to stab them with a dirty syringe. One middle-aged lady swung her purse at me.

But this was worse. I haven't really processed Janice's rejection yet, so I don't know whether to brush it off or feel personally offended. Even though I don't believe in my product, as they say in business, it's still not fun being the target of a stranger's wrath.

1430h: Rick

Claire has decided that I'm not a very competent evangelist, so she took on the next dozen approaches. So far, she's doing better, but I suspect there are other factors in play. Every few minutes, Claire walks up to a group of guys and engages them in small talk. The guys—and it's always the smarmy, sleeveless-shirt and hair-gel types—take this to be some kind of coy flirtation ritual. They sidle up to her, tossing each other looks of smug satisfaction that say: *Dude, that girl is totally into me. No freakin' way, dude, she talked to me first.*

I want to warn the guys telepathically, but it's too late. They smile and nod and answer Claire's initial questions, and then she drops the hammer:

"If a holy and righteous God judged you on the Ten Commandments, would he find you innocent or guilty?"

I've noticed a range of reactions to Claire's hammer drops so far:

- Some people give the hidden-camera-show look. The guys let out a small chuckle, perhaps thinking Claire has just mastered the practice of deadpan irony. Then, when they see her waiting unblinkingly for a response, they sweep the landscape, looking for a tech crew.
- A few people get genuinely angry. One biker said, "If I wanted to hear I was going to hell, I'd call my ex-wife."
- Then there's the you-poor-things response, which thus far has come exclusively from old ladies. When Claire begins her spiel about accepting Jesus Christ as your personal savior, these ladies' faces soften into sympathetic smiles. They listen patiently, like a grandmother hearing a Girl Scout sputter through her

cookie pitch—then they turn Claire down as politely as possible. One woman, who looked like Mrs. Butterworth in a one-piece, asked us, "Now, who put you two up to this?"

Needless to say, Daytona is not the world's easiest place to make disciples. Trucks drive up and down the beach with thousand-watt speakers in the flatbeds blasting Jay-Z. There's an ongoing best buns contest at Spanky's Tiki Bar ($50 cash prize). Claire and I cut a sharp contrast to the bikinied, board-shorted masses in our polo shirts and backpacks stuffed with gospel tracts. So our failure, if not totally expected, at least is understandable.

Claire's other problem is total linguistic isolation. She, like many other Liberty students, speaks in long, flowery strings of opaque Christian speak. When a twenty-something guy named Rick tells Claire he doesn't believe in God, Claire sighs and says, "Listen, Rick. There's a man named Jesus Christ, and he came into my heart and changed me radically. And there is a God who loves you, and who sent his son to die on the cross for you, to take away your sins and my sins, and God shows himself to me every day. When I don't have hope for tomorrow, Jesus never fails. His love is never ending."

While she's speaking, my eyes never leave Rick. I recognize his confused expression as what mine must have been on my first-ever visit to Thomas Road—the same sense that two people, both speaking English, are not exactly communicating. Rick listens to her prattle on for several minutes, and then apologizes.

"Not interested," he says. "But thanks."

Claire thanks Rick and walks away downtrodden, kicking up sand with each step.

1520h: Names Unknown

I approach three girls tanning on beach towels. They're good-looking girls, maybe a year or two out of college. One is reading a Patricia Cornwell mystery, and the other two are on their stomachs, listening to their iPods.

"Hi there," I say, trying to sound as peppy as possible. The Cornwell reader looks up from her book, eyebrows raised, and one of the iPod girls takes out her earbuds.

"I was just wondering if I could give you guys a million dollars."

When Scott was teaching us to evangelize, he gave us several gimmicky icebreakers to use when beginning conversations. This one is a fake million-dollar bill with a message printed in tiny letters on the back:

The million-dollar question: Will you go to Heaven? Here's a quick test. Have you ever told a lie, stolen anything, or used God's name in vain? Jesus said, "Whoever looks upon a woman to lust after her has committed adultery already with her in his heart." Have you looked with lust? Will you be guilty on Judgment Day? If you have done those things God sees you as a lying, thieving, blasphemous, adulterer at heart. The Bible warns that if you are guilty you will end up in Hell. That's not God's will. He sent His Son to suffer and die on the cross for you . . . Please, repent (turn from sin) today and trust in Jesus, and God will grant you everlasting life.

"Sure," Cornwell girl says. "I'll take one."

"But first," I say, "I have to ask you the million-dollar question."

"Shoot."

I take a deep breath. "Do you know Jesus Christ as your personal savior?"

The iPod girl's eyes bulge. "Excuse me?" She pokes her friend, who turns over onto her back, takes out her earbuds, and stares at me.

"Um . . . do you guys know Jesus . . . as your savior?"

Cornwell girl says pointedly, "We're Jewish."

"I'll take that as a no?" I say. They don't laugh. Not even the faintest trace of a smile. I turn and walk away, mumbling thanks under my breath.

As I go, I hear them talking: "What a creep," one says.

After this rejection, I start to get angry. How could Scott make evangelism seem so easy? Doesn't he see that this is torture? When Claire and I return to the Jesusmobile for our appointed meeting time, the rest of the group looks a little shell-shocked. Faces are sullen, postures slumped.

"That was the hardest day of my life," says Samantha.

"Any decisions for Christ today?" Scott asks. No hands go up.

"Well, that's okay," he says. "Decisions or not, we're planting seeds the Lord will water in time!"

Back at the host church, Scott explains that beach witnessing is just half of our agenda. Tonight, we'll get another chance at the nightclubs. We spend half an hour in prayer before dinner. It is, I suspect, the saddest prayer circle ever convened.

"I lift Emmanuel and William up to you, Lord," says James from Baltimore. "They didn't seem interested when I told them about you today, but I pray that they'll think about what I told them, and that they'll come to a saving knowledge of your son, Jesus Christ."

"Lord, I pray for the medical student I met today," says Scott's wife Martina. "Being a hotshot doctor at a big hospital is not going to help her when she has to face you, Lord. Even though she brushed me off, I pray she'll reconsider later."

"I pray, Lord, for the old man who spit on me," says Charlotte, a blonde from Arkansas. "Satan had such a strong grip on him, and I just want to see him know you, Lord."

Claire is the last to pray: "Lord, let them be nicer to us tonight."

2310h: Jason

Around eleven o'clock, the Jesusmobile pulls up to Razzle's. Razzle's is a Wal-Mart-size nightclub with a squadron of earpieced bouncers manning the velvet rope and a set of revolving laser lights that overflow onto the sidewalk. We won't be going inside, Scott says, but we'll stand just outside the rope, witnessing to people waiting in line.

The first surprise is that there are at least two other groups of Christian evangelists here. One group, a youth team from a Florida church, has set up a shaved-ice machine on the sidewalk. They're making sno-cones for the Razzle's patrons, which almost seems like cheating. (Some Christians call this "gastro-evangelism.") The other group, which is affiliated with Campus Crusade for Christ, has done something truly brilliant. A well-funded national organization, Campus Crusade rented the ballroom at a hotel next to Razzle's and set up a fake party inside, complete with strobe lights, a security team, and attractive models paid to stand outside the hotel and gossip loudly about the *great party inside*. When would-be clubbers enter the room, they quickly realize they've been duped—instead of bar specials and trance music, they get gospel tracts and a salvation message.

Our group has no such Trojan horse, just the same Way of the Master routine we used on the beach. (Though at one point, a film crew working on a *Girls Gone Wild*–style documentary sets up their equipment next to us, so we get a nice little assembly line going.) Witnessing at Razzle's, where everyone we meet is either drunk or well on the way, makes communication a little harder. Two conversations I had in the first ten minutes:

"Excuse me, miss. Do you ever think about spiritual things, like heaven and hell?"
"Woooo!!! I love to *party*!!!"

"Excuse me, sir. Would you help me with an opinion poll?"
"Sure, go ahead."
"Who is the greatest person you know?"
"Hmm . . . gayest person I know. . . . I'd have to say Richard Simmons."

We have an odd number of evangelists tonight, and I managed to snag the solo spot. Without Claire watching me, I no longer have to be pushy. I'm just asking people about their religious beliefs and letting them speak if they wish—which clears my conscience a little, and also makes me the worst evangelist in history. One guy I talked to actually said, "You must be new at this."

Meanwhile, others in my group are having more success. I walk over to another part of the sidewalk and catch Scott's wife Martina deep in conversation with a large, muscled man.

"Jason," Martina says as she sees me approach. "Meet my friend Kevin." We shake hands. Jason is slurring his speech and leaning against a palm tree for support, clearly many drinks into his night. But perhaps because of this, he's really opening up to Martina.

"Listen, Martina," he says. "I just met you, and I like you a lot."

"That's very sweet," she says. "Listen to me, though."

He slumps back against the tree, a little maudlin, eyes sloshing around in his head.

"Jason. Are you able to focus on me?"

"Yeah, yeah."

"Jason, if you died tonight, without the blood of Jesus covering you . . ."

"He's all over me."

"Well, how do you know? You don't read the Bible."

"I don't, you're right."

"And you've never been born again."

"No, I haven't. But I still feel . . ."

"Jason, you need to be born again."

"So what if I am? Then tomorrow, I come back out here and go drinking again, and nothing's changed. What good is that?"

"You won't come back out here tomorrow if you get born again. You'll have the Holy Spirit guiding you."

The issue of postsalvation behavior is an interesting one. Claire raised it earlier tonight. "What happens when these people go back home?" she asked Scott over dinner. "Witnessing is great, but I don't want to just look at them as a number."

"If somebody's truly born again," Scott responded, "the Holy Spirit is going to lead them. The most important thing is that they get Jesus."

I thought, when Scott was teaching us to evangelize, that we'd be told to do some sort of follow-up with successful converts, if we had any—guide them to a local church, maybe, or at least take their contact information. But there's no such procedure. If Jason had decided to get saved (he didn't), Martina would have led him through the Sinner's Prayer ("Jesus, I am a sinner, come into my heart and be my Lord and savior" or some variant thereof), she would have let him know he was saved, perhaps given him some Bible verses to read, and they never would have seen each other again. Cold turkey evangelism provides the shortest, most noncommittal conversion offer of any Western religion—which, I suspect, is part of the appeal.

If the new believer backslides, though, like Jason was suggesting he might, Christians are likely to believe that he wasn't really saved. False conversions are a glaring wart on the face of Christian evangelism. In the book that accompanies our Way of the Master program, I found several sobering statistics about the percentage of apparent converts who stay involved with the church in the long term, including one from Peter Wagner, a seminary professor in California who estimated that only 3 to 16 percent of the converts at Christian crusades stay involved.

Those are good statistics for me—they mean that even if I did manage to convert someone with my bad evangelism, there's only a 3 to 16 percent chance it would matter in the long run. But the false conversion rate is profoundly depressing if you believe in this stuff. After all, if we get ten converts during this week—an optimistic number—and our false conversion numbers are consistent with the average, this group has spent a week's worth of twelve-hour days, thousands of dollars, and suffered massive amounts of emotional trauma for what? One more Christian? Two?

There must be an easier way.

1015h: Andrew

On the third day of the trip, my witnessing partner is Caitlin, a blonde sophomore from Oklahoma. She's a sparkly, bubbly girl, which makes her first encounter of the day all the more surprising. She approaches a small Asian man outside a Starbucks.

"Excuse me, sir. If you got hit by a bus today and died and had to stand before God's judgment seat, why would you tell him you deserve to go to heaven?"

Caitlin, I've learned, is a bulldog witness. Last night at our postclub debrief, she castigated the rest of us for being too easy on the people we met.

"It's really great to tell people that Jesus loves them," she snapped, "but you guys need to show them their sinfulness, too. The Bible says that people who are not saved are children of wrath. We can't forget that."

Apparently, success and tact don't go hand in hand in evangelism. Caitlin is the most experienced evangelist in our group. While at Liberty, she started a small student team that goes out to Lynchburg malls and trailer parks to convert the locals. Since her freshman year, by her count, she has converted 235 people.

She certainly doesn't take rejection well. When the Asian man tries to walk away from Caitlin, she follows him down the street.

"In Revelation 21:8, God says that all murderers, fornicators, and liars will have their part on the lake of fire!" Caitlin shouts behind him.

"I don't think I'm going to hell," the man replies, turning to face her.

"Why not?"

"I do good things for people."

"But we're going by God's standards, not yours."

"Yes, but . . ."

"Sir, have you ever been wrong about anything?"

"Yes, but . . ."

"Do you think you could be wrong about this?"

Three hours later, Caitlin and I (mostly Caitlin—she got frustrated with my forbearance after two or three approaches) have gotten maybe fifty walk-aways. Seeing her confront people so coarsely never gets less shocking. Still, I've got to admit, if you have to evangelize, Caitlin is a great partner. After her introductions, nothing I add can offend anybody.

Later in the day, I ask Caitlin why she's so harsh when she evangelizes, especially since she's such a gentle soul otherwise.

"Well," she says, "I want to save as many people as possible. So I don't get into arguments about the facts or evolution or anything. People can look that stuff up. But if I spend twenty minutes arguing with someone, that's four more people I could have approached."

I'm trying to treat Daytona as a weeklong thought experiment. For one, a little mental distance is the only way I can keep myself from feeling like the Grinch Who Stole Spring Break. But more than that, it's the only way I've found to place myself into the moral space of aggressive evangelism, to try to understand how well-intentioned Christian kids—some of the nicest people I've met all semester—can end up on street corners in Florida, shouting hellfire and damnation to the masses.

Part of it, I'm sure, is that these students are convinced that their actions are compassionate and altruistic. All week, we've heard pep talks like this one from Scott at last night's post-Razzle's debrief: "To me, here's the motivation to evangelize: If I'm a doctor, and I find the cure for a terminal illness, and if I care about people, I'm going to spread that cure as widely as possible. If I don't, people are going to die."

Leave the comparison in place for a second. If Scott had indeed found the cure to a terminal illness and if this Daytona mission were a vaccination campaign instead of an evangelism crusade, my group members would be acting with an unusually large portion of mercy—much more, certainly, than their friends who spent the break playing Xbox in their sweatpants. And if you had gone on this immunization trip, giving up your spring break for the greater good, and had found the sick spring breakers unwilling to be vaccinated, what would you do? If a terminally ill man said he was "late for a meeting," you might let him walk away. But—and I'm really stretching here—if you *really* believed your syringe held his *only* hope of survival, and you *really* cared about him, would you ignore the rules of social propriety and try every convincement method you knew?

Maybe you would, maybe you wouldn't. For these students, the choice is clear: the risk of being loathed and humiliated by strangers is far outweighed by the possibility that even one person will see the light and be saved.

Of course, just because the choice is clear doesn't mean it's easy. Tonight, at Razzle's, I see Valentina, the Italian girl from New York, sitting on a curb with a homeless veteran, her arm slung around his shoulder. It's pouring rain, a real torrential storm, and both of them are being pounded by the thick drops. Valentina is witnessing to the bearded, ragged veteran, and she looks frankly miserable. Her hair is dripping, and she has to wipe the water from her face every few seconds. After a few minutes, she stops telling the veteran about God's love and just sits there, holding him. And from across the street, I see her start to cry.

Later, back at the host church, Valentina tells the group about her breakdown.

"I was just sitting there on the curb, and I started thinking about how sad this all is. How sad it is that billions and billions of people are just dying without Christ and how much I wish it wasn't true. I hate it. I hate that hell is a real place, and I hate that sin came into the world through Adam, and most of all, I hate thinking about how all we can do—all anyone can do—is try to tell these people that there's hope out there. They might not want to listen, but we have to keep telling them. For the rest of our lives, guys, we have to keep telling them."

On the last day of our trip, group morale is mixed. On one hand, we've had a pretty good time by ourselves. Between beach crusades and trips to Razzle's, we played beach volleyball, conducted piano sing-alongs, even went swimming for a spell. Everyone on the trip gets along really well, and it's been a faint approximation of a vacation.

On the other hand, our nets are far from full. Caitlin led a high school boy to Christ yesterday, and one woman we spoke to later visited the Daytona host church and got saved under the care of one of their pastors, but that's it. Two people. We've been cheering each other up, saying things in prayer circles like, "Lord, we know we've done a good work here this week, and we trust that you'll follow up in these people's hearts."

Then again, maybe this trip was never all about the spring breakers. Battleground evangelism, it turns out, can be just as useful for the evangelists as for the nonbelievers. For these Liberty students, going to Daytona is a tool for self-anesthetization, a way to get used to the feeling of being an outcast in the secular world. The first forty times someone blows you off, it feels awful. The second forty times, you start reassuring yourself that all of this must serve a higher purpose. By the end of the week, you get the point—you are going to be mocked and scorned for your faith, and this is the way it's supposed to be.

Today, after a hard day of witnessing, Brandon marked off with Post-its all the verses in his Bible that describe early Christian responses to mockery (like 1 Peter 4:14, "If you are insulted because of the name of Christ, you are blessed, for the Spirit of glory and of God rests on you"). Sitting at the dinner table, he read them aloud to all of us. Amber, a shy brunette from Virginia, looked around the table after Brandon was finished.

"Guys, I realized this week that I'm going to be laughed at for being a Christian for the rest of my life," she said.

"I am, too," Brandon said. "We all are."

"Christians have always been laughed at," added Valentina. "We're in good company."

"I love the part in Romans," Brandon said, "where it says we take up Christ's cross, and we bear his suffering. I like that a lot."

Around 8:00 AM on Sunday, eight days after arriving, we pack our suitcases, deflate our air mattresses, and shove it all in the back of the Jesusmobile for the twelve-hour trip back to Liberty. To the last, Scott remains upbeat.

"Sharing Christ is so exciting!" he says as we pull away. "It's a way of life! Man, it's just such a thrill to introduce people to Christ!"

As we cross the Daytona city limits, Brandon turns to me in the backseat.

"Was this a productive trip?" he whispers.

I shrug.

"Unless I go on another mission trip," he says, "I probably won't evangelize like this again."

"Do you think we made a difference?" I whisper back.

"I mean, anything can happen when the Lord is involved. But personally, I don't think us being here was very productive."

Scott looks back from the driver's seat. Seeing us whispering, he smiles warmly.

"Boys and their secrets . . ."

He turns back to face the road, the Jesusmobile presses on, and we never look back, not once, not even to remember the effort.

Near in Their Mouth, But Far from Their Mind

I thought we'd try something new before class today," says Nathan, the Evangelism 101 teaching assistant. "A little cheer."

My roommate Eric turns to me. "God is good. Bet you ten bucks."

Before I can ask what he means, Nathan sets down his microphone and shouts through cupped hands, "*God is good!*"

"*All the time!*" responds the class in unison. Eric pumps his fist.

"Awesome!" says Nathan. "You guys must remember this from your youth groups. Now, let's see if you remember the second part: *and all the time . . .*"

The class shouts back· "*God is good!*"

Nathan waves his arms with brio, conducting the class like John Philip Sousa leading a parade march.

"*God is good . . .*"

"*All the time!*"

"*And all the time . . .*"

"*God is good!*"

I've been back from spring break for two days now, and I'm starting to settle back into my classes. As you might guess from a lecture that begins with a cheer, Evangelism 101 is somewhat of a gut. Our professor, Pastor Andy Hillman, conducts the class like a large, for-credit session of Sunday school, with test questions like:

God wants to be your _____.
a) Slave
b) Best friend*
c) Priest

The ultimate goal of the universe is to show _____.
a) the love of God
b) the glory of God
c) the power of God
d) all of the above*

The upside of an easy class like Evangelism 101 is simple: I'm not failing. In fact, in most of my courses, I'm improving much more quickly than I expected to. Nobody's going to be throwing any Rhodes scholarships my way after this semester, but most of my grades are up in the B-plus range.

Despite it being my worst class grade-wise, I'm still liking my Old Testament class better than any of the others. In addition to the lessons about Deuteronomy and Judges, it's fun to flesh out the oversimplified nuggets of Old Testament lore that make it into secular pop culture. For example: I've heard a million ESPN commentators refer to a lop-sided matchup as a "David and Goliath situation," but I'd never read the Bible's account of the actual battle. I didn't know that Goliath was not only huge—about nine feet tall, with a 125-pound cloak of armor— he was also "uncircumcised," according to 1 Samuel 17:26. This bit of information gives me a leg up on my ESPN-watching secular friends. A juvenile leg, but a leg nonetheless.

I'm finding that my favorite courses, like Old Testament and Theology, have something in common: they're surveys, classes in which the professor's goal is simply to introduce a body of new information. The information always has a literalist slant, of course, but on the whole, the classes are fairly straightforward. You'd find the same thing at a hundred other Christian colleges and Bible study groups.

There's another type of class, though—the agenda-driven class. In these courses, professors aren't teaching new knowledge so much as teaching students how to think about the world around them.

A week or two before spring break, I started sitting in on GNED II, a mandatory second-semester extension of my GNED course. I'm only at Liberty for one semester, so I'll never get to take GNED II for a grade, but people on my hall kept talking about it, and I wanted to get the flavor. The GNED II class I've been going to, like my GNED I class, is taught by Dr. Parks. In it, Liberty students are taught to view socio-political topics like homosexuality, abortion, and euthanasia through an ultra-conservative Christian lens. And unlike its first-semester counterpart, GNED II pulls no punches. Its workbook contains fill-in-the-blank sections like:

What are the consequences of immoral sex?

1. Physical
   - A. <u>Unplanned Pregnancy</u>
   - B. <u>Abortion</u>
   - C. <u>STDs</u>
2. Emotional
   - A. Unrelenting <u>guilt</u> (Proverbs 5:11-14)
   - B. Unwanted <u>memories</u> (Psalm 51:3)
   - C. Less <u>peace of mind</u>

And:

II. Myths Behind the Homosexual Agenda

Myth: The homosexual <u>lifestyle</u> is happy, healthy, and
responsible.

Response: AIDS is most prevalent among gay men and is rising
rapidly among lesbians.

Response: Monogamy among homosexuals is the exception,
not the norm. It is a compulsive lifestyle involving many
sexual partners throughout a lifetime.

Response: The average gay has multiple sex partners during
their gay life, many of which are anonymous encounters in
bathhouses, nightclubs, and porn shops.

In today's GNED II class, Dr. Parks announces that we will be talk-ing about gender roles in the evangelical world. Dr. Parks spends the first ten minutes of class laying out the two main positions evangeli-cal Christians take on gender issues. The first position, egalitarianism, means exactly what you'd expect it to mean—men and women are equal, both in the church and in the home. Women can be pastors of a church, they can teach Sunday school, and husbands and wives share equal authority in marriage. The second position, called comple-mentarianism, means, in Dr. Parks's words, that "God created man and woman with different roles that complement each other." Comple-mentarians believe that only men can be pastors, that only men can teach Sunday school or other Christian education classes (unless it's an all-female class). Complementarians also maintain that the husband should be the head of the household. They quote Ephesians 5:24, "As the church submits to Christ, so also wives should submit to their hus-bands in everything."

"You can obviously tell where I am on this," Dr. Parks says. "I am definitely a complementarian, without apology. I think the egalitarian view is greatly skewed."

Dr. Parks clicks a few buttons on his laptop to start a PowerPoint slideshow. The text is accompanied by photos of white, suburban couples clutching each other, loving gazes plastered on their faces. As the presentation plays, we fill in the blanks in our workbooks:

The role of the husband:

1. <u>Love</u> his wife and <u>sacrifice</u> for her.
2. <u>Head</u> of the wife.
3. Provide for the <u>family</u>.
4. <u>Honor</u> and <u>respect</u> wife.
5. Provide a <u>positive</u> environment for children.

The role of the wife:

1. <u>Submit</u> to her husband.
2. <u>Love</u> her husband and children.
3. Keep the family a <u>priority</u>.

Dr. Parks realizes that to a non-evangelical, the complementarian view of gender roles can sound misogynistic, but he assures us that it's not. Women can still hold high-power jobs under the complementarian model, he says, and they should still get equal pay for equal work. But when push comes to shove, a woman's priority should be her family. "For a woman," Dr. Parks says, "if the career is most important, and the family gets left out, that's a problem."

At first, I couldn't believe Liberty actually had a course that teaches students how to condemn homosexuals and combat feminism. GNED II is the class a liberal secularist would invent if he were trying to satirize a Liberty education. It's as if Brown offered a course called Godless Hedonism 101: How to Smoke Pot, Cross-dress, and Lose Your Morals.

But unlike that course, GNED II actually exists, so I've had to figure out how to process it. I keep thinking back to Marcus Ross, the Liberty professor who was written up in the *New York Times* for his doctoral research on 65 million-year-old reptiles. Ross was able to compartmentalize his brain into two functional halves—a religious half and a secular half—and for a while, I was too. I could sit in History of Life class and hear Dr. Dekker talk about the flaws in Darwinism without going crazy, because I convinced myself that I was just filling an alternate space in my brain. What's the harm in that?

GNED II is different, though. I can't convince myself that those lessons about fornicators and homosexuals are innocuous. For one, whereas I'm not an expert in evolutionary biology, I do have enough experience with gay people to know that homosexuality is not a "compulsive lifestyle involving many sexual partners." (In fact, some of my gay friends at Brown spend a lot of time complaining about how little sex they're having.) But aside from the patently offensive content, my biggest issue with GNED II is the way it bundles political and social issues with religious issues, and what that means for a guy who's trying to give Christianity a fair shake.

Over spring break, I finally finished *Left Behind*, the apocalyptic novel I started a month or so ago. And per my expectations (spoiler alert!) the secular journalist Buck Williams has a religious conversion. I'll spare you the details—it involves a Romanian politician who turns out to be the Antichrist—but suffice it to say that Buck deals with his skepticism, gets down on his knees, and accepts Christ as his savior.

That part didn't bother me so much. The part that worried me was the lead-up to that conversion. A few pages before Buck converts, his thought process is described in these terms: "If this was true, all that Rayford Steele had postulated—and Buck knew instinctively that if any of it was true, all of it was true—why had it taken Buck a lifetime to come to it?"

That middle clause—"Buck knew instinctively that if any of it was true, all of it was true"—is the same rationale Liberty professors use to prove that the earth is six thousand years old, or that wives must submit to their husbands. If the Bible is infallible, my professors all say, and if the parts about Jesus dying for our sins are true, then a host of other things must also be true, including the sinfulness of homosexuality, the pro-life platform, and the imminence of the rapture. In Liberty's eyes, the ultra-conservative interpretation of scripture carries the same inerrancy as scripture itself, and if you don't buy it all—if you're a liberal or moderate Christian—you're somehow less than faithful. That sort of prix fixe theology, where Christianity comes loaded with a slate of political views, is a big part of the reason I've been hesitant to accept Liberty's evangelicalism this semester. Somewhere down the road, I might be able to believe in Jesus as Lord, but I could never believe that homosexuality is a sinful lifestyle or tell my future wife to submit to me as her husband.

I suppose it's weird that I'm more attached to my social and political views than my religious beliefs. Is it really more reasonable to believe that the savior of the world was born of a virgin, lived a sinless life, died for our sins, and was resurrected three days later than to believe that the universe frowns on gay people? On a purely logical level, probably not. But it is what it is, and it does me no good to pretend otherwise. The mind, as we know, is a funny thing.

Wednesday night after curfew, I go to Jersey Joey's room to hang out with Dorm 22's rebel crew. The door is locked. I knock.

"Who is it?"

"Kevin."

"Just you, Rooster? Nobody else?"

"Yeah."

He opens the door a sliver and peers out at me. "All right, come in."

Inside, five or six guys are sitting in the dark, watching an R-rated movie called *The Departed.* Joey and his friends watch a fair number of R-rated movies, and they've never locked the door before, but I understood their paranoia. Everyone on the hall has been a little anxious since last night's *300* incident.

Late last night, eight of my hallmates rented a copy of *300,* the ultra-gory R-rated blockbuster about the Spartan army. They turned the sound down, locked the door, and pushed play. Halfway through the movie, Rodrigo, the religion major from Mexico City, left the room to do his Bible reading. When he left, he forgot to relock the door. A few minutes later, Stubbs the RA came to the room to ask one of the guys a question about a homework assignment. When he twisted the unlocked doorknob and entered the room, he saw a battle scene in progress. In a panic, someone hit stop, but it was too late.

"I think that one locked up the Rep Nazi award for me," Stubbs said the next day. All in all, he dispensed eighty-four reprimands, twelve to each person present. The guys were fined a combined $350, and the DVD was confiscated.

All day today, everyone on the hall has been talking about "The Liberty Way," and debating which of its rules are important to enforce. As a form of catharsis, Joey and his friends have been scouring the Internet for Christian colleges with stricter rules than ours. And surprisingly, there are some. I thought we were on the conservative fringe here at Bible Boot Camp, but apparently, there are places out there with rules that make "The Liberty Way" look lax. Consider:

- At Oral Roberts University, a Christian school in Oklahoma, students are asked to sign an honor pledge that reads, in part: "I will not lie; I will not steal; I will not curse; I will not be a talebearer; I will not cheat or plagiarize. . . . I will refrain from smoking, profanity, gambling, alcohol, dishonesty, and all behavior that might cause Christ to grieve."

- At Bob Jones University, students are required to bring a chaperone when dating or interacting in a mixed-gender group. Unacceptable forms of music include new age, jazz, rock, country, and contemporary Christian music. The BJU dress code is stricter than Liberty's, with rules mandating dresses or long skirts on women except "in and between women's residence halls and when participating in activities where the durability of the fabric is important, such as skiing and ice-skating," in which case pants are allowed. In addition, all clothing from Abercrombie & Fitch and its subsidiary Hollister is banned at BJU, as both have shown "an unusual degree of antagonism to the name of Christ and an unusual display of wickedness in their promotions."

- At Pensacola Christian College, a midsized school in Florida, any physical contact between members of the opposite sex is forbidden. Elevators and stairwells on campus are segregated by gender, and a man and a woman who stop to chat en route to class can be punished. PCC students may not read any books that have not been approved by school administrators and must ask permission to visit websites not appearing on an approved list. According to one website run by ex-PCC students (and here's where it gets weird), "even couples who are not talking or touching can be reprimanded for what is known on the campus as 'optical intercourse'—staring too intently into the eyes of a member of the opposite sex. This is also referred to as 'making eye babies.'"

After scoping out these other schools with the room 201 gang, one thing is clear: we're lucky to be going to Liberty, and we're lucky to be going here in the year 2007. In Liberty's early years, it bore a much closer resemblance to schools like Pensacola Christian College (minus the eye babies, I hope). During the 1970s, for example, Liberty couples had to have a dean's permission to go on a date. Men and women couldn't share a car, and even hand-holding was off-limits until 1991. The most talked-about rule relaxation has been the dress code, which dropped a jacket-and-tie rule for men and a skirts only rule for women sometime in the 1990s.

I thought, from a student's perspective, that all Liberty students would be grateful for the loosened rules. And some are, especially Joey and his rebel friends, and especially in the wake of a massive reprimand bust. But I've found a surprising number of Liberty students who want "The Liberty Way" to be *more* restrictive.

The other day, I stumbled on a Facebook group formed by a Liberty girl, called "Why Is It So Hard For Girls To Follow Dress Code?!?!" The description read:

Hello?!?! What is the DEAL with Liberty girls these days? Is modesty completely out the window??? This group is for anyone who is TIRED of walking around and seeing . . . well . . . everything! Short skirts, see-through blouses, cleavage, and straps everywhere! We have Godly men walking around this campus that can't even stroll down the sidewalk without being distracted by a "woman" that looks like she belongs in a Shakira music video.

Ladies, let's not only protect our brothers in Christ, but our testimonies as well. More of us need to defend what we not only believe is right, but what we KNOW is Biblical!

The idea behind this retro-reformist movement seems to be that unless Liberty returns to a higher behavioral standard, it will become indistinguishable from any secular college in America. Before spring break, I heard a group of guys in the dining hall talking about Liberty students who complain about the rules.

"I don't want curfew moved back," one guy said. "There's no reason to relax the dress code."

"If people want that," said another guy, "they should go to UVA or Radford or some other school."

"The rules set us apart."

"Yeah, man, I thank God every day for the rules here."

Tonight, after I finish watching *The Departed,* I'm hanging out with Fox the RA in his room, and I bring up the subject of Liberty University's rules.

"I think some of them are very important," he says. "The ones about staying out of girl dorms, alcohol, drugs, things like that. On the flip side, I hate enforcing them."

"Why?" I ask.

"Well, I don't mind enforcing the purity rules, the ones that are clearly in scripture. But the Southern Baptist cultural rules, the stuff about hair and dress code, I don't like those rules as much. I mean, I understand why we have them. We need to have a standard to set for ourselves, but I think some of the rules are a little outdated. And, of course, the more rules I have to enforce, the harder my job is."

Being an RA at Liberty is one of the more grueling jobs on the planet. In exchange for a $9,100 annual stipend, RAs have to police every rule in "The Liberty Way" at a 30:1 student-to-RA ratio. They have to dole out reprimands, deal with roommate issues, coordinate sister dorm activities, take attendance at convocation, walk the halls after hours to make sure everyone's in for curfew, and much more.

I ask Fox if he'd rather have fewer duties as an RA.

"They ask a whole lot of us," he says. "But being an RA still provides me the opportunity to make a huge impact in the lives of the guys on the hall. Most college RAs are just tokens. But me, I'm a mom, a dad, a nurse, a policeman, an FBI agent, a professional counselor, a nanny, and a janitor, for $9,100 a year."

Liberty's student lore is filled with stories of power-hungry RAs who take immense joy in making reprimand busts. Fox isn't one of these despots, but he tells me about RAs who camp out at the local movie theater to bust Liberty students sneaking into R-rated movies and RAs who have followed suspected troublemakers off campus to catch them pulling into liquor stores. He mentions an RA named Danny whose Machiavellian streak is the stuff of legend.

"Danny probably has the all-time record for number of reprimands written," Fox says. "I can't even come close. He'll walk around campus giving reps to guys whose hair barely touches their collar or girls whose blouses are a tiny bit too tight. One time, he busted a guy for hair code, and the guy took off running. Danny chased him all the way from Main Campus around LaHaye to East to give him the reps. Got him, too." Fox chuckles. "That's just too strict, you know?"

I look at Fox, a guy I've seen giving my hallmates reprimands for watching R-rated movies, being thirty seconds late to convocation, and saying "hell" in a non-religious context—a guy who, just minutes ago, was telling me that his job description encompassed the duties of a policeman and an FBI officer. Apparently, "too strict" is a relative concept.

Recently, I decided to return all the phone calls I've been avoiding for weeks, the ones from my friends back at Brown. It's not that I don't want to talk to them, or that I don't get lonely at Liberty. It's just that there's rarely a good time to chat. Most of my waking hours are spent shuttling between various classes, club meetings, and choir practices, and when I do manage to get off campus and make phone calls to the outside world, my priority is always reassuring my family that I haven't been tarred and feathered.

But in the past three days, I've caught up with more than a dozen of my secular friends, and although it's been great to talk to them, I've been amazed at how little has changed since I've been gone. Everyone is writing sociology papers and applying for summer internships. A few of my friends threw a roller-skating party at a place called United Skates of America, and three-quarters of the guys in my a cappella group came down with pinkeye, but other than that, nothing stuck out.

Maybe it just seems that way because Liberty operates in hyper-speed. I'm not sure why but things that might take an entire month at Brown seem to happen in two, three days here. Take my friend Paul Maddox, for example. Paul has been dating his long-distance girlfriend Lauren for about a month now, and they're already acting like newly-weds. Even from afar, she has completely consumed Paul's life. When the rest of Dorm 22 is hanging out after curfew, he can always be found sitting on the floor next to the water fountain, hands-free headset plugged into his cell phone, talking to his belle. Every day, he rushes out of class, leapfrogging chairs and sidestepping tables to get into the hall, where he text messages Lauren with the urgency of a SWAT team bomb defuser.

Late tonight, Paul comes into my room.

"Hey, Kev. What's going on?" he says. "Sorry I haven't been around. God's been keeping me busy."

Paul didn't used to talk openly about God, but ever since he re-dedicated his life to Christ during Spiritual Emphasis Week, he's made outward piety a high priority. A week ago, he updated his Facebook profile, adding the Bible to his Favorite Books section and Philippians 3:14 to his Favorite Quotes: "I press on toward the goal to win the prize for which God has called me heavenward in Christ Jesus."

I ask how things are going with Lauren.

"I think she's the one, man," he says. "I think I could marry this girl."

"Dude, you've only been dating for a month."

"Five weeks and two days," he says. "Yo, but look at this." He sits down in front of my laptop, clicks open the browser, and types in the address of a Georgia church's website. "This site is mad cool. They have all these videos about marriage. This one's about how to be a leader in biblical love. This one—oh, this one is good—it's all about avoiding greed in your marriage."

This is Paul's first relationship with a Christian girl, and with his head-over-heels love has come a new desire to impress Lauren with his godliness. Every night, they do half an hour of Bible study over the phone. After that, they pray for their future together. Paul prays for a job coaching high school football, and Lauren prays for a job as a Spanish teacher. It doesn't matter where they live, he says, as long as they're in the same place.

"You might think that's corny," he says. "But I just have this feeling, man."

All semester, I've watched Paul's Christian growth with mixed emotions. On one hand, I sort of miss the old Paul, the Paul who griped with me about Jerry Falwell's intolerance, who would look at me during Friday night Bible study as if to say, "Are you getting any of this?" One of the reasons we became friends, in fact, is that we both felt like outsiders at Liberty.

But tonight, seeing the new Paul—madly in love, spiritually fulfilled—it's clear that he's happier than he used to be. And if he's better off now, with his renewed faith and his ridiculously time-consuming girlfriend, I'm okay with that. This is new for me, counting the religious conversion of one of my friends as a positive change. But under the circumstances, supporting him seems like the right thing to do.

Over the past two months, I managed to convince myself that I didn't need to meet Jerry Falwell.

I was just being realistic. Even though his office is a stone's throw from my dorm, the man remains almost completely inaccessible. He does several TV appearances a week, flies around the country in his private jet to his speaking engagements, and generally seems absent from Liberty's day-to-day operation. Most Liberty students get one picture with Dr. Falwell in their four years, if they're lucky.

But this morning, during Dr. Falwell's convocation speech, I started changing my mind. Liberty, I realized, is a brick-and-mortar extension of Dr. Falwell's personality. Everything that happens here, from the big-name speakers to the courses on offer to "The Liberty Way," is directly attributable to his vision for the school, his personal tastes and goals, his particular slant on morality and theology. To understand Liberty fully, I have to understand him.

So on Friday afternoon, I hatch my grand plan. I walk to the office of the *Liberty Champion*, the campus newspaper, and pitch the faculty editor, a friendly, stout woman named Mrs. Mott, my idea for an article on Dr. Falwell. I propose a full-length feature based on an in-depth personal interview conducted by one of his students.

"It could be called 'Dr. Falwell: Beyond the Pulpit,' " I say.

She ponders it for a few seconds, rocking back and forth in her chair.

"And you want to write this piece?" she asks.

"Well, it would be up to you guys," I say. "But I thought . . ."

She smiles. "I think that'd be wonderful!"

Mrs. Mott introduces me to a student editor named Javier, who also likes the idea, and we spend a few minutes arranging the logistics together. They give me contact information for Dr. Falwell's secretary, and we brainstorm questions for the interview. Ten minutes later, everything is set.

Frankly, I'm shocked at how smoothly things went. Really? I waltzed into a newspaper office, proposed a feature story involving a major national celebrity, and came out with a deadline and a word count? God bless college journalism and its low standards.

When I get back to my room, I write an e-mail to Dr. Falwell's secretary asking if he'd be willing to sit for an interview. Even writing to the secretary makes my hands shake. Despite having spent an entire semester hearing him speak two or three times a week, singing in his choir, and attending his university, the man still terrifies me. But he can't be mean to me, right? After all, for all he knows, I'm one of his own.

Still, if this interview comes through, I'm going to give myself every advantage I can. I'm not sure it'd be proper decorum to show up in a "Jerry Is My Homeboy" T-shirt, but the thought has crossed my mind.

I got my first reprimands today. During convocation this morning, a pastor from some megachurch in the Midwest was giving a fairly platitudinous sermon about obeying God's commandments, and around the twenty-minute mark, I felt my eyelids getting heavy. I put my head back, closed my eyes, and the next thing I knew, Fox the RA was tapping me on the shoulder.

"Sorry, Roose. Sleeping in convo. Four reps, ten bucks."

I couldn't help it. I've been exhausted ever since getting back from Daytona Beach. It was a week of nonstop Bible reading, evangelizing, and prayer-grouping with some of Liberty's most intense students, and I think I'm suffering a bit of a Christian overdose. When I went back to my dorm after convocation, found the door locked, struggled for thirty seconds to open it, and then realized that I had been pushing the remote car-door unlocker in the direction of the keyhole, I decided I needed to give myself a break.

So after classes today, I get in my car and drive four hours north to Washington, D.C., to pay my cousin Beirne a weekend visit.

Beirne is a second-year law student at Georgetown. She's a fast-talking, hyper-intelligent twenty-seven-year-old, and she comes from the ultra-liberal branch of my family, the one that spends family game night playing Class Struggle, the socialist alternative to Monopoly. (If you're curious, the object of the game is to "Win the revolution!" and the box features a drawing of Karl Marx arm-wrestling Nelson Rockefeller.)

Beirne and her husband Adam, who teaches science at a Virginia high school, live closest to Lynchburg of anyone in my family, and they offered to host me whenever I needed an escape. So tonight, we go out for dinner at a Japanese restaurant near their apartment. I spend most of the meal catching them up on my time at Liberty. I tell them about my friends, my classes, and the highlights and lowlights of my semester. After dinner, we sit around in their living room, talking and listening to Arlo Guthrie CDs and drinking oolong tea, and the whole thing feels at once familiar and a bit surreal.

Before I fall asleep on her futon, Beirne tells me, "You know, it's good to see that you're the same person as you were before all of this."

I was nervous about seeing members of my family after being isolated at Liberty for two months, mostly because I was worried that I'd seem different to them. But I suppose Beirne's right. Tonight proved that I can slip back into my secular persona when I need to. I like not having to be back on campus for curfew, and I can laugh along with Adam when he browses my History of Life textbook and pronounces it "a parody of science."

However, there are two things I didn't tell Beirne.

First, when she and Adam were criticizing Liberty students, as opposed to Liberty's core ideologies, I found myself getting defensive. They talked about how I lived with "brainwashed sheep," and although I didn't speak up, I wanted to tell them about Jersey Joey or Paul or any of the other Liberty students I've met who are hardly passive followers. I know Beirne and Adam mean no harm, but it makes me uneasy when people paint Liberty students with a broad brush, just as it would make me uneasy if someone said that all Brown students are amoral, unpatriotic heathens.

Second, things happened inside my head all night that definitely wouldn't have happened six months ago. I didn't pray before eating my chicken tempura at the restaurant, and it made me vaguely uneasy for the next twenty minutes. I saw two men walking hand in hand on the way to the parking deck, and I did an incredulous triple take, staring much longer than politesse would dictate. Most disturbing was when we went on a post-dinner stroll around Beirne's neighborhood. I saw a group of high school–age kids sitting on a stoop, and the first thing that flashed through my mind, before I could quash it, was: *are they saved?*

Ever since being among the spring breakers in Daytona Beach, I've been thinking about my re-entry process, about what life will be like when I'm back in the secular world full-time.

My feeling was this: of course it will be odd to transition away from Liberty. Whenever my college friends come back from their semesters abroad, they spend a few weeks in reverse culture shock, making observations like, "You know, in Portuguese, the word for ceiling is *tecto*." Eventually, though, they readapt to their native surroundings, and life goes back to normal.

But on the drive back to Lynchburg on Sunday morning, I start to wonder. Maybe the transition isn't so smooth when the foreign experiences deal with God. The anthropologist Susan Harding defines a religious conversion as the acquisition of a form of religious language, which happens the same way we acquire any other language—through exposure and repetition. In other words, we don't necessarily know when we've crossed the line into belief. I remember something my friend Laura told me during our pre-Liberty training session. Even though she's been out of the evangelical world for a few years now, she still feels guilty when she takes the Lord's name in vain. "I can't help it," she said. "I don't think I'll ever be able to curse without asking God for forgiveness. I can't get rid of that impulse."

Could it be the same for me? All semester, I've been worried about getting in over my head at Liberty, but what if it's too late?

The Lord Knoweth How to Deliver
the Godly

Here's some unsolicited advice for all the young men out there: If you have to leave an athletic event to go to choir practice, don't make a show of it.

I could have slipped out of Monday's intramural softball game unnoticed, faked a stomachache, or said I had an important meeting, and nobody would have cared, since I'm sort of the Tito Jackson of our team. But for some reason, I felt compelled to share the details of my schedule. It's crazy. Hiding my thoughts from everyone I know all semester? No problem. But give me the one fib that would have spared me weeks of grief, and I turn into a moralist.

"Coach," I said to Jersey Joey, our team captain. "I'm taking off early today. Choir practice."

He peered at me over the top of his aviator sunglasses.

"This is a joke, right?"

I've been pretty quiet about my involvement in the choir, since most Liberty students don't go to Thomas Road, and since even at Christian college, choir singing doesn't carry a lot of social cachet. But I figured there was no harm in telling Joey.

"No joke," I said.

"*'Ey guys!*" Joey shouted. "Rooster is leaving in the bottom of the third to go sing in a choir!"

A day later, this remains the funniest thing anyone on my hall has ever heard. I get greetings like:

"Yo, Roose, are you gonna sing us a song today? Something real pretty, okay? Maybe some Barbra Streisand?"

"Hey, choir boy, you wanna come to the gym with us? Or you got a mani-pedi appointment?"

Or when we went to the Olive Garden for dinner, and Joey saw a dish called Pasta Fagioli on the menu.

"Rooster, you gettin' that?"

I was prepared to shrug it off. After all, with Joey, "homo" is a term of endearment. But ever since the softball game, I've been wondering: are there actual gay kids at Liberty? I almost hope not, for their sakes. In a school this size, though, there must be a few closet cases, if not a whole underground community.

During my mentoring session with Pastor Seth on Tuesday afternoon, I ask him about homosexuality at Liberty.

"Oh, it's huge," he says.

"Really?"

"Absolutely. Huge issue."

He clarifies: same-sex relationships and homosexual acts are definitely forbidden under "The Liberty Way," but the university doesn't automatically expel gay students. That said, "gay" is considered a temporary state here. Many of the Liberty guys who feel attracted to other guys (and Liberty girls who feel attracted to girls, I assume) undergo reparative therapy to change their sexual orientation. For more information, Seth refers me to Pastor Rick Reynolds, Liberty's go-to counselor for gay-to-straight therapy.

"He's been helping those guys for as long as anybody can remember," he says.

I want to get a glimpse of how it feels to be a friend of Dorothy at Bible Boot Camp, so I decide to pay Pastor Rick a visit. I call him to schedule an appointment, and the next day, I walk to his office, a small windowless room in the back of the Campus Pastors Office.

He greets me with a smile. "Come on in, Kevin!"

Pastor Rick is a tall, mustachioed sixty-something man, clad in a red cardigan and low-sitting glasses, who looks like he could have been a reference librarian if he hadn't been called to the ministry. He tells me that he came to Liberty as a seminary student in 1976, after a stint in the military, and stayed on to teach afterward. He's been here ever since, first as a dean and now as the pastor of men's ministries, a post that gives him spiritual oversight of Liberty's entire male population.

Earlier this year, Rick tried to start a group therapy session for his gay disciples (he called it Masquerade), but no one showed up for the meetings. "They didn't want to reveal their struggles," he says. "We're hoping that next year, we can tell guys they don't have to be afraid." So now, he meets regularly with forty gay Liberty students in one-on-one sessions.

For the first ten minutes of our meeting, Pastor Rick asks for an exhaustive rundown of my life—the happiest moments of my childhood, my academic interests, my plans for the future. And as I talk, he smiles knowingly, leaning back in his chair. Midway through my speech, it hits me: Pastor Rick thinks I'm Gay Student #41. Of course he does. When he asked why I had sought his counsel, I said something to the effect of, "I have a lot of gay friends back home, and I want to know what to tell them." God, how flimsy does that sound? I'm sure he hears the "so, I have this gay friend . . ." spiel every day.

Suddenly much less comfortable, I end my autobiographical ramble. Time to turn this conversation elsewhere. I ask Rick my first big question: how does he coach Liberty students out of homosexuality?

"First of all," Rick says, "I don't use the word *homosexuality*. I say *same-sex attraction*. If I say I'm a homosexual, I'm something that I can't help. Now, I may fall into the sin of homosexuality, but same-sex attraction just means I'm attracted to another man."

When I ask if there's any way to read the Bible that permits homosexuality, he shakes his head vigorously and lifts a thick leather Bible from the shelf behind him.

"No, no, no," he says. "Look here: in Romans 1, it talks about the fact that men doing things to other men was not meant to be. Common sense tells me that when God created man and woman he made them different. He gave man a penis, and he created into a woman that which brings a man and a woman together."

Rick wants to back up—he's getting ahead of himself. He says that his job, first and foremost, is to provide emotional support for gay Liberty students. "The problem is, the church has been too busy condemning kids for having these feelings, and now they won't come for help. My pastorate is not like that at all. It's an affirmation. There's a difference between saying 'it's sin,' and saying 'I love you, dude. I want to work through this with you.'"

But working through same-sex attraction, Rick says, isn't as simple as telling a guy to try dating girls. "That's actually the worst thing to do, because if they try it once, and they don't feel any emotional or physical connection, they assume it's because they're gay!"

A proper approach to gay-conversion, according to Rick, involves massive amounts of prayer and Bible study, as well as focused mental exercises. He pulls from his desk a packet titled "Breaking Free," which he distributes to all his mentees. The ten-page packet contains a list of essay assignments designed to instill in them "the confidence to change." On the first page, I see:

1. Describe God's unfailing love.
2. Describe God's great compassion.
3. How does God's unfailing love and great compassion affect me and what I am struggling with?
4. What is David asking for when he says, "Create in me a clean heart?" How can this happen?
5. How can I be cleansed and washed clean from my sin?
6. I am not alone, working through my struggle, for I am upheld by the Holy Spirit. This makes me feel _____.

"It's important to figure out where this same-sex attraction comes from," Rick says. To that end, each of his disciples keeps a journal of childhood memories and reflections, which forms the basis of a sort of neo-Freudian analysis. In these sessions, Rick plays the role of psycho-therapist, working with his students to link their homosexual urges to past traumas.

"One guy I was working with was having trouble figuring out where this stuff came from," he says. "And he called me one day just as I was leaving work, and he said, 'Pastor Rick, you can't go home. I found out where it came from.' So I turned around and went to meet with him. And he said, 'I got it. My dad and I didn't get along. He never abused me, but he was married to his work. He was never there. And I longed for masculine love. That's where it all started.'" Rick shakes his head. "You know, 85 or 90 percent of the time, the problem comes back to Dad."

Twenty minutes into our meeting, I still haven't pinned Pastor Rick down. Here's the confusing thing: his views about the gay lifestyle are no different than the Liberty orthodoxy. He believes the Bible con-demns homosexuality categorically, and he quotes the well-worn verses from Leviticus and Romans to buttress his position. He describes gay relationships as "affectionless," and he criticizes the mainstream media for "glorifying homosexuality" without showing kids dying of AIDS or committing suicide. "They don't show the hollowness or the empti-ness," he says.

But Pastor Rick isn't the whip-cracking disciplinarian I expected him to be. When he talks about his students, in fact, his tone is disarm-ingly compassionate. "You have to understand," he says, "the guys that come to my office, I love them. They always say 'You probably wouldn't want me as a son, would you, Pastor Rick?' But no, I'm proud of them. I think they're doing a great job. It's just a struggle going on inside of them."

Pastor Rick admits that his method doesn't always work. He tells me about a Liberty student named Reggie, who earned two degrees from Liberty's seminary, worked as an assistant to Liberty co-founder Elmer Towns, and went to see Rick for help with his sexuality on the q.t. Today, Reggie is the owner of one of Philadelphia's largest gay nightclubs.

"I know where it's coming from," Rick says. "Reggie had a deadbeat dad, and he was always scared of abandonment. I used to tell him over and over, 'I'm here for you, Reggie. I'm here for you.' And I still tell him that today, even though I know what he does for a living."

At one point, Pastor Rick casts his eyes down at the floor. "I've sat with a couple of guys in the hospital who were dying of AIDS," he says. "And when they found out, who did they call? Me. So my wife and I would go visit them, sit by their beds. There were nights I just sat with them all night. I love these dudes. And I tell them, 'I don't think this is something God intended, but I love you, man.' I can't abandon these guys, Kevin."

Maybe it's retroactive sympathy for Liberty students like Reggie, maybe it's confusion about the coltish paternalism of a guy like Pastor Rick, but this conversation has gotten me emotionally worked up. Before I can catch myself, I wonder out loud if the social atmosphere on Liberty's campus—the incessant homophobic slurring in the dorms, the convocation speakers who lambaste gay culture, the editorials in the school paper titled "Kids Should Pray, Not Learn to Be Gay"—if any of that might make homosexual Liberty students feel, oh I don't know, *abandoned*?

"Maybe not abandoned," he says. "But sure, if I'm a guy struggling with that, and people are calling me 'faggot,' all of a sudden, I start letting them define me. I think that kind of language can push someone further into homosexuality."

Okay, so the problem with calling a gay kid "faggot" is not that it hurts his feelings, but that it might make him more gay. Point taken.

Perhaps sensing my unease, Pastor Rick quickly points out the hypocrisy of people who attack the kids he counsels. "People say you can't struggle with this and be a Christian," he says, extending an angry finger. "Well, I disagree with that. So you're attacking other people for feeling same-sex attraction, but you've been looking at Internet porn and masturbating?"

Here's my honest impression of Pastor Rick: I don't think he's evil. I really don't. I disagree with his line of work, of course. I think the American Psychiatric Association was on target when it warned that the "potential risks of 'reparative therapy' are great, including depression, anxiety, and self-destructive behavior." But despite my basic misgivings about his approach, I can't in good conscience label him an evildoer, and the reason I can't is also the most confusing thing about him: in a ministry that has become the gold standard for venomous anti-gay preaching in America, Pastor Rick seems to have developed a genuine custodial love for his students, if not a theological love for their sexuality.

I still can't puzzle out, though, the means by which he reconciles his message—one of care and (moderate) acceptance—with his job as a pastor at the school founded by Jerry Falwell, who has made a half-century career of flagrant gay-baiting. I ask him about this, and he takes a pregnant pause.

"The world wants us to believe that Dr. Falwell is bashing the homosexuals," he says, catching my eyes in a tight lock. "They want to believe that he's . . . homophobic." He tells the story of a speech Dr. Falwell gave at Exodus International, an annual conference for Christians trying to overcome homosexuality. "When he first got up, people booed him. But he told these people that he loves them and that he wants them to put God in control of their lives, and when he got done, he got a standing ovation." He shifts in his seat. "Is Dr. Falwell homophobic? No, he's far from it."

Of all the soft-spinning and gentle rhetorical massaging Pastor Rick has done today, this move—trying to recast Jerry Falwell as a non-homophobe—strikes me as the most unlikely. In all fairness, Dr. Falwell has come some distance on the subject, and his most intolerant days are probably behind him. Two years ago, during an appearance on MSNBC's *The Situation with Tucker Carlson,* he admitted that he supports equal employment and housing access for gay people, saying, "I may not agree with the lifestyle, but that has nothing to do with the civil rights of that part of our constituency." And it's true that during the speech Rick mentioned—the one Dr. Falwell gave at the 2005 conference of Exodus International, the foremost "ex-gay" ministry—he spoke fondly of an evangelical gay-rights group called Soulforce (though news reports made no mention of the initial booing). But in that same speech, Dr. Falwell also said that Christian parents should be allowed to force their children into gay-conversion programs like Pastor Rick's, comparing allowing a teen to be gay to allowing a son or daughter to play on the interstate.

I have many more questions, but after a long hour of conversation, Pastor Rick seems ready to attend to the other students in the waiting room. But before I leave, he says, "Now, I'm just going to throw this out there: was there ever a time when *you* struggled?"

He waits expectantly, smiling, leaning in close to my face. I laugh nervously and tell him that no, it's not me. It's my friends.

"Let's pray," Rick says, not wanting to force the issue. We bow our heads, he prays for me, and after telling me about a self-help book called *You Don't Have to Be Gay*, which he recommends I give to my struggling friends, we say our goodbyes.

"Oh, and one more thing," he says, stopping me at the door. "Come here." He draws me into a full-on bear hug, complete with side-to-side swaying. "Love ya, dude."

It would be far too easy to emerge from a meeting with Pastor Rick feeling downtrodden and depressed, and I resolved beforehand not to let that happen. If I try hard enough, I can mine some nuggets of hope from the past hour. It's heartening, for example, that Rick shows his students compassion instead of anger, even though he ultimately wants them to change. Love with strings attached seems better than no love at all. And it's a good sign that the person at Liberty who has the most day-to-day contact with real, live homosexuals is also one of the mildest in rhetoric. It affirms my optimism that once Liberty students go out into the world and meet happy, healthy gay people, they'll have a tougher time vilifying homosexuality.

But despite my best efforts, I can't stifle my sadness. I'm sad for Liberty's gay students, who must be going through untold pain. And I'm sad that Pastor Rick, a guy with compassion bursting through his sweater seams, has chosen to put his gifts to use in such an odd way. As I leave the office, I recognize a guy sitting on Rick's waiting-room couch, waiting to go in. He's an RA in a dorm near mine, a musician, a real campus figure, and it surprises me to see him sitting there. He looks down and away, not wanting to be noticed. But it's not quick enough. We make eye contact. He gives me a faintly sympathetic look, as if to say, *hey, we're all in this together.*

When I get back from Pastor Rick's office, I have an e-mail sitting in my inbox from Dr. Falwell's secretary about the interview I requested. Dr. Falwell "would be willing" to talk to me, she says.

As I reread the secretary's e-mail, my hands start to tremble. This is exciting news, but also terrifying. It's extremely rare that a Liberty student gets to spend one-on-one time with Dr. Falwell. What if he doesn't like me? What if one of his staffers background-checks me before the interview and finds out who I am? Or what if he's right about all this religion stuff and he can use his divine powers to see right through me?

This week, I've been spending time with a truly impressive Liberty student. His name is Max Carter, and I met him at a meeting of the Liberty College Republicans. I've been dropping in on the Republicans' Tuesday night meetings for six or seven weeks now, partly to meet Liberty's young politicos and partly because the club doles out free pepperoni pizza.

Max, a broad-shouldered junior who looks a little like NFL quarter-back Tom Brady, first entered my radar when he made a speech at the second Republicans meeting I attended. Whereas most of these meetings are spent hypothesizing about all the ways America would go down the drain if Hillary Clinton were ever elected to the presidency, Max gave a flawless twenty-minute discourse on supply-side economics and the shifting electoral map. It was the kind of speech you'd expect to hear over afternoon tea at the Kennedy School of Government, not while scarfing Domino's off paper plates in Lynchburg.

It made sense, then, when a friend told me that Max is typically acknowledged as one of the brightest, most accomplished students at Liberty. In addition to serving as secretary of the College Republicans, Max is the president of Liberty's Stand with Israel club and the current vice president of the student body. During the summers, he works for a high-powered conservative lobby headquartered in Washington, D.C., and he's planning to apply to top-flight law schools like Stanford, Duke, and UVA. Two weeks ago, he ran for next year's student body president post and won in a Reaganesque landslide.

I've gotten to know Max well this semester, and he's a humble, even-tempered guy. (When I e-mailed him to congratulate him on the presidential win, he wrote back: "It wasn't a very close election. If anything, I sort of feel like a jerk for being ultracompetitive about it.") So on Tuesday, when we go out to lunch at a local restaurant, it surprises me when he begins complaining about Liberty's administration.

"They pretend like student government is a legitimate body, but it's sort of an empty gesture," he says. "We have almost no power."

Incidentally, he's not lying. Student councils in general aren't known for being particularly robust, but Liberty's Student Government Association (SGA) might be the least authoritative governing body in America. I went to an SGA meeting last month, and the members make a good show of it. They wear suits, they debate in parliamentary procedure, they pass important-sounding resolutions. Students campaign for office on issues like relaxing dress code and reducing the number of mandatory convocations per week, but everyone knows it's mostly a moot process. At Liberty, very little change occurs unless word comes from Dr. Falwell's office. While combing the university archives the other day, I found some examples of the SGA's failed efforts through the years. For example, in 1999, back when Liberty women were required to wear knee-length skirts or dresses unless the day's predicted temperature was 34 degrees or below (in which case pants were allowed), the SGA passed a resolution raising the cutoff to 40 degrees. The administration vetoed it. The administration also put the kibosh on a student bill that would have moved curfew back from midnight to 2 AM, and on a 1992 "Dorm Bed Policy Bill" that would have allowed students to move their beds around in their rooms and un-stack their bunk beds.

"It's frustrating," Max says, shaking his head. "We pass a bill, then it goes up to the vice president of the university. He turns it down, no matter what it is."

It's strange that Max would volunteer to serve in what he seems to think is a pretty useless student government. If I had to guess, I'd say he's doing it mostly out of boredom. Max is coasting through Liberty, and I get the distinct sense that he'd rather be somewhere else. When he found out I came here from Brown, he emitted a little sigh, as if to say, "but why?" Every time we hang out, he comes up with a half-dozen more questions about my old school. What kinds of political groups are there? Is the campus nice? How big is the endowment?

Today, he says, "You know, I thought about transferring."

Max tells me that he began itching to leave Liberty after just one semester on campus. His parents had urged him to go to a Christian school, and Liberty seemed like the cream of the crop, but before Thanksgiving had passed, he was filling out transfer applications to schools like Notre Dame and Grove City College. Eventually, though, he decided to stay—too much inertia, too many new friends to pack up and start all over—and over the past three years, he's learned to appreciate Liberty's strengths. He's thankful for the school's Christian environment, he's gotten close with a number of his professors here, and he's optimistic that next year, as student body president, he'll be able to cut through some red tape. Overall, Max says, his Liberty experience has been positive. But it hasn't been perfect.

"Liberty is not the real world," he says. "I mean, take my government classes. There's a debate, but it's not a realistic debate. In class, you have your typical Republicans and your Liberty arch-conservatives. No one would ever tread on moderate or liberal ground."

Part of Max's frustration with Liberty has to do with the law school application process he's preparing to trudge through. He's applying to the nation's top schools, and he's worried that his LU transcript will raise eyebrows among the secular admissions committees.

"There's just such a stigma about being associated with Jerry Falwell," he says. "I'm just hoping that it will work to my advantage. Every law school needs a crazy fundamentalist token, right?"

For the rest of our meal, Max talks more optimistically about his vision for Liberty. He'd like to see a College Democrats club, he says, and an alternative newspaper where students could voice their opinions without faculty censorship. He's been a longtime advocate for a system in which students could appeal their undeserved reprimands to a student court. His ideas seem sound, and he seems confident that Liberty's administration is more willing to hear student input than it has been in the past, but there's still a palpable note of resignation in his voice.

"I hate that I'm so anti-establishment here," he says. "I mean, it's natural to want to go against the grain. But I think I'm going against a grain that I support just because this place indoctrinates people so heavily."

Unlike me, Max is actually qualified to pass judgment on the whole of a Liberty education. He's taken dozens more classes than I have, gone through the entire Government Department curriculum, and he's come out of it thinking, from the sound of it, that Liberty's academic scene could use some work.

I'm inclined to believe him, though I will say this: it's bizarre to be talking to a Liberty student who's more cynical about Liberty than I am. At one point, we're talking about my upcoming interview with Dr. Falwell, and Max tells me that I should ask him about the time he "outed the purple Teletubby." I remember learning that, contrary to popular belief, Dr. Falwell's comments about Tinky Winky may not have been entirely his—they originated in an unsigned editorial in his *National Liberty Journal* newsletter. I bring this up with Max, and then it hits me: I just defended Jerry Falwell to Liberty University's incoming student body president. That's one line I never expected to cross.

On Thursday night, the men of Dorm 22 assemble for Fight Night, our semi-frequent hall tradition.

Once every few weeks, someone on the hall calls, "Fight Night!" Guys emerge from their rooms and gather in the hall in a tight circle. Then, someone shouts out a pairing. The chosen hallmates conduct a shirtless wrestling match while everyone else watches and cheers. When there's a clear winner, another pairing is shouted out. Another fight. This goes on for an hour, or until someone gets hurt. It's not a fancy affair, but at Christian college, anything that keeps boredom at bay is worth doing.

Tonight's Fight Night was well attended, maybe thirty-five guys in total. My name never got called, but there were some decent matchups, including Zipper versus Jersey Joey (Joey won, but it was closer than you'd expect).

After the last match ends, I come back to my room to find my roommate Henry pacing the floor, raging mad.

"I cannot take all the faggots around here," he says. "It's worse than San Francisco in this dorm. These guys aren't even good Christians. Bunch of queers."

As you can see, Henry's all-too-familiar hostile streak is alive and well. In the past few weeks, Eric and I have seen our roommate turn the focus of his vitriol from Paris Hilton and Al Sharpton to something closer to home—namely, he has become suspicious that Dorm 22 is full of closeted homosexuals. Henry sees Fight Night's shirtless wrestling and Jersey Joey's naked skateboarding as instances of a general trend of homoeroticism on the hall, and it makes him very, very angry.

At this point, it's become pretty clear that Henry has some kind of hang-up about homosexuality, or a general issue of paranoia, or perhaps a more serious chemical imbalance. His reputation has gotten so bad that the RAs are afraid to punish him. He didn't show up for curfew the other night, and when Fox came to check on us, he just shrugged, as if to say, "I should give him reprimands, but that guy is *nuts*."

After my talk with Pastor Rick on Monday, seeing my hallmates react so negatively to Henry has been slightly reassuring for me. It's taught me that while being anti-gay is the norm at Liberty, once you start being *too* anti-gay, people wonder what your problem is. Measured homophobia isn't the optimal scenario, but it's better than if Henry's hate speech were greeted with yawns—or worse, with nods of affirmation.

Two things worry me, though. First, although Henry has spent the better part of three months ranting about liberals, gays, and non-Christians (he had a particularly juicy bit about "satanic Jews" the other day), he hasn't actually broken any of Liberty's rules. Racial harassment is prohibited in "The Liberty Way," but almost anything else goes, and unless Henry acts on his feelings somehow, he'll steer clear of Liberty's disciplinary system. Second, I'm worried that both Eric and I seem to have made Henry's list of possible homosexuals. I'm not sure what roused his suspicions—the pink tie I wore the other day? Eric's participation in Fight Night?—but Henry apparently complained to one of our hallmates that both of his roommates were "filthy queers."

Tonight, after Henry's outburst, I go next door to Zipper's room to ask for his advice.

"This just isn't normal," I say. "He's so furious."

Zipper shrugs. "Well, should we pray for him?"

I've asked a number of my hallmates for advice about Henry, and they've all suggested the same thing: pray for him. At Liberty, prayer is seen as a panacea, and with no other options on the table, I suppose it's the only thing I can do.

"Sure. Let's pray."

We bow our heads, and Zipper begins. "Father God, thank you for the perseverance you've given Kevin, the patience not to give up on his roommate. Father, we ask you tonight, light a flame of hope in Henry's heart, God. Teach him to follow you. Teach him to be a peacemaker, and ease the tension in his life. Only you know his heart, God. Bring him closer to you."

The next morning at convocation, a Christian relationship counselor named Dr. Gary Chapman takes to the pulpit.

"This morning, I'd like to speak to you on the cultural phenomenon of falling in love," he says.

Dr. Chapman, a pastor from North Carolina, is the author of the Five Love Languages series, a best-selling book franchise that has become as ubiquitous among Christian couples as *What to Expect When You're Expecting* is among pregnant women. He's a bespectacled man with a classic pastor's comb-over who speaks in a syrupy drawl, and today, he's telling us about a romantic phenomenon he calls "the tingles"—which, in his accent, sounds like "the *tangles*."

"When you see certain people," says Dr. Chapman, "there's something about the way they look, something about the way they talk, something about the way they emote that gives you a little *tangle* inside. It's the *tangles* that motivate you to go out for a hamburger with someone."

We hear love-themed convocation sermons every few weeks, almost as often as sermons about finding God's will for our lives and sermons about America's eroding moral base. Of the three genres, I like the last two best. Not that I'm anti-love, but hearing people talk about dating and relationships always makes me think about Anna, the girl from Bible study.

Things between me and Anna are officially over. We haven't gone on a coffee date in more than a month, and aside from the occasional cordial instant message, we almost never talk these days. I never gave her a real reason for the breakup, so I assume she just thinks I grew uninterested. But since my dorm sits next to hers in convocation, we make eye contact fairly often, and when we do, I always try to give her a look that says both "I didn't mean it like that" and "I'm attracted to you. Really, I am." Apologizing telepathically might not be as effective as, say, opening my mouth and telling her I'm sorry, but I'm not brave enough for that yet. As they say, you go to war with the army you have.

This morning, there was no way Anna and I were going to avoid making eye contact. Not only was the convocation speaker talking about love and dating, but he mentioned eating hamburgers, which was what happened on our first date back in February. When he said the hamburger line, I looked to my right, toward Anna's seat, and found her glancing at me. She looked away, then looked back a second later. Our eyes connected. We both smiled.

Man, this kills me. If Anna and I had met anywhere other than Liberty, I'm almost positive we'd be dating by now. Since I'm in such a peculiar situation here, though, what with my hidden Quakerism and my secret writing project, I just can't bring myself to get involved with her.

Some of my friends have suggested trying to find another girl, but I'm not optimistic about my wooing skills. Most of the Liberty girls I've met seem to like macho, ultra-conservative guys who watch *The O'Reilly Factor* and bench-press hundreds of pounds in their spare time, not English major milquetoasts who drink mango smoothies and listen to the latest Michael Bublé album. For now, singledom seems to be my only option.

Every day, I have a first-time experience that would be old news to kids who grew up in a Christian home. My newest young Christian cliché: being bored in church.

This month, Thomas Road is holding its annual stewardship month, which, if you're not familiar with megachurch life, is sort of the evangelical equivalent of an NPR pledge drive. Every sermon this month has been a thinly veiled and euphemized request for money, and while I realize that a huge operation like Thomas Road needs a lot of cash to operate (and it gets it, to the tune of $12 million a year in tithes and offerings), the ritual fleecing of the flock doesn't exactly make for thrilling sermon material.

To combat boredom, I've developed a few church games to play by myself from the choir loft:

- Spot the Hats: Thomas Road, unlike Liberty's ultra-casual Campus Church, is still largely a formal affair. The elderly women of Thomas Road love wearing ornate hats to church, and from time to time, I like to imagine that the grandmothers are pitted against each other in an intense game of headwear one-upsmanship. Last week, one little old lady who sits about ten rows back wore a round hat with a few colorful feathers on the brim. Today, a lady on the other side of the sanctuary knocked her from her pedestal by wearing a white pillbox topped with what looks to be an entire family of peacocks.

- Sign Language Sleuth: During Thomas Road's services, an interpreter in the front of the sanctuary translates Dr. Falwell's sermons into ASL for deaf parishioners. I spend a few minutes per service watching her, and while my ASL vocabulary is still tiny, it's expanding every week. From what I can tell, *tithe* looks like a thumbs-up, and *homosexual* looks a little like the

197

Fonz combing his hair back, neither of which seems entirely coincidental.

- Name That Secular Tune: A lot of the schmaltzy Christian pop songs we sing in the choir are just secular hits outfitted with evangelical lyrics. "Breathe on Me" sounds to me like a dead ringer for Elton John's "Can You Feel the Love Tonight." "Cry Holy," a massive, escalating rock ballad with soaring guitar solos, is what Journey's "Open Arms" would sound like if Steve Perry had gone to seminary.

- Find Mr. Smiley: There is a man who comes to Thomas Road every Sunday for the eleven o'clock service who looks like the filmmaker John Waters, with a side part in his hair and a thin little mustache. He sits in a different part of the sanctuary every week, and he smiles beatifically through the entire service, no matter what topic is being discussed. I love it. Dr. Falwell will be talking about the demons in hell, and he's out there looking like the star of his own private allergy medicine commercial.

For the first two months of the semester, going to Thomas Road on Sundays was one of the highlights of my week. I loved the adrenaline rush of singing with the choir on national TV, vainly craning my neck to catch glimpses of myself on the Jumbotron screens. I loved hearing the world-class soloists, and the fifteen-piece band that accompanies them. I even began to enjoy watching Dr. Falwell in action, despite the fact that he carries about as much spiritual authority with me as the guy who cuts my bagels at Panera Bread.

I think part of the reason I enjoyed Thomas Road was because it was so novel. Growing up in a Quaker home, I never got to witness a three hundred–person choir, a televised service, or a world-famous preacher. The Quaker services I attended as a kid were held in a little brown house with stone steps in the middle of my town, and when my parents and I went (which wasn't often), we would sit on chairs arranged in a circle and meditate silently for an hour. This is how a Quaker church service—called Meeting for Worship—operates. There's no sermon, no scripture readings, no preplanned music. Unprogrammed Quakerism, as my family's branch is called, is totally free-form. Usually, members of the meeting stand during the hour of silence to give short messages on topics of their choice—ruminations on God, poems about faith, stories somehow related to spirituality. But sometimes, no one is inspired to say anything, and the entire hour is spent in silence.

You can see why I didn't go to meeting much. As a kid groomed on cartoons and video games and Little League, an hour of motionless silence was excruciating. At Thomas Road, on the other hand, there's almost *too* much stimulation. The stage lights, the one hundred–decibel praise songs, the bright purple choir robes, the tempestuous bellowing of Dr. Falwell—it's an hour-long assault on the senses. And all you have to do is sit back in your plush, reclining seat, latte and cranberry scone in hand, and take it all in. It's Church Lite—entertaining but unsubstantial, the religious equivalent of a Jerry Bruckheimer movie. And once the novelty wears off, once the music becomes familiar and the motions of praise become pro forma and mechanized, you start to realize that all the technological glitz and material extravagance doesn't necessarily add up to a spiritual experience.

Today, from my perch in the Thomas Road choir loft, my mind wandered back to the little brown house with stone steps. I think I'd appreciate the minimalist Quaker worship more now than I did as a kid. It didn't have Jumbotron screens or a five thousand–watt sound system or a café in the lobby, and it wasn't run by a world-famous televangelist with millions of followers. But at least it felt real.

There Is Nothing Covered,
That Shall Not Be Revealed

Springtime at Liberty is almost criminally beautiful. The Blue Ridge mountains are filling out with lush greens, purples, and reds, the temperature rarely dips below seventy, and students spend their afternoons playing Frisbee on the lawn in front of Dr. Falwell's office. Construction workers are putting the finishing touches on the mountain monogram, which consists of mammoth piles of rock and brick arranged in the shape of a giant LU on the side of Liberty Mountain. The weather has even brought out a little G-rated mischief. A few days ago, a student prankster poured laundry detergent into the courtyard fountain, turning the whole thing into a huge bubble bath. When the wind blows, clumps of foam break off and float around the courtyard, smacking unsuspecting passersby in the face.

Maybe it's the weather, but I'm finding it hard to study for my classes. My Bible skills are getting better, and I'm fairly confident in my ability to answer quiz questions like "True or False: According to Acts 20:21, both repentance and faith are necessary for salvation." (True, for the record.) Even my History of Life class is getting a bit dull. We've been talking about the fossil record this week, and Dr. Dekker's lectures have been very dry and science heavy, filled with words like *chondrichthyes* and *coelacanth*. I don't get it. Isn't the appeal of young-earth creationism supposed to be its simplicity? If I say I don't believe in evolution, can I get an A and skip the rest of the semester?

With the coming of spring, a wave of romance seems to be sweeping Liberty's campus. And unlike the purity-laced Valentine's Day romance wave, this one doesn't seem to be all sugar and spice.

Last week, I took a walk around campus with Samantha, a girl who came on the Daytona Beach evangelism trip with me. Samantha, a sophomore from Wisconsin with opalescent blue-green eyes and a blonde ponytail, has always struck me as a very typical Liberty girl. Her Facebook profile reads: "I luv God, I luv my family, I luv softball and my dog Sandy!" We've hung out a few times since our mission trip, and she often sends me perky text messages like "hope u have a good day!!!"

So you can imagine my surprise when Samantha told me she had just been busted for violating "The Liberty Way" ban on sexual intercourse.

"I can't believe it, Kevin," she said. "It's the worst thing that's ever happened to me."

Tears welling in her eyes, Samantha told me the whole story. About a week ago, she snuck out after curfew to visit the off-campus apartment of a guy she'd been dating. They fooled around a little, lost control, and ended up having sex. When she returned to campus the next morning, she told her roommate about her sordid affair. Her roommate, after much prayer and contemplation, decided to "do the Christian thing"—she turned Samantha in to the dean of women. Samantha was served with the maximum punishment a Liberty student can get without being expelled: thirty reprimands, a $500 fine, and thirty-five hours of community service.

I couldn't imagine why Samantha was telling me all this. We're friends, but not extremely close friends, and she's the only Liberty girl I've ever heard talking about her sex life. I guess she needed the emotional support, both because of her disciplinary trouncing at the dean's hands and because she was terrified about what her parents will do when they find out.

"Will they be mad?" I asked.

Samantha grimaced and pointed to her purity ring. "Why do you think I wear this? My parents think I'm a virgin. They might have heart attacks."

Samantha's anxiety had an undercurrent of anger, both because she felt betrayed by her roommate and because she felt singled out for committing what is, according to her, a fairly common transgression.

"I know so many girls who have had sex," she said. "Even some of my best friends."

"Would they admit that to me?" I asked.

"No way. There's a double standard at Liberty. If you're a guy, you can have sex and repent for it, and everything's okay. But for girls, if it gets out that you're not a virgin, you're pretty much a leper. No one will date you. Like, now, I have this reputation as a slut! And I had sex with one guy!"

I had no reason to doubt Samantha's claims, but they were still hard to believe. All my evidence seemed to point to a chaste student body. In GNED II class the other day, we had an hour-long discussion of the question "Where should Christian couples draw the line?" Dr. Parks gave us seven choices that ranged from "no physical contact" to "sexual intercourse," and we decided as a class that it would be best to stop at "light touching." According to a schoolwide survey cited in that class, 85 percent of Liberty students have pledged to remain virgins until marriage.

Samantha turned out to be right about at least one thing: Liberty's guys have a lot easier time talking about their sexual histories than their female counterparts. After the conversation with Samantha, I started asking around in Dorm 22 about guys with active sex lives. I expected to get stonewalled, but most guys seemed all too eager to tell me about their exploits. No one told me that they were currently sexually active, but several guys admitted flat-out that they had slept with their high school girlfriends, and several more admitted that they had lost their virginity in one-time lapses. Some seemed repentant, others not so much.

One of the most surprising confessions came from Luke Hatton, a biology major who lives down the hall. He's an ultra-pious Prayer

Leader, and we have lots of instant-message conversations like this one from last night:

> *Luke Hatton: what up roose*
> *Kevin Roose: chillin*
> *Kevin Roose: wasting time*
> *Luke Hatton: maybe you should read God's word*

This afternoon, I walk to lunch at Pizza Hut with Luke, and during an unrelated conversation, he brings up the fact that he only ended up at Liberty because his parents made him come. He actually wanted to go to Duke.

"I'm glad I came to Liberty, though," he says. "I mean, I know I never would have gotten into drinking or drugs at Duke, but I would definitely have gotten into trouble with girls."

"What do you mean?" I ask.

"Roose, I've hooked up with more girls here than ever before," he says. "Can you imagine what it would be like if they could be in the dorms with us?"

I knew Luke was a flirt. I've seen him hitting on girls in the dining hall, but I always imagined him as a hand-holder. Maybe a cheek-kisser on a bold day. What counts as hooking up, I wonder?

"I've had intercourse with three girls here," he says.

I choke on my breadstick.

"I know, it's a sin," he continues. "But . . . yeah."

For the rest of our lunch, Luke tells me all the stories behind his hook-ups, including a reverend's daughter and one girl who had a steady boy-friend. He spares no graphic detail, and after he's exhausted his list, he leans in close and explains that there are three types of girls at Liberty:

- The I'm-dating-Jesus girls, who don't really consider them-selves single. These girls read the book *I Kissed Dating Good-bye*, an evangelical classic that implores Christian girls to skip the dating process entirely, going straight from friendship to marriage. They accept this book as gospel truth—meaning,

Luke says, that "you could be Brad Pitt and you'd still strike out with them."

- The FACS women. FACS, short for Family and Consumer Sciences, is Liberty's home economics department. Women (and it's all women) in the department take classes like Parenting, Families Under Stress, and Psycho-Social Aspects of Clothing. Luke adds, "That's where you look if you want a good wife, not a hookup."
- The closet freaks. "There are girls here," Luke says with a mischievous smile, "who act so virginal, who wear purity bracelets and talk about saving themselves for the Lord, who will knock your socks off."

I probably shouldn't be so surprised to find out that Liberty students aren't as pure as they let on. According to recent studies conducted at Yale and Columbia, 89 percent of teens who pledge to remain abstinent until marriage end up breaking those pledges. The average abstinence pledge, in fact, only delays a young person's first sexual experience by eighteen months. Still, it's disconcerting to hear frank sex talk from a guy who, just a month or so ago, was wearing a white T-shirt to commemorate his Christian purity.

As Luke and I leave lunch, I ask him if Liberty's rules on sexual propriety bother him.

"No, not at all," he says. "I approve of all the rules here." He cocks his head upward and smiles jauntily. "I don't follow them all. But they have my approval."

After my conversation with Luke, I walk around campus feeling dazed and confused. I knew there was rebellion at Liberty, but I thought it was limited to the usual suspects—Jersey Joey, Marco, Travis, et al. I never suspected that my hall's Prayer Leaders were doing the dirty. It makes me worry that I've been blind to my surroundings all semester. What other sub rosa sins am I missing? Is there a secret society of Satanists on campus? Does the basement of Dorm 22 have a meth lab in it?

Luckily, after dinner, I'm reassured that not all Liberty students are closet fornicators. I get a visit from my next-door neighbor Zipper. He's wearing a tie-dyed shirt, a break from his usual Hawaiian prints, and he looks just as exuberant as ever.

"Kevin Rooooooooose!" he says. "Prayer chapel?"

Every few nights, Zipper asks me to accompany him to the prayer chapel, a small, windowless brick building about fifty feet from our dorm. I couldn't turn him down the first time he asked, and he seemed to enjoy it so much that I kept going. We've been four or five times now, and a little routine has coalesced.

Today, Zipper and I sit in the pews and talk for a few minutes about how our lives are going, what's on our minds, what prayers we need. I tell him about my upcoming Old Testament exam, my grandmother's health problems, my issues with lust. He tells me about his upcoming job interview at a restaurant downtown, his application to be an SLD next year, and his blossoming crush on a girl named Emily Jaffee. Then, Zipper refers me to a Bible passage he thinks will help me get through the day, and I pick one out for him. We sit there in the chapel reading our passages silently until we both finish. He prays for me, I pray for him, and we stand up to leave.

The first few times we did this, I was basically humoring Zipper. I sat there and prayed with him, and I even tried to pick out Bible passages that fit his spiritual needs. (When he was nervous about an exam, for example, I picked 2 Timothy 1:7—"For God did not give us a spirit of timidity, but a spirit of power, of love and of self-discipline.") But I couldn't get into it the way he did. For me, going to the prayer chapel was a way to spend time with my next-door neighbor. For him, it was a spiritual fix, the highlight of his day.

But the more we go, the more I'm beginning to understand what Zipper sees in it. I like the feeling of being prayed for. I like setting aside regular intervals of time to pray and read the Bible, undistracted by schoolwork or intramural sports or checking my e-mail. I like the way being Zipper's prayer partner forces me to commit all the minutiae of his life to memory. Zipper's prayers for me are always full of hope and optimism ("Lord, I *know* Kevin can ace this test, I *know* you're going to help him, Lord"), and when I hear that for twenty or thirty minutes in a row, it starts to sink in. In Zipper's world, the glass is always 90 or 95 percent full, and when he's urging you on with that manic cheeriness of his, things start to seem *possible*.

Of course, I haven't worked out the theological kinks of prayer yet. I still don't believe that Zipper praying for my Old Testament exam will get me a better grade. I don't believe that God rearranges the cosmos according to what we say in that prayer chapel. And sometimes, it's hard to overcome those doubts. Couldn't I use my time more wisely than praying to a God who may not even be listening? Should I be doing something that pays more obvious dividends, like studying or doing my laundry or returning my aunt Tina's phone calls?

William James said that the value of a religion lies in its usefulness to the believer, not in the truthfulness of its supernatural claims. And the time I spend in the prayer chapel certainly feels useful. It certainly makes me feel more uplifted, more connected to my Liberty friends. Still, reducing prayer to a pick-me-up doesn't totally satisfy my brain. Does prayer work? Can we change God's mind? These aren't minor questions, and they seem to demand answers. Therefore, my quest continueth.

At this week's Pancake Night, a few girls from the sister dorm are gossiping about one of their hallmates, a girl named Leslie Hawkins.

"Leslie freaks me out," says one girl. "There's just something weird about her."

"She's a feminist," says another. "That's what's weird about her."

I know Leslie. She's a fast-talking, brown-haired junior from Wichita who wears slightly baggy jeans and roomy polo shirts. She's friends with Anna, the girl I used to quasi-date. But I've never heard about the feminist bit. I'm skeptical. A bra burner at the school founded by Jerry Falwell, who once referred to the National Organization for Women as the "National Organization of Witches"? No way.

The next day at lunch, I find Leslie alone in the middle of a dining-hall table. I put my tray down and plop myself down in the seat across from her.

"So Leslie," I say, "I hear you have some interesting views on gender."

Leslie rolls her eyes. "Did you come over here to chastise me for being a feminist?"

"No, no," I say. "I was just curious. So, you're really a feminist?"

"Sort of."

Leslie and I talk for a few minutes about her views. She tells me that she doesn't agree with the "GNED party line," but before she can elaborate, she tells me she's running late for class.

"Could we talk about this more some other time?" I ask.

"Sure," she says. "How's tonight?"

So after dinner, I walk to the sister dorm to hear more about Leslie's feminism. She meets me outside, and we sit on the grass under a large tree.

"First off," she says. "I am not a feminist. I don't want you to think I am."

Hold on. I'm confused. Didn't she say she was?

"No, no. I'm an *evangelical* feminist. Here's the difference: Evangelical feminists don't believe we are better than men. Secular feminists do. They have meetings, and they sit around in a circle and talk about all the bad things men have ever done to them. It's a male-bashing faith system."

Okay, so first things first: Leslie is not your average women's-libber. She's not going to be interning for Gloria Steinem anytime soon. But she explains that she believes in the egalitarian model of evangelical gender relations, the one Dr. Parks dismissed as "greatly skewed" during GNED II the other week.

"I don't believe in role distinctions between sexes," she says. "In my opinion—and I can back this up with all kinds of scripture—everything outside of biology is up for grabs."

Leslie is a women's ministries major, and as such, she hears a lot about the complementarian model. Her degree program includes classes like The Christian Woman, described in Liberty's course catalog as "A study of God's Word as it specifically relates to women today and God's plan and purposes for them in every sphere of life as women, wives, homemakers, and mothers." Leslie knows of only one other girl in her department who agrees with her. "Neither of us is very vocal, because our professor made it pretty clear that if you try to debate her, you don't have a teachable spirit."

When I ask about the other girls in her classes, Leslie laughs. "Honestly, most of the girls in the women's ministries department are just pastors' wives in the making. They're here to get their degrees, get married, and throw church raffles and tea parties for the rest of their lives." Leslie explains that although she doesn't feel called to be a pastor, she would like to be some sort of a traveling evangelist—"stirring up fights in other people's churches and leaving," as she puts it.

"I just can't be that stay-at-home married woman. I love working. It gives me self-satisfaction. I feel like I'm doing something with my life, like I might make a difference for God."

"Does that mean you don't want to get married?" I ask.

"Honestly," she says, "right now, I feel called to be single. Am I open to God calling me in a different direction? Absolutely. Would I love to share my life with someone? Maybe. It's a lot of responsibility. I'm a 'tell it like it is, say what I feel' person, not the 'submit to your husband whatever he says' type."

Leslie is not totally unorthodox at Liberty (she clarifies at least three times that she is not a *feminist* feminist). Still, she's probably the most iconoclastic Liberty student I've met all semester. Though she's "very much pro-life," she describes her views on the "Christian gray areas"— things like drinking, tattoos, smoking—as liberal. She doesn't believe homosexuality is morally wrong. She's the second self-professed Democrat I've met here, and she has harsh words for Dr. Falwell.

"I believe that up until the seventies, he was a racist bigot. And I'm sorry, but I don't think he changed because of God. I think he changed because he knew if he didn't, he wouldn't be as influential as he is now. I think he has a serious power addiction."

I admire Leslie's chutzpah, but I'm also confused. I can't understand why an evangelical-feminist Democrat pro-gay preacher-in-training would choose Liberty. Why not go to a more progressive Christian school?

"I came here to study conservative Christianity," she says. "I knew that I wasn't conservative, but I wanted to know what you guys believe. I wanted to know why we're different."

Leslie would love to talk more, she says, but it's curfew time. She stands up, wipes the grass off her jeans, and heads back inside. I walk back to my dorm smiling. Could it be true? Leslie is doing exactly what I'm doing—learning about the Christian Right, confronting Liberty as an unconvinced student—except she's doing it without a journalistic motive. It hammers home the big lesson from this semester: Bible Boot Camp is a surprisingly messy place.

Halfway back to my dorm, I start to wonder: what did Leslie think about that conversation? I wasn't exactly being subtle back there. In my excitement, I was tossing her softballs, not treating her like the renegade she is. I hope she didn't notice anything fishy.

As it turns out, I wasn't entirely smooth. When I get back to the dorm, I see a string of instant messages sitting on my screen.

> *Leslie Hawkins: why do you ask so many questions but very rarely give any answers?*
> *Leslie Hawkins: do you know what you believe?*
> *Leslie Hawkins: or are you trying to figure that out still?*

Dammit! She's onto me. This is no good. I type, "I have to go, sorry" into the window and hit return. Five seconds later, her response comes back.

> *Leslie Hawkins: fine, but know that this is not over, dude*
> *Leslie Hawkins: ,)*

*   *   *

Last month, I invited a few of my closest friends from Brown to come visit me at Liberty, thoroughly expecting that they would all turn me down. And they did. One by one, the responses came back: "No way." "Not on your life." "When I want to get lynched, I'll give you a call."

My friend David was among those who turned me down on the first pass. It made sense—he's openly gay, radically liberal, and Jewish.

He's a legend at Brown for the huge, creative theme parties he throws (example: the Rubik's Cube party, where everyone comes dressed in multiple colors and you trade clothes with other partygoers until you're clad in one solid color). But a few weeks later, David e-mailed me to say that out of perverse curiosity, he was going to fly down to Lynchburg to see Bible Boot Camp for himself. He's scheduled to arrive today.

I was nervous about letting David into my Liberty life for obvious reasons. If he did anything outlandish during his visit, I'd be guilty by association. But he reassured me that he would try his best to blend in.

"I can pass as straight," he said. "I'll just talk about . . . oh, I don't know, killing animals or something."

His comment was eerily prescient, because killing animals is exactly what we are going to be talking about. Today, I'm taking David to Thomas Road Baptist Church's fourth annual Beast Feast, an outreach event for hunters and fishermen. I'm not much of a sportsman, but when David told me he was coming, I couldn't resist signing us up. The invitation said that "hunters, outdoorsmen and the curious of Central Virginia" were welcome to attend. And at an event like this, who could be more curious than a Quaker pacifist and a gay Jewish liberal?

David's plane is late, so we miss the afternoon seminars on topics like "Planning an Out-of-State Hunting Trip" and "Hunting Strategies Using Modern Technology: Fact vs. Fiction." But we arrive at Thomas Road just in time for the "activity stations," a series of try-it-yourself demonstrations of hunting and fishing equipment set up around the church parking lot. Among the offerings: a BB gun practice range in the shape of a Conestoga wagon, a paintball target shoot, and a contest in which guys try to cast their fishing lures into the center of an old tractor tire.

David and I decide to try the archery station. I had a few archery lessons at summer camp when I was ten, so I figure I should get right back into the swing of things. But this is no recreational archery, judging by the bow. When I get to the front of the line, a man with a white beard thrusts something at me that looks like a prop from *Star Trek*. It's a huge red thing with a liquid level, cushy foam grips, and a complex system of four or five pulleys.

"Take these," the man says, handing me the bow and three arrows, "and hit that." He points to a bank of hay twenty or thirty feet away, with a pair of plastic deer nestled beside it and a paper target taped to the front. Squinting for accuracy, I draw back the string, take my aim, and release. The arrow sails over the hay bank, plinks off the wall of the church, and falls to the ground at the deer's feet. The next arrow goes wide right. I flub the third, and it ends up about five feet in front of me.

"Target's that way, Kev," says David. He slaps me on the back and shoots me a surreptitious wink. "What are you, gay?" This sends the line behind us into raucous laughter.

At dinnertime, the Beast Feast organizers begin herding us into the church gym, which has been decorated with massive mounted animals, including a brown bear, a set of caribou, and a deer the size of a Toyota Camry. For many Beast Feast attendees, the big draw is the dinner. Hunters from Thomas Road have spent months gunning down all kinds of animals for tonight's buffet, including venison, caribou, alligator, and kangaroo. Everything except the alligator and kangaroo is advertised as "local and fresh."

"Who's gonna try everything tonight?" asks the man in charge. Hands go up all around the gym. "Watch out for those guys. They're going to be sick tomorrow."

As we eat, a pastor from Anchorage, Alaska, named Jerry Prevo comes to the stage to deliver the keynote sermon. He's a board member at Liberty, and he served as a high-ranking member of the Moral Majority back in the 1980s. His sermon tonight, he says, is called "Jesus Was a Man's Man."

"Let me ask you a question," Rev. Prevo says. "Why do men follow Jesus Christ? If you're a follower of Jesus Christ tonight and you're not ashamed of it, say *amen!*"

A huge wave of hearty amens echoes off the walls.

"Now, some people have the impression that only women go to church, only women follow Jesus Christ. You know, in Hollywood, they portray Christ as a feminine-acting person, as a sissy, and quite frankly, I get upset about that. That could not be true! Jesus Christ, while he was here, attracted men. In the gospel of Matthew, four thousand men gathered to hear him speak. That's right—four thousand men. That'd be like two hundred thousand today. He was a man's man.

"When he chose people to become his apostles, Jesus chose fishermen. Fellas, in the year 2005, the most dangerous job in the world was commercial fishing. More people get killed per capita doing that than anything else. Jesus chose commercial fishermen to be his apostles. Tough guys. If Jesus had not been a man's man, those guys would not have followed him.

"Unfortunately, there are some sissy ministers out there. But what you need to do is find a man behind the pulpit like Dr. Jerry Falwell, a man's man. When I met Dr. Falwell, he gave me a bear hug and I thought every rib in my chest was broken. How many of you been punched by Jerry Falwell? Yeah, so you all know. It hurts. He's a man's man.

"Some people think that all preachers are wimps and sissies, so once a year I'll get in the pulpit, on my TV show up there, and I'll say, 'Let me say something to you: If you break into my home, and you try to harm my wife or my house, you better come prepared to die. Because if my .357's not enough to kill you, my .45 will. If that doesn't, my .375 rifle will. If that doesn't kill you, one of my other dozen guns will.' You're not going to get a sermon when you break into my house, you're going to get shot at, and I'll read a scripture verse over your funeral service!"

The rest of the sermon is more of the same muscle-flexing, manlier-than-thou rhetoric designed to refashion Jesus as Rambo, and by the time Rev. Prevo prays the closing prayer, I'm feeling sort of guilty about bringing David here. I thought it would be fun to give him an extreme experience right off the bat, but I almost wish I had eased him in. As entertaining and absurd as Beast Feast has been, I'd feel bad if this were his only experience in the evangelical world. I mean, really—Jesus was *a man's man*? What happened to the Prince of Peace? Didn't Jesus weep when Lazarus died? Or was there just something in his eye?

As we walk through the parking lot to my car, David turns to me, looking a little dazed.

"You know that was crazy, right?" he says.

"Yeah," I say.

"Is Liberty always like this?"

"No. I promise, it's not."

He smiles. Somehow, I'm not sure he believes me.

David stays at Liberty for the rest of the weekend, and by the time Sunday rolls around, the oddest thing is happening: he's getting along with my friends.

Nobody here knows anything about him, of course. Things would get interesting if David were to let it slip that he's gay, or if he started a sentence, "See, at *my* bar mitzvah . . ." But so far, he's been pleasantly surprised, like I once was, by how well Liberty students compare to their stereotype. He's spent time with Jersey Joey, Zipper, Eric, and Paul, and everyone seems to be on good behavior. There's been no overt gay-bashing, no anti-evolution rants, no condemnation of non-Christians. They've all been treating him warmly and normally.

On Sunday night, David and I head to the campus gym with a few guys from Dorm 22. I do my usual twenty minutes on the treadmill, leaving David with my hallmates, and when I emerge from the cardio room, I see that they've invited him into their pickup basketball game. David's laughing and high-fiving and trash-talking right alongside them.

I stand there watching David run down the court with my Christian friends, and all the unexpected revelations from the past week come flooding into my head. Liberty students who struggle with lust. Secular Quakers who enjoy prayer. Evangelical feminists who come to Bible Boot Camp out of academic interest. I used to think that my two worlds were a million miles apart. But tonight, the distance seems more like a hundred thousand miles. It's not a total improvement, but it's not meaningless, either.

I Made a Covenant with My Eyes

Every Monday before convocation, I eat breakfast with Pastor Seth, my spiritual mentor. Our meetings are usually pretty relaxed. We head to the local Panera Bread to talk theology, go over my Bible-reading assignments for the week, and keep each other abreast of the goings-on in our lives.

Today, though, he has an agenda.

"Let's talk about lust."

In our first discipleship meeting, Pastor Seth asked me what specific sin struggles I was having. Lust was the first thing that came to mind. I figured it was a fairly typical collegiate vice, and we put it on the back burner. Now he wants to tackle the issue head-on.

"How would you say your lust expresses itself on a day-to-day basis?" he asks.

I shrug. "I mean, I look at girls . . . lustfully . . . sometimes."

Seth sets down his coffee cup.

"Let me cut to the chase: do you have a problem with masturbation?"

"Uh," I stammer. "I guess it depends how you define *problem*."

"Well, how many times a week do you masturbate?"

Man. We haven't even finished our chocolate-chip muffins, and he's already asking me a question I'm not even sure I'd answer under a

214

grand jury subpoena. Am I really supposed to tell an evangelical pastor? Plus, there's a family with young children in the next booth over. Is there no decency?

But in the spirit of full disclosure, I make a ballpark estimate. (I'll spare you the exact number, but if you're really curious, it's somewhere between zero and my current shoe size.)

Pastor Seth nods. "It's a widespread struggle."

You might think that Liberty, with its unforgiving rules about sexual contact between students, would look kindly upon masturbation as a safe, solo alternative. You'd be wrong. As I learned during orientation week, evangelicals of the Liberty ilk frown heavily upon self-love. The problem, in their eyes, lies not with masturbation proper, but with lust, coveting, and the other sins that typically accompany the act.

"If you can find a way to masturbate without thinking lustful thoughts, I suppose it wouldn't be sinful," Pastor Seth once told me. "And if you do, you'll want to take your number out of the phone book. Christian men will be overloading your circuits."

Today, after a brief discussion of my libido, Seth recommends I check out Every Man's Battle, Liberty's on-campus support group for pornography addicts and chronic masturbators.

To be clear: I am nothing close to a chronic masturbator, nor am I even remotely addicted to pornography. In fact, a semester in Liberty's neo-Victorian sexual climate has caused a significant and perhaps irreparable falling out with my loin parts. But Seth wants to make sure I have the tools to combat lust should it ever turn into a serious problem, so he recommends that I pay a one-time visit to Every Man's Battle, a self-help group so bizarre in premise that to acknowledge its existence is to wonder whether this whole school isn't someone's idea of a practical joke.

That night, I head to the Campus Pastors Office to attend the weekly meeting of Every Man's Battle (which I've taken to calling Masturbators Anonymous). The group convenes in a small, fluorescently lit conference room. When I walk in, I see eight guys seated around the table, talking to Pastor Rick—yes, he of the reparative therapy for homosexuals. Apparently, Pastor Rick is also the leader of Every Man's Battle.

Lovely. Now he thinks I'm a self-denying homosexual *and* an inveterate masturbator.

"Come on in, Kevin!" he says.

I take a seat next to Pastor Rick, and after several minutes of idle chatter, he prays to open the meeting.

"Lord, we pray that in the process of coming together as a group, we will hold each other accountable. As we finish the school year, Lord, I pray that these guys will be able to get their work done without letting down their guards. I know it's hard, but I know they can do it."

Next, the guys go around the table in sequence to talk about the Bible reading they've been doing. A muscled guy in a camouflage shirt has been going through the book of 2 Peter. A husky mustachioed guy next to him has been reading a devotional book about God's will. A hipster with Buddy Holly glasses and an "I [Heart] Jesus" sticker on his Nalgene bottle is immersed in the gospel of Matthew.

For the first ten minutes, Every Man's Battle seems no different from my Friday night Bible study. The guys are drinking iced tea and passing Doritos around the table as they talk. Nary a mention of porn or sexual sin. I begin to wonder if I stumbled into the wrong room.

"Okay," Pastor Rick says, thumping his Bible on the table. "Victories and falls. Let's hear 'em. Brett, start us off."

Brett, the mustache wearer, begins. "This week has been a mixed bag," he says. "For a long time, I was having a lot of victory. My time with the Lord was awesome. Then I got sick a week ago, and laying in my bed, my thought life started to go down the drain. On Saturday morning, I was praying, I was reading the Bible, but I knew something was missing. Then God sent me a sign. Saturday afternoon, I started feeling really, really sick. I ran to the toilet and started puking everywhere. I mean, I didn't think God was punishing me or anything, but hey, if he has to stick me to the toilet with a stomach virus to get me to think about holy things, so be it."

"Praise the Lord!" Pastor Rick says. "Any victories?"

"I've been putting up some safeguards," Brett says. "I found myself making an account on a website to post photos that I had taken, and I caught myself looking at other people's beach pictures. I thought, whoa, this is not going anywhere good, so I deleted it."

"And what can you do to make sure you don't fall again?"

Brett shrugs. "I've been trying to find some filter software for Macintosh. I've started to leave the windows open in my room. I've stopped changing into an undershirt and boxers when I get back to my room. I put worship music on really loud and make sure the door is open."

Pastor Rick nods, and we continue around the circle. Alex, a timid, skinny guy who hasn't looked up from the ground since I arrived, says that he masturbated for the last time sixteen days ago.

"I had a rough night the other night, but I managed to get through it," says Alex. He points to Shawn, his roommate. "Luckily, this guy was in the room. And we always joke with each other when we're on our laptops."

Shawn laughs. "I'll be like 'Hey, buddy, whatcha lookin' at?'"

"And I'll stutter, and be like 'Uh, uh, nothing. Uh . . . Jerry Falwell pictures! Right here!'"

"And then he'll get the message and put away his laptop."

"It really helps."

Pastor Rick smiles and points to the next guy, a tall black man named Horace.

"I've been using this software on my laptop," Horace says. "It's called XXXChurch.com. It keeps a log of every site I visit, and then it e-mails the log to my youth pastor at home. So if I visit anything raunchy, he hears about it. And that ain't good."

The guys chuckle. Pastor Rick gives Horace a golf clap.

"But I did have a small fall yesterday," Horace continues. "I saw a girl in class the other day, and I kept telling myself, 'Close your eyes, that's not your wife.' She was looking good, though."

After Horace finishes, Pastor Rick points to me. I decide to talk more generally about my problems with lust. Pastor Seth is one thing, but I'm not ready to reveal my onanistic habits to a bunch of strangers.

"Well," I say. "It's getting warm outside, so girls are wearing less clothing . . ."

This half sentence is all it takes to send the room into groans.

217

"Dang, man, I hate this time of year," says Horace. "I wish it was cold again."

"Spring is my Achilles' heel," says a guy named George.

Brett chimes in with a story.

"Just yesterday, I was walking in the hallway on the way to chemistry, and there was this girl walking right in front of me. Now, I don't know how this girl passed dress code at all. Her skirt was the size of a washcloth. So I kept looking down at the ground, repeating to myself 1 Corinthians 6:18, "Flee from sexual immorality." Flee, flee, flee. And it wasn't working, so I decided to grab my stuff and run ahead of her so I wouldn't have to look at her backside. So I zip past her, and she says out loud, 'Hey, where's that guy going?'"

Brett lets out a hearty laugh. "I just kept walking, thinking 'Boy, I'm not gonna have her walking in front of me!'"

After a few more stories about sin avoidance, Pastor Rick gives us the "Nine Fs to Victory" (Feed on the Word, Follow Christ, Faithfully pray, Fall in love with Christ, Fellowship, File away sins, Flee, Foresee, and Fortify). Then, he asks for our "battle plans."

Shawn says, "Well, my parents were planning to get a wireless router, but I asked them not to. Our only Internet access right now is next to a big picture window that looks into our neighbor's house, so I'm not tempted to do anything bad because they might see me."

"We have wireless Internet in my house," says George. "I struggle at night. I'm going to turn my bed around so it faces the door, so people who walk in can see what I'm looking at on my laptop."

"I think that's a very good idea," says Pastor Rick.

We spend ten more minutes brainstorming ways to keep ourselves pure over the summer, including avoiding the beach, keeping a small Bible in our pocket at all times, and setting up regular meetings with an accountability partner. At the end of the hour, Pastor Rick doles out hugs and parting words of encouragement.

"Love you, man," he whispers in my ear, clutching my head to his chest. "Hang in there."

On the walk back to my dorm, I start to feel a number of the same emotions I felt after I went to see Pastor Rick about his conversion program for gay Liberty students. Sadness for the guys of Every Man's Battle and the epic wars they're forced to wage against their hormones. Mild disappointment with Pastor Rick, who sees managing these struggles as his divine calling. Frustration with a religious system that gives issues of personal sexuality higher spiritual priority than helping the poor or living a life of service.

But I also feel a new sort of empathy. I can't really identify with a gay Liberty student working to become straight, but I can identify with these guys. After three months here, I know how it feels to struggle against temptation. I can sympathize with the Liberty students who pray for stricter rules, for longer skirts on girls, for stronger Internet filters. I've felt the guilt that comes with a moral lapse. I keep replaying in my mind what Alex, the smallest and shyest of the guys at the session, said about his masturbation struggle: "Right after you fall, you feel like everybody's looking at you. And you're thinking, what if they knew what I just did? You go to church on Sunday feeling so dirty. You feel like you're throwing mud on the Lord."

All semester, whenever I've seen Liberty students beating themselves up over minor piccadilloes, I've wanted to grab them by the shoulders and shout, "It's okay! It's really okay!" I've fantasized about whisking them away to the secular world, where they'd be free to lust and covet with the rest of us. And part of me still dreams of staging some sort of intervention. But maybe these guys need to be here. Maybe they need each other. As frustrating as the fight for purity may be, I suppose it's easier when you've got company. After all, it's not One Man's Battle.

Two days later, after my Wednesday night choir rehearsal, I walk into Paul Maddox's room to ask him about the due date of our Evangelism 101 paper. When I knock on the open door, he looks over, sees it's me, and waves me into the room.

"Yo, Kev, you got a minute?"

I nod.

"All right, all right, close the door."

I sit down on Paul's bed, and he brings his chair over next to me.

He's shirtless, with a gold chain around his neck, and he's rubbing his hands together anxiously, like he has something pressing to tell me.

"Man, I need your advice," he says. "I'm having this problem with Lauren, and I don't know what to do about it."

He looks down at the floor, then back up at me.

"She's . . . bi."

Last night, Paul explains, he was browsing his girlfriend's MySpace profile when something made him look twice. Under Orientation, Lauren had listed herself as "Bisexual." Paul assumed it was either a joke or a typo, but just to make sure, he brought it up during their nightly phone call.

"Baby, you're not bi, are you?"

"I'm dating you, aren't I?" she replied.

"Yeah," he said. "But if we broke up, would you date guys or girls?"

"I don't know," she said. "Maybe both."

Paul had to adjust his ears. "Baby, you're joking."

"I'm not," she said. "Why would I joke about something like that?"

Paul was floored. Bisexual? They read the Bible over the phone every day! How could she do this to him?

"I just don't understand it," he tells me. "I mean, I've been doing everything right since I gave my life to God. I found a Christian girl-friend, and I've been giving everything to this girl, man. And now she's bi? It doesn't make any sense."

Over the phone, Paul tried to explain to Lauren that she couldn't follow God and be a bisexual at the same time. He read her Bible verses like 1 Corinthians 6:9–10, "Do not be deceived: Neither the sexually immoral nor idolaters nor adulterers nor male prostitutes nor homo-sexual offenders nor thieves nor the greedy nor drunkards nor slander-ers nor swindlers will inherit the kingdom of God."

"And what did she say?"

"She didn't believe me. She was like, 'Maybe I was born like this.' And I told her: 'No, baby, you weren't born like this. If you were meant to be with a girl, you would be a boy.' And she was like, 'Well, God works in mysterious ways.'"

Paul takes his head in his hands and rocks back and forth.

"What do I do, Roose? I mean, I love this girl, and I'm not gonna break up with her for this. I don't want to break up with her. But I know in my heart that what she's doing is wrong. And I want to help her change."

I sit there with Paul for four or five minutes, listening to him weigh the pros and cons of breaking up with Lauren and offering whatever emotional support I can. I tell him that he should wait until he's calmed down to make a decision. I don't think I'm helping him much. As I talk, he's still rocking back and forth in his chair, head in hands, emitting quiet groans, like he's being hit in the stomach with a series of tiny fists.

Paul is in an understandably tough spot. His Liberty classes have taught him that bisexuality is a sin—and not just any sin, but a sin above all sins, a lifestyle choice that represents a total disregard for God's will. As a new Christian who has struggled to grow in his faith all semester, Paul can't afford to be "unequally yoked" with a sinner, as the Bible says. Still, he isn't prepared to end his relationship with Lauren over it.

This conversation brings up a question I've been thinking about a lot today. Namely, what happens when a Liberty student's instilled values clash with his personal experiences? What happens when the moral system we're taught in our classes—a system in which everything is clear-cut, black or white, good or evil—comes into contact with the messy, complicated world? Do the values flex to fit reality? Or is Liberty's theological inculcation so powerful that it can convince its students—people like Paul—to override their social inclinations?

What originally brought this to mind was a conversation I overheard last night between Jersey Joey and his roommate Jonah, the strait-laced pastor's kid. Joey and Jonah were talking about Travis, their non-Christian roommate. Jonah was prodding Joey to witness to Travis, but Joey seemed reluctant.

"I don't know about all that," he said. "I mean, I know what the Bible says about Jesus being the only way to heaven, but I feel like Travis is making his own path, you know?"

"But how can you make your own path to heaven?" said Jonah.

"God made heaven. God's in charge. And he said, 'I am the way and the truth and the life. No one comes to the Father except through me.'"

"Don't preach at me, Jonah," said Joey. "I know what the Bible says. All I'm saying is that, look, my grandfather's not saved. He's the best person I know. Just a fantastic human being. And I've tried witnessing to him tons of times, but he's not getting it. He just doesn't want to believe it. So tell me this: how can the meanest old Christian who's the biggest dick—who gossips, lies, beats his wife—how can he go to heaven over a guy like my grandfather? I don't get how that happens. It doesn't make sense."

"It just happens, Joey," said Jonah. "I mean, it's hard for me, too. I have a lot of unsaved people in my family. Aunts, uncles, cousins. And I've tried to witness to them, too. I wish so badly that they would just accept it."

"So you think your aunts and uncles are going to hell?" Joey asked.

"I mean, yeah," said Jonah. "Jesus is the only way. I wish it wasn't the case. But it's not our choice. It says it in the Bible."

"I guess you're right," said Joey. "But I just hate it when people say, 'Oh, Mother Teresa is in hell, the Pope is in hell. I have a lot of Catholic friends back home, and that offends me. It's not for us to judge. I mean, yes, you have to accept Christ, but let God decide, you know?"

Just as Paul is struggling to plug Liberty's teachings on same-sex attraction into his relationship with Lauren, Joey is struggling with the interpretation of scripture that sends all non-evangelicals to hell. It seems too harsh. It's not something a loving God would do. And he's willing to bend Liberty's bedrock beliefs to bring them more into line with his own values.

Does it mean that Liberty students are straying from conservative theology? Probably not. At the end of the day, Paul is still convinced that bisexuality is wrong, and his first inclination upon hearing that Lauren is bisexual is still to help her change. Joey still believes that the only way to heaven is through Jesus, even if he's not happy about it. I wouldn't say that these conversations indicate a hidden ecumenical streak at Liberty or a new move toward tolerance. But it is nice to see that once in a while, amidst the hard-line dogmatism of a Liberty education, human decency still shines through the cracks.

The next day, I'm on the phone with my friend Einat, a loveable Jewish girl in my class at Brown. Einat mentions that she's taking a trip to Israel next week, and the Middle East being what it is, she's getting antsy about her safety.

"I'll pray for you," I say.

There's a long pause on the other end of the line. Like all of my other secular friends, Einat has never heard me talk about prayer. I picture her gaping, open-mouthed, into the phone.

"Sorry," I say.

"No, no, it's okay," says Einat. "That's sweet of you. A little weird, but sweet."

I couldn't help it. I decided about a week ago that since I was getting so much out of my prayer chapel sessions with Zipper, I ought to start praying on my own. So I did, and I think I may have gotten a little out of control.

What opened the door for me was a conversation I had with Pastor Seth. During last week's breakfast discipleship meeting, I brought up prayer. I told him I still had a bunch of questions about the practice. Like, how does it work? Do prayers actually change God's mind? If so, then why do so many prayers go unanswered? Why does Liberty's football team lose any games? Why is the dining-hall food still terrible? And if prayer doesn't change God's mind, why do we pray at all?

Pastor Seth smiled.

"First," he said, "I want you to think about it this way: God is our father, and we are his children. How would you feel if your children didn't talk to you? A relationship with God isn't a one-way street. God wants us to ask for things, even if he already knows what's going to happen. We have to supplicate, to put ourselves in his will."

His second point was even better. "Prayer may not always be entirely about God," he said. Here, Pastor Seth quoted the famous Christian author Oswald Chambers, who wrote: "It is not so true that prayer changes things as that prayer changes me and I change things."

"When you pray for other people, your own heart will be transformed," Pastor Seth said. "You'll find yourself living for others, making decisions with others in mind, putting the concerns of others ahead of your own. It's a way to connect to other believers in the way God wants you to connect."

Pastor Seth's pep talk helped me get over my hesitations about prayer. Even if God wasn't listening to my requests, I reasoned, the process of making those requests would be good for me and good for the people around me. So this week, I committed myself to praying for half an hour a day, an amount of time my Evangelism 101 professor recommended.

It's not easy to fill thirty minutes with prayers, and I don't always make my quota, but I'm getting close. I pray the Lord's Prayer when I wake up. I pray the ACTS method (Adoration, Confession, Thanksgiving, Supplication) in the shower. At lunch, I go through the daily list of prayer requests my GNED professor sends out on behalf of the students in our class (e.g., "Elizabeth's uncle passed away, pray for family; Ashley's stepfather was in mine accident, pray for health; Michelle's grandmother having hip replacement, pray for doctors"). Before bed, I pray for my family. When I run out of family members, I pray for friends from Liberty. When I run out of those, I move to friends from Brown, friends from high school, friends from middle school, celebrities, politicians, colleagues of my parents, right on down to the helpful baristas at the Lynchburg Starbucks.

And by the time I've spent my day like this, dredging up every person in my life who could possibly be undergoing any amount of hardship or strife and praying for their needs, a few things happen.

First, all my problems snap into perspective. Compared to a girl whose stepfather was in a mine accident or an old lady having her hip replaced, nothing in my life seems all that pressing. Instead of obsessing over the History of Life quiz I bombed or the parking ticket I got, I'm focusing more and more on people with real hardships. I put myself in the shoes of a guy on my hall who just totaled his car on the freeway or my aunt Cindy, whose house in California just burned down. Eventually, I go back to worrying about my tiny problems—I can't help it—

but for those thirty minutes, I'm at least going through the motions of compassion.

Second, the compassion I dig up during those thirty minutes sometimes carries over to the rest of my day. This past weekend, for example, I was praying for Mike, a guy in my a cappella group at Brown. Mike was having a terrible week: a messy breakup with his long-term girlfriend, a bad stomach flu, and a bout of the pinkeye that was being passed around Brown's a cappella community. And after praying for him, I felt myself wanting to write him a letter. I never write letters, but on a whim, I sat up in bed, tore a page out of my Theology notebook, and began to scribble. I wrote about how I hoped his pain would turn into something positive, how I thought the struggles he was going through would make him stronger in the end. Halfway down the page, I almost quit—Mike and I have an ultra-sarcastic friendship buffered by a lot of macho restraint—but I forced myself to keep going. I sent the letter off, and today, Mike wrote me back. His message began: "I got your letter the other day, and it brought tears to my eyes." He continued to say how unexpected it had been and how much it had lifted his spirits.

For the next two or three hours, I walked around campus glowing, doing all the small acts of kindness I typically overlook. I held open doors. I said, "Thank you, ma'am" to the lunch lady, whom I typically greet with a nonchalant grunt. I felt a metaphysical connection with everyone—and everything—around me.

I'm still not totally settled on prayer. Part of me still thinks it's a waste of time, and another part of me wonders whether I could be increasing my levels of compassion some other way—watching Nancy Grace every day, maybe, or reading news stories about famine in third-world countries. It's probably a bad sign if the only way I can tone down my narcissism is by forcing myself to believe that God is monitoring my thoughts. But for now, it doesn't seem to be hurting anyone, so I guess I'll keep at it. When I think of the benefits I'm reaping, a little cognitive dissonance seems like a small price to pay.

*　　*　　*

After our sex-themed chat last week, Luke, the smooth-talking lothario of Dorm 22, decided that I needed to meet some girls. He figured that unless he stepped in, I'd be destined for eternal bachelorhood. So he set me up with his friend Aimee.

"You guys will get along really well," he said. "She's sort of the Paris Hilton of Liberty."

An interesting way to describe an evangelical girl, I thought. How is that even possible? Is she an heiress? Has she starred in grainy sex tapes?

"No, no," Luke said. "She's just very popular. Kind of a socialite."

I understood when I looked at her Facebook profile. Only a freshman, Aimee already has eight hundred friends at Liberty. And judging by her picture, she's very attractive—long brown hair, slender frame, and a pair of dark, pouty eyes. Her profile reads:

> *Basically, here's me in a nutshell: I love God, and I'm committed to*
> *His service for the rest of my life. I love to have fun, and I'm ALWAYS up*
> *for hanging out. :)*

Luke was right. I do need to get out more. And although I'm not sure why he thought a socialite would be a good match for me, Aimee sounds like a fun date. So last night, after Luke introduced us, I sent her a Facebook message asking if she wanted to grab a bite to eat. She responded this morning: "Aww that's sweet. Yeah, I'd be down for hanging out."

Tonight, I drive over to Aimee's dorm to pick her up. She emerges from the building with a smile on her face. She's wearing a billowy purple blouse and tight black pants.

"I brought something for you," she says. "Don't laugh." She takes out her purse and extracts a business card. The card contains her name, e-mail, and the URL of her MySpace profile, all surrounded by a border of red roses.

"What's this?" I ask.

"It's my card," she says. "My mom made them for me before I came to Liberty. She wanted me to meet a boy, so she made me a box of 250, and I'm supposed to give them all away by the end of the semester."

Before our date tonight, Luke warned me that Aimee was on a "serious husband hunt." He told me that by going on a date with her, I'd be putting myself on her radar of possible spouses. But the way Aimee tells it, the husband hunt wasn't her idea.

"I told my mom, 'No, Mom, I don't have a boyfriend yet, and that's okay.' She didn't understand why I didn't want to get married at the age of eighteen."

For dinner, Aimee and I head to a local T.G.I. Friday's knockoff, the kind of place with faux 1940s kitsch on the wall—wooden tennis rackets, Radio Flyer wagons, Rosie the Riveter signs. We sit down in a corner booth, order two sandwiches, and get down to the business of introducing ourselves. Very quickly, it becomes clear that we have absolutely nothing in common. Aimee is a homeschooled navy brat, I'm an anti-war Quaker boy. Her mom went to cosmetology school, my mom barely owns makeup. She's a chocoholic, I'm lactose intolerant.

Midway through the meal, she tells me about *Click,* the Adam Sandler movie she just saw, and how it reminded her of the sin of pride: "The main character was a greedy, ambitious businessman, and he ended up with nothing," she said. "And while I was watching it, I was thinking about all the people out there who don't know Christ, who live completely for themselves, and how I just wish they could know that there's something better for them. If they follow God, they'll have something else to live for."

Tonight isn't the first date I've been on at Liberty. There was Anna, of course, but after things ended with her, I spent some time with Bethany, another girl from the sister dorm. Bethany, a short, tomboyish girl with a pair of deep dimples, was just as poor a match for me on paper as Aimee. She's a pastor's daughter, she's demure and shy, and like Aimee, she seems to mention God in every other sentence.

Neither Aimee nor Bethany appeal to me in the same way Anna did. They're both engaging and adorable, but they're too pious, too innocent for me to consider dating seriously. I need a girl with a little irreverent sass. Plus, the religious disparity is just too much. Anna I can handle—she's a bit milder in her beliefs—but I'm not sure I could ever date a girl who firmly believed my entire family was bound for hell.

That said, there are some things about Liberty's dating scene that I sort of enjoy. At first, I thought "The Liberty Way" and its rules against physical contact would ruin the dating experience. But strangely, I'm not feeling frustrated on these dates. In fact, having preordained physical boundaries takes a huge amount of pressure and anxiety out of the process. Think about it: at the end of tonight's date with Aimee, I won't have to worry about how to secure a good-night kiss or an invite to her room. My friend Luke might be able to seduce innocent Liberty girls, but for me, it's just not happening. No chance. And that's a very freeing feeling. When dinner dates aren't just preludes to hooking up, you end up truly *listening* to each other. The conversation is the centerpiece, and what emerges is deeper and more intimate than if you had been spending your time trying to Don Juan your way into her bed.

Recently, I've been reading *I Kissed Dating Goodbye*, the book Luke mentioned during our sex talk last week. The premise of the book is that Christian teens should, as the title suggests, stop dating. We don't actually get to know the people we date because we're caught up in the pursuit of physical intimacy. Christians should replace dating with "courtship," close platonic friendship that leads right into engagement.

Now, that last part scares me. Going straight from friendship to marriage seems reckless, like buying a house sight unseen. But I'm thinking about a line I read the other day that resonated with me. The author writes: "Dating creates an artificial environment that doesn't require a person to accurately portray his or her positive and negative characteristics."

One of my secular friends called me the other night for girl advice. He's pursuing a girl at his college, and he's going through the classic "tell her I like her without telling her I like her" phase. He wanted to know how to seduce this girl without seeming like he was trying too hard.

"I have to make her think I'm interested, but not that interested," he said.

This is a popular notion in dating circles at secular college—the idea that to be an effective Casanova, you've got to employ a little bit of circumlocution and trickery. Hedge your enthusiasm. Make the girl work for your affection. If she asks you to buy her a drink, say, "How about *you* buy *me* a drink?"

I have to say, after talking to my friend, it was hard not to feel like I have the better deal at Liberty. Sure, it's frustrating not to be able to relieve sexual tension, but with that option off the table, I'm free to be totally transparent. The whole interaction feels more honest, more straightforward. In the words of *I Kissed Dating Goodbye,* "our entire motivation in relationships is transformed." I've said things to Aimee tonight that I would never say to girls back in the secular world for fear of alienating them. Strange things to say to a girl who looks really beautiful—like, "You look really beautiful."

Tonight, Aimee and I stay at our antique-decorated restaurant for almost three hours. The waiters eventually stop coming back to refill our water glasses, and we sit there in our booth, talking, laughing, and generally having a wonderful time. At the end of the date, when I drop her off at her dorm, I have a fleeting thought about what it would be like to venture back out into my old world, the mélange of frat-party hookups and free-flowing sexuality, and say to a girl: "Listen, I just want to get to know you. No physical stuff."

I'm guessing she'd laugh. Or assume I was doing method acting for a revamp of the *40-Year-Old Virgin.* But after tonight's success, I decide I'm going to try it, just a few times, just to see how it feels.

The next Sunday is Easter, the most important day on the entire Christian calendar, the commemoration of the risen Lord.

I've always loved Easter. When I lived at home, my parents and I would drive over to my maternal grandparents' house in the Cleveland suburbs for Easter dinner. As churchgoing Episcopalians, my mom's parents were the most traditionally religious people in my family, and I remember eating my grandmother's lamb-shaped Easter cakes after dinner. We'd all hold hands around the table while my grandfather said grace, a stock Episcopalian blessing he rattled off so quickly that it sounded like one long word: "BlessolordthisfoodtoouruseandustothyserviceinJesusnameamen."

I suspect this year's Easter celebration will be less cake, more Christ.

Earlier this morning, Liberty held a special SonRise church service on the lawn outside Dr. Falwell's office. It was scheduled for 6:30 AM, and I was planning to go, but I stayed up too late on my date last night, and by the time I managed to pry myself from bed, I was an hour late. So I contented myself with the 8:30 service at Thomas Road, which, as a member of the choir, I'm required to attend anyway.

Easter morning at Thomas Road is a momentous occasion. The normally bare stage has been filled with beautiful white lilies, and silhouettes of three giant crosses have been projected on the wall above the choir loft. The crowd is standing-room only for the first time since Dr. Falwell's "Myth of Global Warming" sermon, and so many choir members showed up that, for the second time this semester, I got stuck with a comically large robe. This one isn't as enormous as the one I got on my first day, but it's big enough that I have to bunch the excess fabric in my hand when I walk, which keeps the bottom hem safely off the ground and also makes me look sort of stupid, like an Elizabethan duchess making her way to the ball.

The way Thomas Road celebrates Easter, you'd think no one had ever heard about this Jesus-rose-from-the-dead thing before. As choir director Al leads us in resurrection-themed hymns ("Christ the Lord Is Risen Today," "Jesus Is Alive," "He Lives"), the scene out in the sanctuary looks more like a Rolling Stones concert audience than a Baptist congregation. People are smiling open-mouthed, clutching each other lovingly, waving their hands in the air like windshield wipers. The camera zooms in on a middle-aged woman jumping up and down in pious joy while her teenage son looks on in mild embarrassment.

Today, Dr. Falwell's sermon is titled "The Fact, Force, and Faith of the Resurrection of Christ," and it's mostly standard Easter fare—a brief recap of the empty tomb story, a few unnecessarily graphic details of Jesus' crucifixion ("his lacerated body hung limp on the brutal cross, the thorns had been crushed into his skull, the blood and spittle dripped from his lifeless form," et cetera, et cetera), and a short lesson about what the resurrection should mean to us as believers. It's over in about thirty-five minutes, and after the altar call, the choir sings again as the Thomas Roaders file out of the sanctuary.

To accommodate the massive Easter crowds, Thomas Road is holding two identical services today at 8:30 and 10:30. And during the second service, while I'm singing the same three resurrection hymns I sang last time, I find myself getting swept up in the mass joy. During the last verse of "He Lives," the soloist hits the climactic high note, and I feel a little tingle start in my fingers. The tingle works its way up my arms, into my shoulders, and up my neck into my head, and pretty soon, I feel euphorically light-headed.

I've gotten this sensation twice this week. The first time was during Wednesday's Campus Church. This week, in honor of Holy Week, Liberty held a special communion service in the basketball arena. It was a pretty spectacular sight. A hundred-foot cross was constructed on the floor of the arena, with thousands of grape juice–filled plastic cups and industrial-size buckets of communion wafers sitting on top. The whole thing was spotlit from below, which gave it a strange ethereal glow.

The communion service itself wasn't particularly memorable. A campus pastor gave a bland sermon on the resurrection, we all filed down the aisles to take our juice and wafers, and on the pastor's cue, we partook in the Lord's Supper. Afterward, the campus praise band played a song called "Make a Joyful Noise to the Lord." It's a catchy, upbeat number, and the only thing that distinguishes it from the twenty other catchy, upbeat numbers in the praise band's repertoire is that this one has built-in audience participation—when the front man sings the title line, the congregation whoops and hollers, literally making joyful noises.

That's when it happened. When I heard thousands of Liberty students erupting in joy all around me, in a dark arena with a huge glowing cross, I got that same tingling sensation. This time, it began to feel like there was a string connected to the top of my head, and it was being pulled slowly upward, toward the ceiling. Pretty soon, I was joining the rest of my classmates in shouting and cheering—not out of any duty or desire to blend in, but because in that moment, I couldn't restrain myself.

What's happening to me? Two weeks ago, I was bored out of my skull in church. I was getting as much spiritual nourishment out of my Sundays at Thomas Road as I get from clipping my toenails or reading *Harper's* on the toilet. And now, I'm finding myself actually looking forward to services. I smile when I put on my choir robe. I chuckle at Dr. Falwell's hacky political jokes (e.g., "Chelsea Clinton was interviewing a marine coming back from Iraq, and she asked him what he was most afraid of. He replied, 'Osama, Obama, and your mama.'"). Last week, I went to Thomas Road on Sunday evening, even though I'm only required to attend the morning service.

If I had to guess, I'd say that the meaning of *church* is changing for me. I used to define church as a series of events—the sermon, the worship music, the collection, the altar call. Now, when I think of church, I think of George, the elderly man in the choir who greets me with a "hello there, Mister Kevin" every week. I think of Mac, the sixty-five-year-old tenor who always updates me on his son and daughter—an engineer in Gary, Indiana, and a sales representative in Charlottesville. On Wednesday nights, I think of Campus Church as the guys I sit with—Jersey Joey, Paul, Eric, Zipper—instead of the laser light shows or the fog machines.

The benefit of this is obvious: it's much easier for me to enjoy church when I conceive of it as a gathering of people. I still don't agree with Dr. Falwell's sermons, and I still have serious problems with some of the doctrines being preached at these things, but I can appreciate the feeling of singing in a choir with three hundred other people. I can appreciate the comfort of having a stable, predictable period of diversion every week at exactly the same time, and I know why it's appealing to take part in a communal activity, to feel like I'm part of something bigger than myself.

The downside of thinking of church this way is that it's not always easy to separate the feelings of joy from the beliefs that give rise to them. When thousands of Liberty students are all praising the Lord at the top of their lungs, it's hard to step back and ask myself: what exactly are they so happy about? Does it really have anything to do with a sandal-wearing rabbi who lived two thousand years ago? Would they be praising just as hard if Liberty were another kind of religious school, and the song lyrics said "Buddha" or "Gaia" or "Allah" instead of "Jesus"? Would it still seem so attractive to me?

There's a difference, it seems to me, between the form of religion and the content of religion. Right now, I've got all of the form and not much of the content. I pray like a Liberty student, I read the Bible like a Liberty student, and I sing in the choir like a Liberty student. I even go on dates like a Liberty student. And for the most part, I've enjoyed living this way. But I still don't believe the same things Liberty students believe about God. I still don't believe, as Dr. Falwell said during Easter services this morning, that "the resurrection of Christ is an indisputable fact." And yet, the possibility is entering my mind.

Earlier this week, I reread a book by the anthropologist Susan Harding. One of her points hit particularly close to home. Harding says that although most people think of religious conversion as a one-step process, it's really two steps. First, you pass into what she calls the "membrane of belief." That happens when you absorb the language and mannerisms of a religious community and begin to frame your thoughts and actions the way the community does. After that, you pass out of the "membrane of unbelief." You decide to abandon your skepticism and make the community's creed your own, becoming a true believer. The second step is a conscious choice, says Harding, but the first step often happens without your knowledge—or permission.

I used to think that I had control of my spirituality. I pictured a mental spigot that regulated the flow of faith into my brain. But I'm starting to understand that it doesn't work that way. Not for me, at least. I'm not a perfect rational being. I'm susceptible to the same emotional tugs and visceral urges as my Liberty friends, and I'm capable of shoving logic aside to make room for transcendence. And if Harding is right, the fact that I'm realizing these things means I'm probably much closer to conversion than I think.

Give Us Aid Against the Enemy

After my shower on Monday morning, I check my e-mail and see a message from Liberty's administration with the subject "Urgent Prayer Requested for Virginia Tech."

As I'm opening it, Jersey Joey bolts into my room.

"Rooster, you have to see this."

He reaches over my shoulder, types "CNN.com" into my browser, and reads me the breaking news.

"Thirty-two dead at Virginia Tech," he says. "A student gunned 'em down during their morning classes. It's a freaking Van Damme movie."

It's true. This morning, the deadliest school shooting in American history was conducted at Virginia Tech, only an hour and a half's drive from Lynchburg. As Joey and I read on, it only gets worse. The disturbed, introverted gunman. The Holocaust-survivor professor who blocked a door and took a bullet to save his students. The deed was perfectly scripted, perfectly executed, and perfectly awful. We sit in silence for two minutes.

Within half an hour, Liberty is in emergency prayer mode. Signs are posted all around campus saying PRAY FOR VA TECH. Facebook groups sprout up: "Pray for Virginia Tech," "VT in our prayers," "Liberty is

234

praying for VA Tech." Outside my window, ten or twelve students are kneeling in the grass, holding an impromptu prayer circle for the victims.

I stay in my room all morning, missing my classes because I can't bring myself to leave my bed. Maybe it's because I'm living in the same state as the shooting, or maybe it's because I have a few friends at Virginia Tech (all safe, thankfully), but today's news hit me incredibly hard. I can't watch the news without wanting to curl up in a ball for the rest of the month.

In mid-afternoon, Liberty's campus pastors call an emergency prayer vigil in honor of the victims and their families. I need some way to process my feelings, so I decide to pull myself out of bed and go. When I get to the prayer room where the vigil is being held, twenty or so students are already seated on the floor. As I slip in beside them, one guy is praying softly.

"Father, I pray for those injured and killed at Virginia Tech. Bless them and heal them, Father. I pray for the families. I pray for the school, for the leaders having to deal with this chaos."

When he finishes, a brunette with a thin, wispy voice says simply, "Father, please help the people there."

We proceed around the circle in order, each person praying in turn. And halfway around the circle, I find myself choking up. This is really awful. There is nothing in the world more unnerving, more senseless than a school shooting. Of all the answers I've found this semester, I still can't fathom why things like this happen. I've got nothing.

Prayer seems to be helping everyone else in this room cope with their sadness, but I'm having problems mustering any petitions of my own. After all, if God really is listening to these prayers, if he really is an omnipotent micromanager, then why didn't he just prevent the killing in the first place? If comforting the victims' families isn't too much to ask of God, why couldn't he have spared them their grief altogether?

Of course, I'm hardly the first person to ask these questions. For thousands of years, an entire branch of Christian theology, called theodicy, has been devoted to the question of why an omnipotent, omniscient, and omnibenevolent (all-loving) God would allow human suffering. Job wrestled with the question in the Bible itself. And need-less to say, millions of believers have made peace with the issue using a variety of theological work-arounds (for two well-reasoned—and opposing—perspectives on theodicy, I recommend the books *God's Problem* by Bart D. Ehrman and *The Problem of Pain* by C. S. Lewis). But I can't do it. For me, no amount of theological massaging can resolve the central issue—if God could have stopped the Virginia Tech killings from happening, he would have. I can't see any way around it.

At Liberty, where almost everyone believes in an omnipotent, omni-scient, omnibenevolent God, there seems to be two kinds of responses to tragedy.

The first kind is the blind prayer for healing—people simply saying, "God, I don't know why you would let something like this happen, but I pray that you'll help the people who are hurting." Most of the prayers I've heard today have been of this ilk. And even though I'm having a lot of trouble believing in a God who could allow this, I can see why it's comforting to think that someone is looking out for the victims and their families.

The second kind is the one I don't understand at all. This is the kind of prayer that says, "God, you let Virginia Tech happen, and I know ex-actly why you did." These prayers assume that God has an ultimate plan in mind, and that any event—even a horrifically tragic one—should be considered either a judgment of God or a strategic move on his part. Halfway through today's prayer vigil, the proceedings take a turn in this direction.

It starts when one of the campus pastors concocts a prayer that makes me wince: "Lord, we know that you use catastrophes like this to bring people to you. What happened at Virginia Tech today was awful, but I pray that you'll use this situation to make people see their need of a savior. I pray that you would send believers to Virginia Tech, to spread the gospel to people who are grieving right now."

"We talk about the separation of church and state a lot," says another campus pastor. "But as soon as something like Virginia Tech happens? Even *liberal Democrats* are saying 'We're praying for the families.'"

"Let's keep things in perspective," says a skinny guy with a bowl cut in the corner of the room. "This was only thirty-three people. Millions of murders happen in the United States every year through legal abortions."

"Yes," says the pastor. "Can't forget that."

I sat in the prayer vigil fuming. This sort of opportunistic partisanship is the same thing that happened after 9/11, when Dr. Falwell used the opportunity to claim that the Twin Towers had been hit because God was judging America for its sins. It's the same thing that happened when the Rev. Pat Robertson stated that Hurricane Katrina was a blessing insofar as it distracted the American public from the impending Supreme Court nomination of John Roberts, saying that "out of this tragedy, the focus of America is going to be on these victims" and that opposition from Democratic senators during Roberts's confirmation hearings was "just not going to play well now."

The twin responses to today's tragedy point to one of the central issues I've been struggling with all semester. At Liberty, I've met hundreds of people whose lives have been made better and more virtuous by their faith. But I've also seen a process whereby some reasonable, humble believers are taught to put their religious goals above everything else. This is how you get gentle Christian kids condemning strangers to hell in Daytona Beach, and it's how you end up with a group of Liberty students sitting around a prayer room talking about the ideological crops that can be reaped from a national tragedy.

This dark side of Liberty reminds me of a passage from one of my favorite Nathaniel Hawthorne novels, *The Blithedale Romance*. At one point, Hawthorne's narrator reflects on the inhabitants of Blithedale, an experimental utopian community whose goals were ultimately derailed by quarreling and infighting among the leaders. Hawthorne writes of their flawed ideology:

> [It] grows incorporate with all that they think and feel, and finally converts them into little else save that one principle. . . . And the higher and purer the original object and the more unselfishly it may have been taken up, the slighter is the probability that they

can be led to recognize the process by which godlike benevolence
has been debased into all-devouring egotism.

Twenty-four hours later, I'm still depressed and anxious. All the
major news networks are still in wall-to-wall Virginia Tech coverage,
and people on campus are still worrying, praying, and crying about the
tragedy there. I haven't heard any more of the "school shootings are a
blessing from God" rhetoric, but I haven't really been looking for it,
either. I've been busy calling my mom in various stages of agitation,
biting my nails to the stubs, and going on nervous eating binges.

Oh, and I've been fighting with my roommate. That's another reason
my mood is unusually dark this week. Henry, my twenty-nine-year-old
crank of a roommate, has decided very recently that he hates me.

I still barely know Henry. Three months as his roommate, and I
don't know whether he has siblings, or what his favorite ice cream flavor is, or why he came to Liberty in his late twenties. He's never volunteered the information, and I've never felt comfortable enough around
him to ask.

The one thing I have known for some time is that Henry is obses-
sively homophobic, an extreme case even by Liberty standards. First,
you'll remember, there was his conversation with Eric, during which
he spoke in favor of beating gays with a baseball bat. Then, there was
Fight Night, when he decided that most of the guys on our hall are gay.
Now, I think he's added me to his list of closeted homosexuals.

Mind you, Henry doesn't think I'm gay for the reasons people have
always thought I was gay. It's not the fact that I used to sing in an a cappella group that tipped him off, or the fact that I have a subscription to
Details. It's not even the fact that just a week ago, my friend David—
a real, live homosexual—was sleeping in our room at my invitation.
(Not that I told Henry about David's sexual orientation, but you'd
think a guy with a homophobic streak like that would have a halfway
decent gaydar.) In the end, what made Henry suspect I was gay was that
I defended my Evangelism 101 professor, Pastor Andy Hillman.

Henry has always harbored a secret suspicion that Pastor Andy is gay
on account of his high-pitched speaking voice and penchant for semi-

tight sweaters. But I like Pastor Andy. He's one of my favorite professors on campus—a bright, somewhat neurotic guy who seems genuinely kind and non-threatening. So last night, when Henry and I got back to the room from our Evangelism 101 section and Henry kept referring to Pastor Andy as "that queer," I felt I had to say something.

"Hey, man, go easy on him. He's a good guy."

Henry's lip curled. "You think Andy Hillman is a good guy?"

"Yeah," I said. "I think he has a good heart, and I don't think he's gay. In fact, I'm sure he's not gay."

"Why are you defending him?" Henry snapped. "You've seen him prancing around that classroom. Come on, man. Put two and two together."

Henry sounded angry, so I didn't press my case, but I gave him what I considered to be sufficiently judgmental looks for the rest of the night. Then, this morning, as I was brushing my teeth in my boxers, I heard his voice boom down from his bunk bed.

"Put some clothes on, faggot."

I looked up to glare at him, but he had already rolled over onto his stomach. He didn't say anything to me for the rest of the morning, and he hasn't said anything to me since.

It's easy enough to write Henry off as a basket case. Between his inexplicable anger and his bizarre episodes of gay panic, he's obviously struggling with something much bigger than he's letting on, and I'm certainly not assigning myself the job of psychotherapist. What's amazing, though, is that he's not being disciplined—even mildly reprimanded—for any of this. Guys on the hall know he's odd, and they talk about him in wary tones, but they're certainly not concerned enough to take any sort of action.

This semester, I've developed a numbness to homophobia. I don't like it, but it's unavoidable when you're in a climate like this, where homosexuality is talked about at near-Tourettic frequency. Every day, I've heard someone worrying about gay people, praying for gay people, talking about the scientific evidence against the alleged "gay gene." I've heard ten times as many conversations about homosexuality at Liberty than I ever heard any place where gay people existed in the open.

Kurt Vonnegut once wrote that there were two things about American culture a Martian anthropologist would never understand. Upon visiting the United States, his Martian's first comment was: "What is it, what can it possibly be about blow jobs and golf?"

I'm utterly convinced that the same Martian, invited to Liberty, would take one look around this campus and say, "What is it, what can it possibly be about two dudes kissing?"

Wednesday morning, I wake up to a buzzing campus. Today's convocation speaker is Sean Hannity, host of FOX News's *Hannity and Colmes,* longtime friend of Dr. Falwell's, and apparent hero of the Liberty student body. All morning, the parking lot behind the Vines Center is packed with photographers, autograph seekers, and a group of guys from a neighboring dorm who made a twenty-foot-long sign reading "YOU'RE A GREAT AMERICAN, SEAN!" which they plan to unfurl during his speech. Most of our guest speakers get polite applause, but when Hannity walks to the lectern, a rafter-shaking roar fills the arena. Students throw streamers and blast air horns, and the standing ovation lasts for nearly a minute.

"You know, there's a lot of pessimism about the youth in America," says Hannity. "It's pretty inspiring to come to Liberty University and see people putting God first in their lives."

It's hard to imagine a more receptive audience for this speech than the LU student body. After a few sincere remarks about the Virginia Tech tragedy, Hannity—who looks a lot more like Fred Flintstone than I remembered—cracks a few Ted Kennedy jokes, then veers into a lengthy assault on liberalism paired with a drooling paean to Ronald Reagan. It's not a particularly inspired speech, but with this crowd, Hannity could draw an encore by reciting his grocery list. When he mentions FOX News, everyone cheers. John Kerry, everyone boos. ("See why I love Liberty?" he says.)

I've been thinking a lot about politics this week, both because of Sean Hannity's Harold Hill—esque campus visit and because right now, Liberty students are starting to talk about the candidates for next year's presidential election. It's not yet clear who the GOP nominee is going to be, but none of the front-runners seems to have a particularly large fan base on campus. I used to think this was because all three viable candidates at the moment—John McCain, Mitt Romney, and Rudy Giuliani—have thus far gotten tepid support from the evangelical community. But this week, I began to wonder whether I might be seeing symptoms of a more general political apathy at Liberty.

Let me explain. When I arrived here in January, I thought I was coming to America's most politically active university. I pictured ten thousand future White House staffers, right-wing think tankers, and budding conservative lobbyists. I assumed that "Champion for Christ" was coded language and that Dr. Falwell really wanted to train an army of Republican policy wonks. But that hasn't been my experience at all. Liberty students have political opinions, of course, and I'm sure most of them will vote for the Republican candidate no matter who gets the nod, but I've come to expect a certain detachment from my Liberty friends when it comes to the actual machinations of the political process.

I started to feel this way after I read a *New Yorker* article several weeks ago about Patrick Henry College, a small evangelical school in Purcellville, Virginia, that was started as a training ground for conservative Christian political groups. According to author Hanna Rosin, Patrick Henry students spend a lot of their free time talking about arcane legislation, watching polls, and beefing up their political résumés. Liberty students, on the other hand, don't seem consistently interested in actual Beltway politics. If you press them, they can all tell you where they stand on the left/right spectrum (actually, it's more like the right/far-right spectrum), but issues outside the evangelical voting trinity of abortion, gay marriage, and school prayer rarely come up, and I can count on one hand the number of *McLaughlin Group*–caliber political discussions I've heard this semester.

I had lunch the other day with Max Carter, Liberty's whip-smart incoming student body president and a guy with both feet firmly planted in the civic process. He agreed with me about the backseat nature of Liberty's politics.

"It's hard to get into a discussion of conservative policy here," he said. "Even with the professors, it's all about the same two or three so-cial issues. Very few people can tell you anything about the arguments for limited government or the nuances of fiscal conservatism. There's political activism on campus, but it's all sort of shallow."

To the extent that Dr. Falwell seems to be training front-line con-servatives, rather than simply reliable Republican ballot-punchers, his efforts seem to be focused on two groups: the debate team and the law students. Liberty's debate team consistently ranks among the top in the nation, has a six-figure budget and a full scholarship program, and was profiled in a 2006 *New York Times Magazine* feature called "Ministers of Debate." Dr. Falwell speaks fawningly of the debaters and openly hopes for many of them to become conservative politicians. The Lib-erty School of Law has only been in operation since 2004, but it's al-ready becoming another central component of Dr. Falwell's political mission. At the law school's opening, he said that his intent was to "infiltrate the culture with men and women of God who are skilled in the legal profession."

Liberty's law school is hardly huge, though—only about two hun-dred students—and the debate program is much smaller, which leaves thousands of Liberty students who aren't being explicitly trained as professional culture warriors. Maybe that shouldn't be surprising. After all, according to pollsters who have a handle on this stuff, to-day's young evangelicals are much less attached to the Moral Majority–style culture war than the evangelicals of their parents' generation. I read a book the other day called *unChristian*, written by the president of the Barna Group, an evangelical polling firm. According to the book, 47 percent of born-again Christians under age forty think "the political efforts of conservative Christians" are problematic for America. Add to that a recent Pew Research Center study that revealed that the percent-age of white evangelicals between the ages of eighteen and twenty-nine who identify as Republican has decreased from 55 percent in 2001 to 40 percent in 2007, and evangelical college students aren't looking so monolithic these days.

So what about Liberty? Is Bible Boot Camp on the verge of becom-ing a haven for liberals? Somehow, I doubt it. Liberty students may be less involved in the political scene than in years past, but between the GNED curriculum, Dr. Falwell's political legacy, and the fact that the university is overseen by the Thomas Road Baptist Church, it's pretty likely that in ten years, your average Liberty student will still be staunchly conservative, even if his politics only revolve around a few issues.

My suspicion is bolstered at the end of today's convocation, when Dr. Falwell steps to the lectern. He announces that he has a piece of breaking news for us, something we'll all want to hear.

"I just got a text message," he says. "The ban on partial-birth abortions went before the Supreme Court today, and about ten minutes ago, according to my text message—and I hope it's true—the U.S. Supreme Court upheld the ban, 5–4."

Students in the rows around me look at each other in utter shock. Then, as if every seat in the arena had simultaneously caught fire, they rocket to their feet. The ovation lasts for one minute, then two, then three. People are high-fiving and cheering at the top of their lungs. The video cameras zoom in on Sean Hannity, who looks a little taken aback. I guess you don't see manic pro-lifers every day—not even at FOX News.

During Thursday's lunch, Marco plops his tray down on the table with a thud.

"Okay, guys. Deep theological discussion time."

Guys look at him quizzically. This is not the right place to have a deep theological discussion, nor the right crowd to be having it with. I'm sitting in the middle of the dining hall with Jersey Joey, Travis, and several other members of Dorm 22's rebel crowd, and for the past ten minutes, I've been listening to a lust-filled conversation about Christine, a girl in the sister dorm who has apparently been blessed with a rather sizeable bosom (or, as Travis puts it, "huge chesticles").

Luckily, Marco is kidding. The deep theological discussion he wants to have, he says, is simple: "Hottest Disney princess . . . go!"

"Belle," says Ernest, a quirky music major from down the hall.

"Jasmine," says his friend Patrick.

"Belle, no doubt," Ernest repeats.

"Pocahontas," offers Travis.

"Little Mermaid," says Jonah.

"Dude, it's got to be Belle," says Ernest. "Did you see her in that yellow dress? Plus, she's a sweetheart. She didn't judge the Beast on his looks."

"Shut up, Ernest," says Travis. "She knew he was a king. That's why she hooked up with him!"

"Pocahontas is better looking anyway," says Marco. "Her butt, dude? You could see the bulges in her butt."

All in all, this lunch is pretty standard fare for the room 201 guys. The only bizarre element is Jersey Joey, who sits quietly at the table, eating his cheeseburger, saying nothing the whole time.

After lunch, I go to Joey's room to check on him.

"Hey, man, is everything okay?"

He's sitting at his desk, staring at the wall, looking a little shell-shocked.

"Rooster, do you think I'm a douchebag?" he says.

I laugh.

"No, I'm serious, do you think I'm a douchebag?"

"No," I say. "But why?"

Joey explains that earlier this week, after a conversation with his friend Rodrigo, he got inspired to read Ecclesiastes, one of the Bible's wisdom books. Joey almost never reads the Bible on his own, but when he started Ecclesiastes, he couldn't stop. He finished the book in one night.

"It really opened my eyes," he says.

Ecclesiastes isn't a particularly fire-and-brimstone-heavy book, but Joey felt convicted when he read verses like "As dead flies give perfume a bad smell, so a little folly outweighs wisdom and honor." After finishing the last page, he began to wonder if his rebellious streak was damaging his relationship with God.

It didn't help that the next day, while Ecclesiastes was still fresh in his mind, one of Joey's female friends called him a douchebag.

"At first, I was like, 'whatever, screw her.' But then, I started to wonder if I should take the cocky stuff down a notch. Maybe I should. I don't want to get a reputation, you know?"

Another reason Joey is considering changing his ways is because Travis, his roommate, still hasn't become an evangelical Christian. Joey thinks that if he can reform in front of Travis's eyes, perhaps it will help convince him that Christianity is worth his faith.

"I mean, you never know," he says. "I should be a good example for him."

As for what being a good example means, he's not so sure. Yesterday, when one of his friends invited him on a cigar-smoking trip, Joey turned him down. He's going to keep reading the Bible and praying for guidance, and he's going to try to stay away from temptation when he goes home to Hoboken.

"There's this girl at home," he says. "We made out a little over spring break, and she's been texting me, like, 'Oh, Joey, I can't wait to hook up with you this summer.' I think she's going to try to have sex with me. She's smokin' hot, Rooster. Beautiful, beautiful girl. But I know I shouldn't."

Of all the people I expected to have a moral awakening this semester, Joey was at the bottom of the list. Liberty does this to you, though. It tempts you with the constant possibility of personal realignment. Joey can refashion himself as a Champion for Christ, and everyone will applaud him for it. And if that applause is loud enough to drown out the voice in his head telling him to stick to his guns, it might be enough to convince him that he made the right decision.

Frankly, it's a little weird to hear Joey talking about piety and moral self-control. I love the guy, and I'll support him no matter what, but I hope one Bible-reading session didn't turn him into my next-door neighbor Zipper.

"So you're really turning your life around?" I ask.

"I guess," he says, looking down at the floor.

"Are you happy about it?"

"I mean, I should be happy about it. It's the way God wants me to do things."

"You think it'll stick?"

"It might be hard to keep this up over the summer, especially because I won't be around Christians. My friends from home won't want to hang out with some pious Liberty kid."

Joey winces, suddenly realizing everything he's going to have to leave behind if he wants to stage this moral makeover. He'll have to be careful around his friends. He'll have to give up drinking. He won't be able to go out to hookah bars, his favorite activity back home. He'll have to stop cursing, and he'll have to keep holding on to his virginity for dear life.

"Rooster," he says. "This is gonna be a bitch to pull off, isn't it?"

As exam time approaches, my classes are getting unbearably hard.

In Theology, we're studying ancient ecclesiology, the history of the Church from Jesus' death up until about the year 600 AD. It's not an easy subject, even for the seasoned Christian kids in my class. We've had to memorize the details of tiny historical movements like the Marcionites (who denied the validity of the Old Testament and most of the New Testament, and primarily followed the writings of Paul), the Montanists (an early charismatic renewal movement), and the Novationists (a truly hardcore group of Christians who believed that if you denied Christ even once, you were doomed to hell forever, with no second chances).

In Old Testament, we're learning about the structure of the Bible's poetry. Dr. Thompson is teaching us that all of the Psalms and Proverbs fit into one of a half-dozen rhetorical modes. For example, Psalm 49:1 ("Hear this, all you peoples; listen, all who live in this world") is an example of synonymous parallelism, meaning that the first clause ("Hear this, all you peoples") is simply reworded in the second clause ("listen, all who live in this world"). This is not to be confused with synthetic parallelism, which means that the second clause amplifies or complements the first (as in Psalm 55:6: "I said, 'Oh, that I had the wings of a dove! I would fly away and be at rest' ").

See what I mean?

In addition to cramming massive amounts of material into my skull, I've been thinking a lot about my classes in general and about the characteristics of a Liberty education. I've been pondering the conversation I had with Max Carter the other week, the one in which he inveighed against Liberty's educational one-sidedness.

I think I see what he means when he criticizes a Liberty education as undemanding. I'm struggling just to tread water in my Liberty classes, but for a Christian college student with a huge amount of intellectual curiosity, going to Liberty could be a frustrating experience—not because the classes are too easy or the professors are incompetent (which, by and large, they're not), but because Liberty seems to have a conflicted view of the academic process itself.

Several weeks ago, after a lecture about the age of the earth, Dr. Dekker, my History of Life professor, projected a passage on the board. The passage, which comes from the pen of Dr. Kurt Wise, one of the world's foremost young-earth creationists, goes as follows: "I am a young-age creationist because that is my understanding of the Scripture. As I shared with my professors years ago when I was in college, if all the evidence in the universe turns against creationism, I would still be a creationist because that is what the Word of God seems to indicate. Here I must stand."

"Ultimately," Dr. Dekker said of the passage, "what Dr. Wise wrote there is the same thing I'm saying: when it comes to the age of the earth, it becomes a question of what the Bible says."

Say what you will about young-earth creationism (I think I've said enough already), but there's something depressing about a credentialed, university-level scientist who freely admits that he wouldn't budge in his beliefs even if *all* the evidence in the *universe* contradicted one of his scientific theories. Never mind that Dr. Dekker is talking about creationism—can you imagine a physicist saying that about the Heisenberg uncertainty principle? Or an English professor saying that about his theory of late Victorian poetry? It might be honest of Dr. Dekker to admit that his views are impervious to evidence, but it should probably disqualify him from any sort of university-level teaching.

Another worrisome statement came during a guest lecture in my Evangelism 101 class by one of Liberty's campus pastors. At the end of the lecture, the pastor addressed the two hundred–plus students in my class this way: "I just want to say this, Liberty students. My biggest worry about you, about all of you, is that you'll become educated beyond your obedience."

This, too, struck me as depressing. What he was saying, in effect, is that there's a cap on a Liberty education, a point at which knowledge becomes dangerous rather than useful. And once you're aware that some Liberty administrators feel this way—or at least one Liberty administrator feels this way—the signs appear everywhere you look. You realize that the reason Liberty's GNED professors cherry-pick quotes from Kant and Nietzsche and insert them in workbooks rather than assigning entire texts is that reading non-Christian philosophers in the originals might cause some Liberty students to stumble in their faith. You start looking back at Liberty's institutional history and realizing why, for example, the school library wasn't built until a regional accreditation board mandated it. And you start to wonder if the Facebook joke, "You know you went to Liberty if . . . you learned more about tithing than your major," might actually have a kernel of truth to it.

It's not that there aren't smart people here. In fact, with very few exceptions, I've been impressed by how bright and intellectually engaged my Liberty friends are. The problem is in the system. Liberty is a place where professors aren't allowed to take chances with their course material. It's a place where academic rigor is sacrificed on the altar of uninterrupted piety, where the skills of exploration, deconstruction, and doubt—all of which should be present at an institution that bills itself as a liberal arts college—are systematically silenced in favor of presenting a clear, unambiguous political and spiritual agenda.

I wish I could claim these criticisms as my own, but I'm just echoing things I've heard my friends and hallmates say all semester. A few weeks ago, I took a walk with Stubbs, the RA from Dorm 22, who sits next to me in Theology class. Stubbs is an exceedingly smart guy with an encyclopedic grasp of Christian doctrine, and outside of class, he spends a lot of time complaining to me about our professor.

"It's not that I don't agree with Mr. Watson," Stubbs said. "It's just that I wish he allowed alternative points of view in class."

"Why?" I asked.

"Well, because without skepticism, without challenging our own views, what we're learning is lifeless. I mean, there are some major issues Christians should all agree on: the infallibility of scripture, the atonement of Christ for all men, things like that. But I wish our professors would branch out a little."

I've always known that I'll be leaving Liberty after this semester, which is why I think I've been so forgiving of Liberty's academic flaws. But Stubbs doesn't get to leave. Max Carter doesn't, either. For both of them—and for the rest of my friends here—Liberty's institutional shortcomings are no minor business. This is their college education, and for their sakes, I can't help wishing that Liberty would purge itself of the attitude that education is an enemy of faith.

Admittedly, there are a few positive signs on the horizon. After thirty-plus years of an untenured faculty that could be fired for straying from the party line, Liberty gave out its first tenure position in 2004. Rules on academic freedom among professors are being loosened, and I've heard some things in my classes this semester that, while not heretical, were definitely unorthodox. (One faculty member, whom I'll refrain from naming even under a pseudonym, told me that Dr. Falwell's approach to Christian doctrine struck him as "overly reductive").

There may be other signs, but until anti-intellectual attitudes like the ones I've heard in History of Life and Evangelism 101 are dealt with, I'm afraid Liberty will continue to wallow in academic mediocrity. Me, I'm praying for a turnaround. As people like Stubbs and Max Carter have taught me, education and piety are not mutually exclusive, and the sooner this school's higher-ups take this to heart, the sooner Liberty students can go about the business of loving God with their minds.

Late Friday night, Jersey Joey comes knocking at my door.

"Rooster, come to my room. We're watching old Van Halen videos on YouTube. The ones with the hot chicks in bikinis."

"I can't," I say. "Sorry."

"Why not?"

"Too much work."

"Fine, be that way."

I don't actually have any homework tonight. In fact, I've been browsing Facebook for forty-five minutes, and I've got no plans to do anything more productive. But I didn't want to tell Joey the real reason I couldn't watch lascivious music videos with him, because, well, it's sort of embarrassing. Namely, I'm trying to stop masturbating.

In this week's discipleship meeting with Pastor Seth, I told him about my trip to Every Man's Battle. He asked what I had learned by going, how it felt to talk so openly about my lustful habits, and what the experience had motivated me to do.

"What do you mean, motivated me to do?" I asked.

"Well, I've been thinking," Seth said. "And I think we should work on cutting out your masturbation."

I was mortified. Cutting out my masturbation? I went to Every Man's Battle strictly out of curiosity. I wasn't expecting to join the fray myself. Also, what's this about *we*? Curtailing my self-love is going to be a corporate effort?

"Here's the plan," Seth said. "First, I want you to try all those tips you heard in the group. Keeping your door open, making sure you play Christian music when you're alone in your room, things like that. Second, when you feel like you're about to fall, I want you to text message me."

Oh, really?

"Really. Any time of night, if you feel a tingle down there, text me. I'll stop everything and help you through it."

I tried to laugh it off, but Seth was serious. He really wanted to help me stop masturbating. And since I really had no other option—what was I going to say? "No thanks, I think I'll keep touching myself"?—I nodded in agreement. The apex of awkwardness between us had long passed. What did I have to lose?

"Now, don't be shy," Seth said. "If I haven't gotten a text from you in a week, I'll assume you're hiding something from me."

Calling Pastor Seth and telling him I masturbated is by far the most uncomfortable hypothetical I can imagine, so for the past four days, I've been mounting an all-out campaign against lust. I deleted my TMZ.com bookmark, I deep-sixed my *Esquire* magazine with Halle Berry on the cover. Whenever Jersey Joey has tried to show me something racy— a Van Halen video, a picture of Britney Spears flashing her nether regions to the paparazzi—I've politely declined. All in all, I'm dominating my libido.

But tonight, without warning, it all hits the fan. My roommates are gone for the night, and I'm sitting at my desk typing an e-mail when I start having these intense, two-second-long visual flashes. *Girls in bikinis. The Victoria's Secret catalog. The alto two seats over in choir.* I try to make the thoughts go away. I get up from my computer. I leaf through *Walden.* I make lists in my head. Baseball teams, soft drinks, European capitals. But nothing works.

I think briefly about relieving myself and not telling Seth. Then I think of what he said: he'll know I'm lying if he doesn't hear from me this week. Man, the guy drives a hard bargain.

My fingers shake as I text him.

Red alert.

I wait nervously, phone in hand, for a response. Ten seconds later, I hear the new text ding.

Gotcha.

The phone rings.

"Kevin, it's Seth. I got your text."

"Hey. Yeah . . . I'm having some, uh, trouble over here."

"Sorry to hear that. Are you alone in your room?"

"Yeah."

"Where are your roommates?"

"Away for the night."

"Uh-oh. Well, that's okay. Everything's okay."

Seth's calm sounds rehearsed, like a crisis-line operator talking a guy down from a bridge.

"Have you gone to the gym today?" he asks.

"No."

"Well, you should head over there. Work it off. And listen to some music or something."

"Okay, sounds good."

251

"Oh, and Kevin: remember to keep the door open tonight."

"Will do."

"And maybe invite a friend to sleep in your room."

"Okay."

"Good. And call me if anything, uh, *comes up*."

I hoped that battling my sexual appetite would lead me to new levels of spiritual growth, or at least to a greater level of empathy with my Liberty friends. But truth be told, I still don't get it. Masturbation seems like a victimless crime if there ever was one. And from the Christian perspective, allowing a Liberty student the freedom to do it would seem to lessen the chance that they'd be experimenting with actual sex.

Most of all, I feel sorry for Pastor Seth, who—in addition to winning the double entendre prize of the century—has worried himself sick about whether or not I'm touching myself. I can think of very few people, at Liberty or anywhere else, who would call me on a Friday night to help with any of my personal problems. That level of support is something I've rarely felt before, and I don't take it for granted.

It comes back, I guess, to the difference between the form and content of Liberty's religious system. I love the way Pastor Seth's faith motivates him to help me in my struggles. I admire his compassion and selflessness. I just wish he were calling to see whether I was returning my mom's phone calls, or whether I had left good tips at restaurants, or whether I had been nice to everyone I met today. Working on masturbation when I have so many other flaws seems like putting fuzzy dice in a car whose transmission is falling apart. I suppose it's better than nothing, but it doesn't feel like a particularly good use of anyone's time.

One King Shall Be King to Them All

Every afternoon around three o'clock, Dr. Jerry Falwell drinks a bottle of Diet Peach Snapple very, very quickly. I know this because he told me so, and because right now, I'm watching him in action. First, he removes the plastic seal over the cap with a utility knife. He cuts horizontally, then vertically, then horizontally again, straining and struggling for the proper angle. It takes a little while, but he succeeds eventually, and once the cap is off, it's five seconds, tops, before the empty bottle is set back down on the table. I've never seen anything like it. He pours that stuff down his throat like a genie appeared in his office and said, "I'll grant you three wishes, but only if you can kill your drink before I finish tying my shoe."

Today is my interview with the chancellor for the *Liberty Champion*, and this speed-drinking spectacle is a probably a good distraction. After all, marveling at the way Dr. Falwell guzzles his iced tea is a lot easier on my nerves than contemplating the reality of who he is. When you're sitting five feet away from a man who has held the ear of five U.S. presidents, a man whose Moral Majority changed the course of modern American politics, whose life work has won the adoration of millions of people and the fear and loathing of millions more, it's good to have a little mental distance. So . . . the Snapple.

I was actually feeling mildly relaxed about this interview until I checked my e-mail this morning and saw the flood of panicked notes from my friends and family in the secular world, who apparently consider a tête-à-tête with Jerry Falwell about as safe as a lox brunch with Hannibal Lecter. The e-mails said things like "PLEASE be careful with him" and "Be aware that he is crazy like a fox." Then there was the one from Mrs. Mott, the *Champion*'s faculty advisor, who seems to have realized that what she did in my case—assigned a major feature to a student she doesn't know from Adam—isn't exactly standard protocol. She wrote: "Normally, such interviews are granted to senior staff members to whom much trust has been given. As a new reporter, you will want to conduct the interview in a professional manner."

Armed with all that emotional support, I put on a shirt and tie and walked over to the chancellor's office, which is housed in an opulent white estate in the middle of campus (Liberty students call it "the Mansion"). When I arrived, Dr. Falwell's secretary escorted me past the reception area, where a portrait of Ronald Reagan hangs high on the wall, to the waiting room, where I spent ten sweaty-palmed minutes staring at a bookshelf that contained titles like *Falwell: The Autobiography*, *Jerry Falwell: Aflame for God*, and *Strength for the Journey: An Autobiography* by Jerry Falwell. (A secular friend of mine quipped that this shelf could be called "Barnes & Ignoble.")

When the secretary came for me, I wiped my hands on my pant legs and followed her down the hall through a thick wooden door, around a quick bend, and into a cavernous room where Dr. Falwell, clad in his signature black suit and red tie with a shimmering "Jesus First" lapel pin, stood to shake my hand.

"Come on in, Kevin!" he bellowed.

The first thing to know about Dr. Jerry Falwell is that his office is damn nice. The walls are lined with rich, dark wood, the high-back leather chair looks like it was plucked from Donald Trump's personal collection, and there's a private powder room next to the door. The shelves are smattered with portraits of Dr. Falwell's personal heroes, men like Mickey Mantle and Winston Churchill, and carved wooden eagles and antique globes fill the space behind his desk. Everything is neat, tidy, polished to a shine. Dr. Falwell's moral platform may be up for debate, but his taste in office décor is fairly unimpeachable.

The second thing to know is that at the moment, Dr. Falwell is tired. After he drank his Snapple, he slouched down in his chair, splayed his legs out in front of him, and hasn't budged since. As I introduce myself and tell him about the premise of my interview, he closes his eyes and breathes slowly and heavily, as if meditating.

I don't blame him. It's been a hectic few weeks in the Falwell empire. After the Virginia Tech disaster, Dr. Falwell had to scramble to organize a prayer service at Thomas Road and comfort the Liberty community by e-mail. ("During times like these when unexpected tragedy strikes," he wrote, "I tend to refer to 1 Peter 5:7, which tells that we worship a God who is wholly concerned about us."). In addition to his usual slate of media appearances, he's been busy denouncing the Emergent Church, a growing branch of evangelicalism that de-emphasizes political issues like abortion and gay marriage and seeks to return to a more spiritual form of Christianity. This afternoon, he'll be conducting a groundbreaking ceremony for a new Religion Department building on campus, and he's still fending off media pressure to endorse a candidate for the 2008 presidential election. Carrying out any one of these roles—megachurch pastor, theological gatekeeper, university president, conservative political icon—would exhaust most seventy-three-year-old men, and even though Dr. Falwell is a renowned workaholic (one *Newsweek* profiler wrote of his nineteen-hour workdays fueled by a dozen cups of coffee), I can't imagine he has a lot of energy to spare.

So today, I'm giving him a break. With the *Champion*'s permission, I'm planning to ask Dr. Falwell all the questions Anderson Cooper would never bother with—the ones that have nothing to do with gay marriage, abortion, or the war in Iraq. Instead, I'll ask about his personal life. What are his hobbies? Where does he take his wife out to dinner? Does he have an iPod?

"We'll do it," he says. "Ask anything you want."

It might sound like a sophomoric way to interview a major American religious figure, but I figure sticking to small topics will help me humanize Dr. Falwell. By this point in my semester, I've read all of his biographies, visited the museum bearing his name, and lodged a few dozen of his sermons in my brain. I might know more about Dr. Falwell than I know about my own grandfather, and yet, in my mind, he's still a larger-than-life movie villain, no more relatable than Vito Corleone or the Terminator. So today, I'm asking him questions so lowbrow and banal that he'll be forced to peel off the Superpastor mask and expose his baseline humanity. That's the plan, anyway.

In twenty minutes, I learn the following things: Dr. Falwell owns between forty and fifty red ties, his favorite TV show is *24*, and he has recently learned how to send text messages on his cell phone, although he has never used Facebook or MySpace. His favorite dessert is vanilla Häagen-Dazs, and when not on the job, he likes to ride four-wheelers with his sons. (For the record, he does not have an iPod.)

Surprisingly, Dr. Falwell doesn't seem to mind my line of questioning. In fact, he seems relieved to be asked about something other than his controversial political and religious opinions. He even helps me debunk some popular campus myths. The rumor that Liberty's administration is planning to legalize dances? False. ("Not while I'm living," he chuckles.) The legend that he drives a bulletproof SUV? Also false—although he did have a bulletproof pulpit installed at Thomas Road during the Moral Majority's heyday. ("There were people who wanted to do us harm," he explains.)

Bulletproof pulpit aside, the in-person Dr. Falwell reminds me of every other septuagenarian I've ever known. He coughs a lot, he's obsessed with his grandchildren (at one point, he lists all eight in order of age), and he's an early riser. "I wake up a little before six, and I go right to my study," he says. "That's where I do my daily reading of the Oswald Chambers book, *My Utmost for His Highest*. I've read that day by day for fifty years now. I have a one-year Bible, too. I read the Old Testament, New Testament, Psalms, and Proverbs every day. I'm at work by eight or eight-thirty, and when I get home every night, my wife and I walk around the lawn. We have dinner together, and then we spend most of our evenings alone."

Shooting the breeze with Dr. Falwell is a bizarre experience, because when you keep him on benign topics, the patriarch of the Religious Right is actually a likeable guy. He slouches low in his chair, making his points while jabbing the air with his index finger and saying things that, while not particularly newsworthy, seem altogether reasonable. Consider what he tells me about Liberty's dating scene: "I think Liberty students ought to date a lot without commitment in mind. If you're thinking commitment—and you probably shouldn't until you're a senior— you don't want to start your marriage off under the constraints of poverty and schooling. I see it all the time: kids get here, fall in love the first year, and it prevents them from getting the best education possible. Sometimes, they drop out of school. When that happens, it's usually the girl, and she doesn't feel good about that later on."

Things get even stranger when I bring up his widespread reputation as a prankster.

"Oh, yes," he says. "The pranks."

An admitted no-goodnik in his youth, Dr. Falwell wrote in his autobiography that he still savors a good practical joke "like some people savor old wine." When I quote this line back to him, he spends ten minutes regaling me with decades-old stories about hot-wiring his colleagues' cars and blowing up mailboxes with M-80 firecrackers. His back comes off his chair as he tells me about the time he placed a stink bomb under the chair leg of Bob Jones, Jr., the then-president of Bob Jones University, at a conference of pastors.

"When he sat down, the bomb broke," he says, his belly rising and falling with laughter. "And in a crowded auditorium, it got pretty rank pretty quick. Everyone was choking for ten, fifteen minutes."

A juvenile sense of humor is an unexpected thing to find in a religious zealot. It's hard to imagine James Dobson telling "yo mama" jokes or Pat Robertson making fart noises with his armpit. And yet, I have to admit that Dr. Falwell's blend of religious authority, preening confidence, and irreverent wise-assery—equal parts Billy Graham, Henry Kissinger, and Walter Matthau—makes for a fairly pleasant package.

After he finishes with his prank anecdotes, Dr. Falwell tells me a story about an African American family that lives next door to him.

"This family has young children," he says, "and one of the lads knocked a baseball over my fence one day. I have an eight-foot fence around my property, and my security officer found the ball and showed it to me. I said, 'See if you can find out who lost it, and get it back to him.' A few days later, a young boy came around to the gate and said, 'I lost my ball.' The guard said, 'All right, you can have it back . . . if you talk to Dr. Falwell.' I met him. He was a fine young man. I asked him, 'Where are you going to go to college?' He didn't have any idea. I said, 'I'll tell you what. I'm going to write on this ball.' "

So Dr. Falwell took a permanent marker to the ball and inscribed *This ball entitles you to a full four-year scholarship at Liberty University, whether I'm dead or alive. —Jerry Falwell*

As anyone who has spent time in evangelicalism's inner orbit knows, there are really two Jerry Falwells. One, of course, is the frothing, shameless fundamentalist most Americans have seen on television, the man who once denounced homosexuality as "a vile and satanic system" and the feminist movement as "a satanic attack on the home." This is the Jerry Falwell who not only blamed the terrorist attacks of 9/11 on a long list of domestic minorities (homosexuals, feminists, pagans, abortionists, et cetera), but who also tried to cash in on the public outrage over those remarks by telling his supporters—in a letter signed by his son Jonathan—that he was being victimized by "a vicious smear campaign" and asking them to send "a special Vote of Confidence gift . . . of at least $50 or even $100."

The other Jerry Falwell, the one I'm seeing today, is more akin to a religious Willy Wonka—a whimsical, mercurial figure who delights in unexpected acts of generosity and trickery. This is the Jerry Falwell who gives away college scholarships to kids who hit baseballs over his fence, who plays lighthearted pranks on uptight fundamentalists and speaks adoringly of his grandchildren. This Jerry Falwell has made some unlikely friends over the years, including Senator Ted Kennedy and *Hustler* publisher Larry Flynt, both of whom praise Dr. Falwell as a decent human being while condemning his political views.

What both Jerry Falwells have in common is a rock-solid streak of self-confidence. Dr. Falwell is almost universally described as a man who never wavers, never waffles, never second-guesses his beliefs in the open. In his autobiography, when writing about the day he became a Christian, Dr. Falwell wrote, "I accepted the mystery of God's salvation. I didn't doubt it then. I haven't doubted it to this day."

That certainty dominates his management style as well. During our interview, he gets a call from Jerry Falwell, Jr., a lawyer-cum-businessman who, along with his brother Jonathan, is being groomed to take over the Falwell empire someday. Jerry Jr. is calling, it seems, because he needs his father's approval for a new bookstore being proposed for Liberty's campus. The elder Falwell listens to his son rattle off the pertinent facts and figures, looks up at the ceiling while performing a series of quick mental calculations, and slams his empty Snapple bottle on the desk.

"I'm for it!"

That's it. No committee meetings, no focus groups, no spreadsheets. Dr. Falwell runs his university like a Tammany Hall politician, with direct edicts, micromanagerial governance, and an organizational chart shaped like an upside-down T.

When applied to his evangelical faith, that gut-based conviction leads to a worldview that is almost preternaturally unshakable. When I ask him the famous Proust question—"What do you want God to say to you at the pearly gates?"—he smiles and leans back in his chair.

"That's easy. He'll say, 'Well done, good and faithful servant.'"

It's not a wishful answer—Dr. Falwell feels absolutely, 100 percent sure that when he gets to heaven, the Lord will thank him for his service and usher him swiftly in. A television interviewer once asked him what he'd do if he turned out to be wrong—if, when he got to heaven, God thanked him for his ministry, but chastised him for getting involved with the homophobes and the misogynists and the people who want to use Christianity as a battering ram. Dr. Falwell responded, "I wouldn't think it was him I was talking to."

Earlier this semester, I caught a glimpse of Dr. Falwell walking through the central corridor of DeMoss Hall, one of the busiest areas on campus. He was on his way to a meeting, but once he was spotted, a hundred Liberty students swarmed him immediately, creating a George Clooney–esque frenzy in the space across from the school bookstore.

Some students clamored to shake his hand. A few snapped cell phone photos. But most just shouted their prayer requests from afar.

"Dr. Falwell, can you pray for my uncle George's pancreatic cancer?"

"Dr. Falwell, I'm trying to decide whether to go into the ministry, and I need your prayers!"

"Dr. Falwell, will you pray for my financial aid for next year?"

What struck me about that encounter is that while evangelical theology teaches that God considers all prayers equal, no matter who the petitioner is, these students seemed convinced that Dr. Falwell's prayers would have more oomph than their own. In other words, his cocksure confidence and his Wonka-esque unpredictability had combined to make a figure who seemed to straddle the line between prophet and publican, biblical hero and fallible mortal.

Almost an hour into our interview, I've learned what Dr. Falwell's favorite meal is (steak and baked potato, no butter) and where he gets his hair cut (Lynchburg's A-Plus Barbershop), but I still haven't glimpsed any mystical, quasi-divine side of his personality. Maybe, I decide, I should be asking him about bigger, more consequential things.

"What's the biggest cultural deficit in America today?" I ask, holding my breath for some fire and brimstone.

"The breakdown of the family," he replies. "We have a 50 percent divorce rate. Seventy-five percent of all African American children born in the United States this year will grow up in a single-parent home. The trend is going the wrong way, not the right one."

Huh? What about gay marriage?

"That's serious," he says, "But frankly, I think we've got it pretty well hedged in now. Of course there are gays, but you can't make laws against that. They just have to meet the Lord."

Spending time alone with Dr. Falwell in his office hasn't made me a convert. When I look at him, I still see a man who has used his charisma and razor-sharp business acumen to spread the worst form of religion. He may be friendly and compassionate with his followers, but making a judgment of him based on how he treats the people in his flock seems a little like complimenting the builders of the Death Star for their solid metalwork. It might be true, but it's sort of beside the point.

All that said, I can certainly see why die-hard liberals like Larry Flynt and Ted Kennedy have been able to forgive Dr. Falwell for his sins. In person, he beats you over the head with his folksy charm, his relaxed confidence, and his polished interpersonal skills (in the last hour, he's started almost every sentence, "Well, Kevin, you see . . ."). And in the end, you're ultimately cajoled into liking him, even if you still hate everything he stands for.

So who is the real Jerry Falwell? Is he a rabid, hate-spewing fundamentalist? Or is he a dutiful family man, a talented preacher, and a competent administrator? Was John McCain right when he called Dr. Falwell an "agent of intolerance" during the 2000 presidential campaign? Or was the *Wall Street Journal* right when, in 1978, it described him as a "man of charm, drive, talent, and ambition"?

Well, in a way, both are right. In fact, that's the overwhelming impression I get from the time I've spent watching Dr. Falwell this semester and talking to him this afternoon: he's a complex character, but he's not hiding anything. He may be a blundering, arch-conservative provocateur, and he may spew anti-gay venom more often than most people brush their teeth, but I honestly think he believes every word he preaches, and I wouldn't be at all surprised if he really does stay awake at night worrying about the homosexual agenda, the evils of abortion, and the imminent spread of liberalism. He really does think America needs to be saved.

Realizing that Dr. Falwell isn't a fraud—as troubling a notion as that is—has helped me solve one of the great mysteries of this semester. For months now, I've been puzzled by the thousands of good, kindhearted believers at Liberty who follow a man who seems, to my mind, to be almost unredeemable. They like him, I'm learning, because he's a straight shooter. In a half century of preaching, Dr. Falwell has said some outrageous things, and he's angered Christians and non-Christians alike, but he's never revealed himself as a hypocrite. He's never been caught in sexual sin, and he's been as transparent in his financial dealings as you could reasonably expect. And in the world of televangelism, a world filled to the brim with hucksters and charlatans and Elmer Gantry–type swindlers, a little sincerity goes a long way.

261

After an hour or so of talking, Dr. Falwell sounds like he's ready to wrap things up, but first, he says he'd like to pray for me. And who am I to refuse? So right there in his office, he bows his head while I bow mine, and in his godlike basso profundo voice, he calls down the heavens on my behalf.

"Father, I pray for Kevin. I pray that your anointing will be upon him in a very special way. And Lord, if you want him in journalism, I pray you'll put him in key places where he can make a difference in the culture. God, give him a great family and children that he'll raise up in the nurture and admonition of your Son. I put Kevin in your hands, that you'll make him a special tool, a special instrument in your kingdom. For Christ's sake, Amen."

He shakes my hand and signs my Bible ("To my friend Kevin, Phil.1:6, Jerry Falwell"), and when I'm almost out the door, I hear his voice boom behind me.

"Kevin!"

I turn around to find him holding his empty Snapple bottle with two hands, the label pointed toward me.

"Make sure to tell 'em that every afternoon, I drink a peach tea," he says. "Diet peach tea. Make sure to tell 'em that."

I assure him that I will. He smiles, and I smile back, and then I turn and walk away.

After leaving Dr. Falwell's office, I feel a little woozy. All things considered, I think the interview went pretty well. But man, do I need to decompress.

Luckily, today is the next-to-last intramural softball game of the season, so I'll get to run around for a few hours and calm my nerves. My hall's team, the Billy Goats, has done fairly well this year. We're a few games above .500, a record I take pride in despite the fact that I contributed very little to it. After a game in which I struck out swinging two times in a row, Jersey Joey gave me the nickname "AC."

"AC?" I asked.

"Yeah, Rooster, AC. Air-conditioning. You're making a lot of breeze with all that whiffing."

Since then, I haven't done much to redeem myself. First, there was the choir practice incident, which I still haven't lived down. Then, there was the time I stole second base. During a game a few weeks ago, when the opposing team's pitcher wound up for his delivery, I put my head down, sprinted as hard as I could, made a sleek, well-timed slide into the bag, and rose up proudly, brushing the dirt off my legs. The pitcher gruffly reminded me that there's no base stealing in intramural softball, and would I please go back to first?

These days, Joey usually puts me in for a few innings per game, but only if we're winning by seven or eight runs. And when I'm playing, my teammates' expectations of me are so low that anything I do right is grounds for completely disproportionate enthusiasm. I catch one fly ball, and they're hooting and hollering like I just made an unassisted triple play while curing the common cold and fighting the mujahideen.

Today, though, I raise my profile. Our regular second baseman is sick, so I was called up to play his position. For most of the game, things are going along fine—a few runs here, a few fly-outs there—when, in the third inning, a guy from the other team wallops a ground ball in my direction. Actually, it's headed a good fifteen feet to my right, smack dab between me and the shortstop.

Normally, I'd stand and watch as it careened into the outfield. But for whatever reason, I get a quick flash of optimism. I decide to go for it. I make a soaring, acrobatic, slo-mo-worthy dive to my right, and somehow, the ball ends up in my glove. Without thinking, I fire it across the field from my knees, where it reaches the first baseman on one hop, a millisecond or two before the runner reaches the base. He's out.

"*Rooster!*" shouts Joey from right field. "*Where the eff did that come from?*"

No one can believe it. My teammates look at me with the stunned expression you'd give a three-year-old who began quoting Molière, and then they erupt into applause. By some act of God, I've just made a play befitting a Division I starter, not a klutzy choir singer. The impossible has been rendered possible.

My second big moment comes at the end of the game. We're down 5–4 in the ninth with two outs, and we're up to bat. Our last hope is

Jonah, the pastor's kid who rooms with Jersey Joey. Jonah has runners on first and third, so if he can just get a base hit, we'll tie the game and send it into extra innings.

Jonah swings and misses on the first pitch, then again on the second.

"Come on, Jonah," says Marco, our first baseman. "Don't be a choke artist, buddy. We need this."

The third pitch comes, and Jonah winds up for a mammoth swing. It's a meaty pitch right over the center of the plate, and he misses. Strike three. Game over. Groans and boos erupt from the dugout.

Normally I try not to rejoice at the failings of others, but in this situation, I can't help feeling like the pimple-pocked loser in middle school whose emotional load is lightened when an even more unfortunate kid—pimples *and* braces—moves into town. I'm no longer the worst player on the team. Now, Joey and his friends will be picking on Jonah instead of me, making gay jokes about Jonah instead of me.

"So, Coach," I say to Joey, on our way back from the game. "How'd I do?"

"You were pretty good, AC. I didn't expect that at all."

"Guess I should change my nickname to Amazing Champion, huh?"

Joey laughs and looks me over top to bottom, from my gloriously unathletic khaki shorts to my T-shirt, emblazoned with the name of my old a cappella group.

"How about Adores Cock, Rooster? That work for you?"

Wednesday night, I walk into Thomas Road for the second-to-last Campus Church of the semester, and there's a party going on. Well, not really. But it's close. All around the sanctuary, students are standing in the aisles, cheering and yelling, snapping photos with their cell phones. It takes me a few seconds to realize that everyone's attention is directed upward at the pool.

Tonight is Baptism Night. A few times per semester, the first half of the regular Campus Church service is replaced with baptisms for Liberty students who have never been baptized or who want to get rebaptized. The baptismal pool at Thomas Road is lofted high above the sanctuary, built into the wall in about the same spot as the seats of those two bickering cranks on the *Muppet Show*. The pool is filled waist high with unnaturally blue water and fronted with a pane of glass so the cameras can show the facial expressions of the baptizees as they get dunked.

"This is Brandon from Dorm 8," announces the pastor standing in the pool. He and Brandon are both clad in long black robes, which gives the whole thing a wizards-stuck-in-fish-tank aesthetic. Brandon's name and hometown flash on the Jumbotron, prompting wild screams from his friends on the floor below.

"Yeah Bran-Dogg!"

"Yeeeeeeeaw!"

"That's my roommate!"

"Brandon, have you accepted Jesus Christ as your personal savior?" the pastor asks, shouting over the crowd noise.

"You bet I have!" yells Brandon, provoking more hoots and catcalls.

"Well then, Brandon, upon profession of your faith, and in obedience to Christ's command, I baptize you, my brother, in the name of the Father, and of the Son, and of the Holy Spirit."

He dunks Brandon backward into the pool . . .

"Buried in the likeness of his death."

. . . and lifts him out.

"Raised in the likeness of his resurrection."

I know one of the girls getting baptized tonight—Valentina, a girl from my Daytona Beach evangelism trip. Halfway through the service, she wades into the pool, smiling nervously.

"This is Valentina from Dorm 13," the pastor says. "Valentina, have you accepted Jesus Christ as your Lord and savior?"

"Yes, I have."

This morning, Valentina told me she was worried about looking her best for her appearance on the Jumbotrons. She said she spent "an ungodly amount of time" primping, straightening her hair, and buying special waterproof makeup, and her effort isn't lost on me. As I watch her being dunked in the water, coming up with her hair dripping, the wet robe gripping her body, I can't stop my mind from wandering to that Denise Richards pool scene from *Wild Things*. Which probably means I'm not ready to get baptized, come to think of it.

After Valentina's turn, the pastor continues with the assembly-line baptisms. Students file into the pool, and they're in, under, and out in less than a minute apiece. Everyone gets a hearty round of applause, and when the line runs out, the pastor dries off, and we move on to church as usual.

Earlier this week, I got a call from my friend Laura, the one who helped me prepare for Liberty. She knows that my semester is coming to a close, and she asked me what I'm going to miss.

I told her that, if anything, I'll miss the nights like tonight, when Liberty students come together to lift each other up in celebration. Because isn't that what this is? Take away the religious symbolism, and Baptism Night is a giant group hug. It's six thousand Liberty students saying, "We affirm your membership in this community. We value you." And as mawkish and sentimental as that sounds, it's true.

The French sociologist Émile Durkheim wrote about "collective effervescence," a special type of energy that forms around mass gatherings —concerts, raves, political rallies, things like that. Liberty, for all its flaws and quirks, fosters more collective effervescence than any other place I've ever been. Every Wednesday night and Sunday morning, you feel it at Campus Church. Three times a week, you feel it in convocation. You feel it in dorm-wide prayer meetings, at Christian rock concerts, and during Spiritual Emphasis Week. It's the sensation you get when your mind is swallowed by a sort of group mind, when the hundred-decibel worship music and the laser light shows and the people jumping and screaming and hollering all around you combine to form a social organism that takes on a life of its own.

It's sort of sad that most secular colleges have no real substitutes for this kind of ecstatic group activity—or at least none that occur weekly, involve the whole student body, and are enjoyable while sober. At most schools, the social, intellectual, and spiritual components of the college experience are confined to separate experiential spheres. We party, we learn, and we contemplate the metaphysical, but we rarely do all three simultaneously and en masse. And maybe that's just as well.

Maybe secular college shouldn't be in the business of collective effervescence, and maybe most college students aren't looking for mass spiritual euphoria from their schools. But after all I've seen this semester, I can't say I blame the ones who are.

The next morning, I get a call from my aunt Teresa.

"Kevin!" she says. "You're almost free!"

This is how most members of my family talk about Liberty—in prison parlance. For my aunts Tina and Teresa especially, experiencing my Liberty semester from afar has been torturous. When I told them I was coming here in the first place, they winced. When I told them I didn't hate it here, they shivered. When I told them I was sitting down for an interview with Dr. Falwell, it was all they could do not to go into paroxysms.

In fairness, my family has tried very, very hard to see things from my point of view. My mom, for example, has been watching Thomas Road's church services on TV every Sunday morning to see what all the fuss is about. Several aunts and uncles have sent supportive e-mails, and a few weeks ago, my aunt Tina told me that she didn't blame me for enjoying myself at Liberty. "It's natural to connect with people on a human level, even if you do disagree with everything they say." She added, "You *do* disagree with everything they say, right?"

In short, although they hate the fact that I'm here, my family has been treating me a lot more civilly than I'd be treating my hypothetical son if he spent a semester with my ideological enemies. If we're talking biblical family conflicts, I'm somewhere between the prodigal son, who ran off to squander his inheritance money, and Absalom, who formed an army to rebel against his father's empire. I'm sure I'm causing them a lot of heartache and anxiety, and yet, they're still treating me with the same amount of love and compassion they always have. It's amazing, really.

In fact, I'm starting to think that after this semester, I should do something to compensate my family for all the pain I'm putting them through. Today, Teresa made a suggestion for my next project.

"You should spend a semester living with a gay-rights group in San Francisco," she said.

It's worth a thought, anyway.

With less than two weeks left to go in the semester, I figured it was time to start telling people that I'm not coming back to Liberty next fall. So I did. And so far, I've gotten a range of responses.

My roommate Eric just shrugged, told me he'd miss me, and wished me well wherever I ended up. Fox the RA spent ten minutes trying to convince me to change my mind. My next-door neighbor Zipper gasped, shook his head, and asked why I didn't want to stay. I told him that I missed my friends from my old school and added, "I just don't think this is the place I'm supposed to be." He nodded, sighed, and said he hoped I would come back to visit.

Even Jersey Joey took the news well. When I told him that I was planning to go back to Brown in the fall, he asked me a few questions and then slapped me on the back.

"Well, you gotta do what you gotta do, Rooster."

The most unexpected thing about the reaction to my news was that no one seemed at all suspicious. None of my friends were troubled to hear that I'm leaving Liberty after only one semester, even though I've displayed no signs of unhappiness. I gather, though, that quick turnover is not altogether unusual at Liberty. Here, people come and go all the time, often on short notice. Some are expelled, some get married and drop out, and others simply feel called elsewhere. Maybe I'm just another transient soul.

Or maybe it's that everyone else is preoccupied by their own worries. After all, summer vacation is coming up, and for a lot of my friends, spending three months away from Liberty's rigid spiritual structure is a nerve-wracking proposition.

Last night, when I went into Jersey Joey's room to watch TV, I found him at his computer, looking through a girl's Facebook photos. The girl, a tall, thin, Eva Mendes look-alike, was wearing a small red bikini and making the college-girl kissy face.

"This girl is trouble, Rooster," he said.

"She's cute," I said.

"I know. She's hot as balls. She knows me from high school, and she just sent me a message saying that we should hook up when I get back to Hoboken."

For the past week, ever since he read Ecclesiastes in one sitting, Joey has been test-driving his Nice Christian Boy persona. He prays more these days, and he's been doing things like kicking his friends out of his room at midnight so he can do his Bible reading in solitude. But his reform attempts haven't been entirely successful. He still curses, he's still playing pranks on our hallmates, and he hasn't been able to stop smoking cigarettes. Last night, he started to worry about losing his virginity.

"I should probably turn this girl down," he said. "I need to hold on to my v-card for a couple more years. But man, it's not gonna be easy to say no."

These days, when Joey tells me about his summer plans, he gives me two scenarios: what he wants to happen and what's going to happen. He wants to turn down party invitations, but he knows he's going to accept them. He wants to avoid going to hookah bars with his friends, but he knows he's going to give in to peer pressure. He wants to keep his virginity, but he's going to sleep with the hot Latina from Hoboken. He's not proud of his moral foibles, but he doesn't particularly feel like fighting them, either.

My friend Paul is having similar woes. For the past few weeks, Paul has been repairing his relationship with Lauren, his no-longer-bisexual girlfriend. Through scripture reading and prayer, Paul was able to convince Lauren that she wasn't truly attracted to women, and he felt confident enough in her heterosexuality to continue the relationship. That problem solved, Paul has focused his worries back on himself and his spiritual life.

"I'm scared that I won't be able to keep this up over the summer," he told me earlier today.

By "this," of course, Paul means his religious transformation, which has been enormous even by Liberty standards. When I remember the Paul I met on the first night of school—a sarcastic, womanizing football player who struggled to say "Lord" during prayer groups—it's hard to believe today's Paul inhabits the same body. His is the ultimate Liberty success story, the kind of thing Dr. Falwell must have dreamed of when he started this school thirty-six years ago. One semester at Liberty, and Paul has a marriage-track Christian girlfriend, he reads the Bible furiously, and he's begun sharing the gospel with his secular friends. But he's scared that without the presence of a strong religious community, he'll lose all the growth he's undergone this semester. The "summer slide" is a frequent topic of conversation among Liberty students, and it's a widespread joke that the first few weeks of the fall semester are spent repenting for the things that happened during June, July, and August.

These summer slide conversations with Joey and Paul raise another one of the big questions I've been mulling all semester. Namely, what happens to Liberty students after graduation, when they leave the safe confines of Bible Boot Camp and move out into the messy, sin-filled secular world? What happens when there's no more "Liberty Way" to keep them on the straight and narrow?

Like everything else about Liberty, I suspect it depends whom you ask. For Jersey Joey, who wants to work as a firefighter someday, graduation will be a glorious emancipation. I'm sure he'll be a life-long churchgoing Christian, but it's probably unreasonable to expect that he'll stay devout when he's not being prodded into piety by his classmates. People like Max Carter, the student body president-elect who wants to go into Republican politics, have already recognized that they'll need to make their faith more private to be taken seriously by a community that includes non-evangelicals.

On the other hand, Liberty students who are committed to a Christian career—missionary work, church planting, getting a seminary degree—may not feel much of a change at all. Zipper, my next-door neighbor, is in this group. He wants to be either a youth pastor or a Christian camp director when he grows up, and last night, when I asked him how he planned on keeping his faith strong in the secular world, he told me, "Look at it this way. A Christian's best friends should always be other Christians. Jesus didn't shy away from nonbelievers, but he had his twelve disciples as his core group. Of course, we need to be going out into the world and acting as the salt of the earth, and I'm excited to do that, but my core group of friends will always be Christians. I need that support system."

Most college students, myself included, talk about entering the real world with a certain level of wariness. But I suspect Liberty students have more reasons to worry than I do. When I'm no longer in college, I might be surprised to discover how hard it is to make a living wage or raise a family, but Liberty students going anywhere outside Lynchburg's city limits will soon find their whole cosmology shaken. They'll meet people who believe in evolution, people who don't believe in Jesus, people who mock them for having attended Jerry Falwell's college. What's more, they'll see that those people bear no resemblance to the heathen masses they learned about in their GNED classes. For Liberty students who have spent four years hearing from their professors about how unfulfilled, relativistic, flimsy, and hedonistic the real world is, meeting hordes of happy, principled, morally sound non-Christians will come as a shot between the eyes. And to be honest, I'm not sure how they'll take it.

Last night, in a moment of uncharacteristic candor, I asked Zipper how he thought he was going to fare in the world outside Liberty.

"Well, it's not going to be the same, that's for sure," he said. "I know things are never going to be as easy as they are here. I mean, I guess there's only one thing I can do, and that's rely completely on God. I think he'll . . . well, I *hope* he'll help me out."

Test Me, O Lord, and Try Me

Tuesday night, Dorm 22 holds its last hall meeting of the year. As always, we sit along the walls facing each other while Fox and Stubbs pace back and forth in the middle of the hall.

"We're doing white gloves this week, gentlemen," says Stubbs.

Everyone groans. In a white-glove inspection, the RAs don pairs of latex gloves, run their hands along the baseboards of your room, and tell you to keep cleaning if the gloves come up anything less than spotless. It doesn't sound all that hard, but if you're dealing with a year's worth of built-up grime, polishing a small room to a shine can take a few hours.

To cheer us up, Fox and Stubbs announce that they have special certificates to give out—the Dorm 22 Gag Awards.

"First up is the Sister Dorm Award," says Stubbs. "This one goes to the guy most likely to marry a girl from Dorm 33 . . . Mark Mitchell!"

Everyone chuckles at the joke. Mark, a shy math major from Memphis, almost never hangs out with the girls from the sister dorm—or any girls, for that matter. He's as likely to marry a Dorm 33 girl as I am to be picked in the first round of the NBA draft. Mark blushes as the guys cheer and catcall him, and then responds with a gag of his own: "Stubbs, I didn't know your mom lived in Dorm 33."

The rest of the meeting is filled with more funny awards and frat-boy repartee. The Honeymoon Sex Award goes to Brad Miller, who is getting married in July, the Biggest Deuce Award goes to a freshman named Toby who allegedly forgot to flush the toilet last week, and the Dorm 22 Man of the Year Award is given to Rodrigo, the kindhearted sophomore from Mexico City.

When the last award is given out, Fox sighs.

"Well, guys, that's all we've got. It's been a great year."

"We're really going to miss you guys," says Stubbs.

An announcement is made that James Powell, this year's Spiritual Life Director, will take over as an RA next year. About half of this year's residents are coming back to Dorm 22, and among the half who aren't, some are graduating, some are switching dorms, and some are moving off campus. Then, there's me.

"As most of you guys know by now," Stubbs says, "Roose is leaving Liberty."

Jersey Joey puts on his best mock-agonized voice and wails, *"Say it ain't so, Rooster!"*

After the laughs die down, Fox says, "Roose, we'll miss you, buddy. We're sad you're leaving, but we're happy that the Lord is taking you where you're needed."

Last week, I wrote an e-mail to my family. In it, I said that I was 85 percent excited to be done with my time at Liberty and 15 percent sad to be leaving. But in truth, it's more like fifty-fifty. For lots of reasons, I'm looking forward to leaving Liberty. I'm excited about seeing my Brown friends again, living in a laxer environment, and getting some semblance of my old life back. But for every reason I'll be glad to leave, there's another thing I'll miss. These hall meetings. Late-night conversations in Joey's room. My prayer group. Fight Night. The list goes on and on.

Earlier today, a dozen guys from Dorm 22 went out for lunch at T.G.I. Friday's. Over lunch, Fox the RA announced that just for kicks, he wanted to hear everyone's confessions from the year. He promised us amnesty in exchange for our juiciest rule-breaking tales.

The first few confessions were relatively tame. Steve, a junior from

Pittsburgh, confessed that he went dancing with a girl last semester. Tony, a sophomore from Miami, said that he faked absence slips for convocation and watched R-rated movies "almost every night." Six or seven guys admitted to having snuck out after curfew. Eventually, the confessions got more sordid, and even the RAs got involved. Fox admitted that he had gone to the Smoker's Hole to share cigars with his friends. Stubbs confessed that he hadn't exactly followed Liberty's rules about guy/girl contact.

"I can't count on my fingers how many times I've kissed my girlfriend this year," he said, laughing. "A hundred? Two hundred? I don't know."

As funny as it was to hear the secrets of my Liberty friends brought out in the open, the confession lunch made me feel a little guilty. After all, I had an actual confession to make—the big confession about who I am, what I believe, and why I came to Liberty. But I couldn't bring myself to make it.

All semester, I've made peace with my Christian façade by telling myself that I needed to keep it up in order to blend in here. And a lot of the time, it wasn't that hard to stay silent. After a month or two, when my hallmates stopped asking about my faith and when acting like a Liberty student became second nature, I sort of forgot that I was hiding anything. But now, with a week and a half left in my semester, I'm starting to panic. Should I tell them everything before I leave? How will they react? Will I be run out of town? Will Dr. Falwell condemn me from the pulpit? Will there be a GNED exam next year that reads, "Kevin Roose can be best described as (a) a fraud, (b) a Tartuffe, (c) a tool of Satan, or (d) all of the above"?

I hope not, but I'm honestly not sure. I've gotten in pretty deep on this hall. Yesterday, Fox the RA told me he considered me a "true man of the Lord." Before he knew I was leaving Liberty, Zipper asked me if I wanted to be a Prayer Leader next year. I don't know how, but I think I managed to convince most of these guys that I was a strong, faithful evangelical. And while solid fakery on my part might have made my semester more successful, I also realize that I'm setting these guys up for a big disappointment.

I didn't expect to care so much about the people I met at Liberty, but I had no choice. For all their foibles and all our differences, my hallmates are an amazing bunch. I hope I'll find a way to let them down gently, and I hope, in time, they'll forgive me my trespasses.

Of course, I won't miss everyone at Liberty. For example, I'm really looking forward to leaving Henry, my angry twenty-nine-year-old roommate who, as of this writing, still thinks I'm a homosexual.

I admit, I'm still holding out for a fairy-tale ending to the Henry saga. Things have been tense ever since Henry brought my sexual orientation into question, but I keep imagining a final heartwarming turn of events, a rapprochement that erases all his animosity toward me. In my mind, it goes something like this: after a heated argument, Henry stares at me, I stare back, his face softens as he recognizes a spark of human unity between us, and he bursts forth with a final, made-for-TV line. Like, "You know, brother, maybe we're really *not* that different." Or maybe, "Well, we're *all* just struggling to make it in this crazy world, brother." Something involving brothers.

The semester is almost over, though, so I've had to kick my efforts into overdrive. Luckily, I've gotten some help from fate. Earlier this week, while getting a soda out of the vending machine, I accidentally pressed the wrong button. Instead of the Diet Pepsi I was aiming for, out popped a Mountain Dew. Aha! A sign! Mountain Dew is Henry's favorite drink, and this was just the olive branch I needed. I brought the bottle upstairs to Henry, offering it to him with outstretched hands.

"Henry, I bought this Mountain Dew by mistake," I said. "Here, I want you to have it."

"No thanks," he said.

"You sure?"

"Yep."

Having failed at outright bribery, I tried a simpler approach. I started saying hello to Henry every time he entered the room. I hoped I'd show him by sheer persistence that I wasn't content to remain on his bad side.

For several days, he ignores my greetings. But today, when I say hi, he stops in his tracks.

"Why do you always talk to me?" he asks.

"Just to be nice," I say.

The face he's making is one of genuine puzzlement, like he simply can't understand why I'm still making an effort to repair things between us. Is he softening? I think so! Here it comes! The moment of reconciliation! Brotherhood!

"Well, save it," he growls.

Henry shuffles over to his desk, thumps down in his chair, and pulls his curtain tight across my sight line, mumbling something that sounds a whole lot like "faggot."

After failing in my last attempt to befriend Henry, I sit at my desk wondering why exactly I still care what a nasty, intolerant fundamentalist thinks of me. The problem obviously lies with him, since I don't think I've done anything to provoke his ire. So why bother mending fences? Is it because the Quaker in me wants to make peace with my enemies? Is it because I didn't want to be on his bad side if he snapped? It's probably some of both. But most of all, I think I saw a friendship with Henry as the last frontier of empathy—like, if I could just get along with the angriest, most outlandish fundamentalist at Liberty, I'd have done my job this semester. I'd have bridged the God Divide right in my own room. Of course, that never happened. And with a week left in the semester, I don't think it will.

In an odd way, having Henry as a roommate has probably been good for me. Whenever he went on a vituperative, unprovoked rant against homosexuals or feminists or Al Sharpton, I was forced to step back and remember: *oh, right . . . this is Liberty University*. It was a constant reality check. I felt the same emotions when talking to Henry that I feel whenever I see the footage of Dr. Falwell's 9/11 remarks or when I hear my hallmates condemning non-Christians to hell. It's my reaction to a certain kind of arrogance I've seen among Liberty students—and religious fundamentalists of all ages—who claim to have all the answers.

At the same time, it was reassuring to see how the rest of my hallmates reacted to Henry. When I got to Liberty, I assumed that a guy like him would fit right in. Weren't Liberty students all angry, ranting ideologues? Well, no, it turns out. And what's more, a guy like Henry has a hard time making friends.

The approaching end of the semester has made me want to encapsulate my Liberty experience in tidy, feel-good morals, and I put my finger on a good one today while thinking about Henry. Namely, one of the most humanizing things I've learned this semester is that even at Liberty, personality trumps ideology. Ask even the most conservative, hard-line Dorm 22 resident who he would rather hang out with—a grouchy, misanthropic evangelical like Henry or a funny, kindhearted atheist—and he'll pick the atheist without blinking. Liberty students like being around fellow believers, but not at the expense of everything else. When it comes down to it, no matter how pious or like-minded he might be, a Christian jerk is still a jerk.

I almost missed convocation on Wednesday. I've been nursing a head cold, and I was close to hitting the snooze button, rolling over, and going back to sleep. I'm glad I pulled myself out of bed, though. If I had skipped, I'd have missed the highlight of my semester.

During his sermon this morning, Dr. Falwell said, "A young man from the *Liberty Champion*, Kevin Roose, interviewed me last week."

I jerked up in my seat. Me? A loud cheer went up from the rows around me, and heads snapped in my direction.

"Kevin wanted to know personal things," Dr. Falwell continued. "He asked how many red neckties I had. I said somewhere between forty and fifty so I can wear a red tie every day of every month. And then he asked me questions about my practices—what I do and how I do it."

The weekly edition of the *Champion* came out today, with my profile of Dr. Falwell inside. The editors gave it a two-page spread with sidebars, jumbo-size photos, and a giant headline: EXCLUSIVE INTERVIEW WITH THE BIG MAN ON CAMPUS. The article has only been out for a few hours, but it's already caused a minor sensation on campus. I've gotten stopped in the hallway a few times by friends and acquaintances, and my e-mail inbox is full of congratulatory messages. I never expected Dr. Falwell to mention me in convocation, though. He almost never singles out individual Liberty students by name, and when he does, they've usually done something spectacular, like broken a state record in the 1600 meters. But me? All I did was write an article, and not a very good one at that. I've known all along that the *Champion* gets vetted for unflattering content by a Liberty administrator, so I had to write my profile with kid gloves, describing Dr. Falwell in terms like "a decision-maker and a thinker" with an "uncanny" business sense. I felt a little traitorous, but I couldn't very well back out of my assignment, so I gritted my teeth and wrote. And apparently, it turned out well enough for Dr. Falwell's taste.

After convocation ended, my hallmates swarmed me.

"Oh my gosh! Jerry said your name, man!"

"What was it like to talk to him?"

"How did you get him to like you?"

The strangest development in this whole *Champion* saga is that in my last official week as a Liberty student, I'm becoming known as a journalist on campus. All day, students have been coming up to me, slapping me on the back, and saying, "Hey, Roose, I didn't know you were a writer!" The first few times that happened, my breath shortened and my pulse spiked to two hundred beats per minute. Then I realized: *ohhh*, they're talking about the *Falwell* article.

Since the article came out, it's become harder for me to keep my two identities neatly compartmentalized in my mind. It's all blurring into one secular/evangelical/journalist/student amalgam. Usually, I never take notes in public, but tonight at Campus Church, I wanted to write down a few details about the sermon, and I figured, "What the heck. If they ask, I can just tell them I'm working on a story." So I whipped out my notebook and jotted down a few sentences. I got away with it that time, but I'm starting to worry that I'm getting too cavalier.

After curfew, I'm playing video games with Jersey Joey, and he brings up my article.

"You had never written for the *Champion* before?" he asks.

"No," I say.

"And they let you interview Falwell?"

"Yeah."

Joey stares at the wall, squinting in deep thought.

"So . . . wait. You're leaving Liberty after one semester, and you're going back to Brown. Are they even going to accept your transfer credits?"

"I don't know," I say. "Probably not."

"So you just wasted an entire semester basically."

"I guess you could look at it like that, yeah."

Joey glances up at the ceiling, then shoots me a suspicious, sideways glare. Oh no. I know that look. I've been afraid of that look since the day I got here. That's the look of a guy who is putting together the pieces of a puzzle. Right now, Joey is thinking: *student journalist . . . came to Liberty from secular school . . . scored an interview with Dr. Falwell . . . leaving after one semester . . .*

"You know, Rooster," he says, "I almost feel like you're a mole, and when this semester's over, you're gonna go back and write an article in *Rolling Stone* about being different at Liberty."

I laugh—an involuntary, nervous laugh—and stammer, "What . . . do you mean . . . *different?*"

"You know," Joey says. "Gay."

This semester, Joey has called me gay approximately ten thousand times, but this time sounds different. He's not exactly serious, but I don't think he's joking, either. It's as if "gay" is a placeholder for some other descriptor he can't quite put his finger on. Part of me wants to tell him that he's right, that he's figured me out as an outsider. The other part of me knows that the semester isn't over yet, and that I need to squirm out of this somehow.

"So . . . are you?" he asks.

"Gay?"

"Or a mole."

We stare at each other for fifteen seconds, tension filling the space between us. Head spinning, gut churning, I spurt out the first thing that comes to mind.

"You got me, Joey. I'm a gay mole. Actually, I work for Elton John. He sent me here to recruit innocent Christian kids for his army of homosexuals. He told me to become friends with the Liberty students who seemed like closeted gays, and I picked you. Want to join us?"

Joey laughs. "Suck my balls."

He turns back to our video game, chuckling, apparently convinced of my innocence for now. Five minutes later, he looks at me again, shaking his head.

"Man, Rooster, you are one weird bastard."

Liberty's final exam period is officially under way, and campus anxiety is running high. This morning, when Zipper and I went to the prayer chapel for our usual session, we found the place jam-packed. Thirty or forty people were squeezed into the pews, all of them praying for their exams. One girl, a leggy brunette with a pink scrunchy wrapped around her ponytail, kneeled on the floor with her back arched and her arms extended straight overhead, in the I-just-won-Wimbledon pose. "Fill my head, Lord!" she pleaded in audible whispers. "Fill my head!"

I had my first exam yesterday, though I didn't know it at the time. You know that classic anxiety dream where a student goes to class one day and is informed that the final exam is being given, even though by some freak miscalculation, he hasn't even begun to study? Well, that happened to me. Yesterday afternoon, I walked into my History of Life class a few minutes late and noticed that everyone was sitting silently in their seats, pencils at the ready. I asked the guy seated next to me what was going on, and he shushed me.

"It's the final, man."

I thought he was kidding, but sure enough, as soon as I sat down, Dr. Dekker began passing out our final exam, a multipage monstrosity as thick as a piece of French toast. How could this have happened? It's not even finals period yet! As the exams circulated through the rows, I remembered something I'd heard Dr. Dekker say earlier in the semester: since History of Life is a two-credit course (most courses are three), its exam is held a week early.

I was apparently the only calendar-challenged idiot in the class—everyone else went right to work, scribbling their answers to questions about the scientific classification of Neanderthals, questions that used science-speak like *Homo ergaster* and *Homo rudolfensis*. I did my best, recalling what I could from Dr. Dekker's lectures, but it wasn't pretty.

By the end of the test, I had left about a third of the questions blank, and I was sympathizing with the *Australopithecus*, an ancient hominid whose brain capacity was one-third of that of the modern human (and who, according to young-earth creationists, was not a human ancestor at all).

Today, I get a tough exam of another sort. After lunch, my phone buzzes with a call from Pastor Seth, my spiritual mentor.

"Are you free this afternoon?" he asks.

The last time I met with Pastor Seth for our usual breakfast discipleship session, I told him that I wasn't planning to come back to Liberty next year. He didn't take the news well. We spent most of that hour talking through my reasons for leaving, with him trying to convince me that I would fall into sin if I left and me trying to change the subject. Since then, I think he's accepted the fact that I'm not going to reverse my decision, but he's been calling me all week with offers to hold a special prayer session on my behalf.

Today, I take him up on it. After my New Testament review session, I go to Pastor Seth's office, where we spend half an hour in prayer. We pray for all kinds of things—my summer, my future job, my future family, my final exams next week, his upcoming hunting trip—and as always, it's a good feeling to be prayed for. Then, after the final amen, he rolls his office chair a few feet closer to me.

"So, Kevin," he says. "We've been doing discipleship for a while now, but I'm still not really sure where you are with God. Talk to me, man. Tell me where you are."

People's reactions to my departure seem to be coming in two waves. First, they either accept it or they try to convince me out of it. Then, after the news sinks in, people start wondering if I'm leaving because I haven't totally bought in to Christianity. That's when the interrogation starts. This morning at convocation, Paul Maddox asked me how my prayer life was going and if there was anything I needed help with. Then, at lunch, Zipper offered to pray with me over the phone this summer. It's the most passive-aggressive Inquisition trial in history.

Similar questions are also beginning to trickle in from secular friends and family members who want to know what my semester at

Bible Boot Camp has done to me. Yesterday, I got an e-mail from my friend Janine. She wrote: "Are you a Bible-thumper now?"

The short answer, as you might guess, is no. I'm not a Bible-thumper, and I'm not a conservative evangelical. There were moments this semester when I felt myself being pulled in that direction, sometimes quite strongly, but in the end, there's still a rather large gap between my beliefs and the beliefs of my Liberty friends. Am I glad that they hold those beliefs? Yes, for the most part. Do I find their faith compelling and beautiful? When it's not being used to offend or exclude people, sure. But I'm not where they are.

Coming into this semester, my family's biggest concern was that I'd develop an evangelical persona that would compete with, and eventually overtake, my secular persona. And in a sense, that has happened. When you're at Liberty full-time, immersed in this spiritual environment, it's impossible to keep your objective reference points intact. Everyone around you is talking about how God changes their lives, all the worship songs are about God "completing" and "filling" and "renewing," and after a four-month fusillade of that stuff, it sinks in. You start to see your old secular self as incomplete. You wonder if maybe accepting Christ would be worth it just so you could be as happy and bright-eyed and earnest as everyone around you.

What holds me back, ultimately, are all the disappointingly predictable things. As I said a while back, the all-or-nothing approach to salvation is prohibitive for me. I could never become an evangelical if it meant condemning homosexuals or proselytizing aggressively to non-Christians or believing that the Bible is infallible. And although I know that many, many evangelicals don't condemn gays or go "fishing" in Daytona Beach, that's the way Christianity has been presented to me this semester, and I haven't been convinced by it.

That said, this semester has definitely changed the way I think about God. I've always gone through brief phases of belief, but now, I find myself believing in some sort of divine presence more often than not—maybe 70 or 75 percent of the time instead of 30 or 35 percent. Part of this is wishful thinking, I'm sure. I hope there's a God so that all the praying and Bible reading and spiritual struggling my Liberty friends do isn't pointed toward an empty sky. I hope Jesus was truly resurrected from the dead because I have a couple hundred friends who have oriented their lives around that story. I hope there's a God so that all the good deeds being done in this world are being recorded somewhere— and, if I'm being perfectly honest, so that the bad deeds are being punished. My God is still much more similar to the inner light God of Quakerism than a God who answers prayers and heals sicknesses and helps football players catch passes. But there's something there, some belief in a divine caretaker, and I'm okay with that.

Pastor Seth wouldn't be okay with that, of course. In his eyes, and in the eyes of most Liberty students, it's all about Christ. Over and over this semester, I've heard it said, "There are only two types of people in the world: saved and unsaved." And if that's true, all my personal changes this semester have amounted to squat. If the only things that matter about a person are whether he's prayed the Sinner's Prayer and accepted Christ as his savior, I suppose I'm no better off than I was in January.

Here's the thing: I don't believe it. I know what the Bible says, but I don't believe the world is arranged according to a two-category binary. It can't be. Just look inside the saved category, for example. All semester, I've been exposed to the vast range of personalities at Liberty, and I've seen the complexity of what I used to think was a unified whole. For every Zipper who fits neatly into the norms of evangelical culture, there's a Jersey Joey carving his own path. For every Liberty student growing in faith, there's another one lying in bed at night wondering if all this God stuff is just made up. Once you dig under the surface, Liberty is every bit as messy and diverse as any secular college, and lumping everyone on this campus into a single category seems irrational and simplistic.

In the same way, lumping me into the unsaved category along with the Rational Response Squad atheists also seems overly reductive. I'm not an evangelical, it's true, but I've found that I have a lot in common with Liberty students. This semester, I've learned to interpret the world the same way Liberty students do. I've learned to think about love and grace the way they do. I've learned to call bad things "sin" and good things "blessed" and to expect that there's a cosmic difference between the two. Most of all, I've learned that faith, worn correctly, can be amazing and life-changing. Having met Liberty students who use their faith to improve their lives and the lives of the people around them, I can say with relative certainty that although I don't always believe in God, I believe in belief.

Back in Pastor Seth's office, he's still waiting for an answer to his question: where am I with God? I decide, for the sake of brevity, to keep it simple.

"Honestly," I say, "I'm struggling. I don't know where I am. I wish I did, but I don't."

Seth laughs.

"That's weird, because *I* know where you are."

"You do?" I say.

"Of course I do. Kevin, I remember you on the first day we met. You were skittish and nervous, and you couldn't look me in the eye without flinching. But now you're being genuine with me. You tell me that you're struggling with faith, and I believe you."

"And you don't think you wasted your time on me?" I ask.

"No!" he says. "Not at all. Listen, you're in a period of transition. You're still struggling to find your spiritual identity, and there's no shame in that. God doesn't make everything clear for us right away. We have to engage our faith, wrestle with it, make it ours. Otherwise, it's dead."

I'm not sure if Pastor Seth meant what he said, but I hope he was being genuine. It's not every day you meet a conservative evangelical pastor who tells you that being a Christian is more about doubt than dogma. It might not have been completely orthodox, and it certainly wasn't typical of Falwell-style fundamentalism, but today it was exactly what I needed to hear.

On the Friday night before exams, Liberty holds its annual Junior/Senior Banquet, which is sort of like prom, except no dancing is allowed. All around campus, couples are getting dolled up in dresses and tuxes, taking group photos on the steps of DeMoss Hall, and speculating about the particulars of this year's banquet.

I'm not going to the banquet. For one, I'm not a junior or a senior, which means I'd have to find an older girl willing to take me as her date. For another, the only girl I'd really want to take is also a sophomore, and even if I could ask her, I'm not sure whether she'd say yes.

That girl, of course, is Anna, the brunette from Bible study. I still haven't been able to get her off my mind. We see each other in passing a few times a week, and every time, there's a weird, elephant-in-the-room tension that revolves around our relationship's past. Since I was never able to explain the real reason we aren't dating, things between us are still unsettled. A week or so ago, during lunch at the dining hall, I told a few of Anna's hallmates that I still had a thing for her, hoping that they'd relay the message back to her, but I'm not sure if they ever did.

Tonight, watching all the upperclassmen in Dorm 22 don their tuxes and take their corsages out of their mini-fridges, I knew how I had to spend my last pre-exam weekend at Liberty. Saturday morning, I find Anna on my cell phone's contact list and hit the green button.

"It's Kevin."

"Kevin . . . hmm . . . ," she says. "Rings a bell."

"Can we talk?" I say.

"In person?"

"Yeah."

"Sure!" she says. "My dorm in five minutes?"

Two and a half minutes later, I'm sitting in my car outside Anna's dorm, and she emerges wearing slim-fit khakis and a ruffled top. She's smiling.

"Hey there," she says. "Want to go up to the monogram?"

Last week, a construction crew finally finished building Dr. Falwell's mountain monogram, the enormous LU emblazoned on the side of Liberty Mountain. It's still accessible only by climbing the mountain, but Liberty placed a small white gazebo at the top, where students can sit and take in a panoptic view of the Blue Ridge mountains. I haven't been there yet and neither has Anna, so we decide to take a little hike.

On the way up the mountain, Anna and I catch each other up on the developments in our lives. I tell her about my exams, my Falwell interview, and the fact that I'm leaving Liberty after next week. She tells me that she's spending the summer as a counselor at a Christian camp in Maryland and that she's thinking about transferring, too.

"I don't think I can handle four years of this place," she says. "It's great for some people, but I think I need a change."

By the time we reach the top of the monogram, we've reverted to our old levels of flirtatious mockery. (Me: "You sure you can keep going?" Her: "Shut up, you're the one breathing heavy over there, Darth Vader.") And maybe I'm delusional, but I think our chemistry is bubbling up again. Lots of coy smiles being passed back and forth. I brush up against her side by accident, and she playfully returns it a few seconds later.

From up on the mountain, Liberty's campus looks like something out of *The Sims*. The cars in the parking lot are just little colored dots arranged in rows, and the dome of the Vines Center is no bigger than a golf ball. The soccer team scrimmaging on the varsity field looks like a human version of foosball. The Blue Ridge mountains form a spectacular, Kodak-ready panorama in the background.

After spending a few minutes sitting on the gazebo bench, looking upon this scene, I turn to Anna.

"Listen, I'm sorry about what happened a while back. I really wanted to keep seeing you, but I couldn't, and it was totally my fault. Please don't think it was about you."

She laughs. "I mean, it was pretty obviously not about me. I'm perfect!"

Slowly, she puts her hand on top of mine.

"It's okay. Really. Things happen, and I know you didn't mean any harm."

She keeps gazing off into the distance, smiling, while her hand sits gently on top of mine. I sort of forgot how it feels to touch a girl, even if it's only our hands touching. It's electric. All the energy in my body has been transferred to those five fingers.

"I should go soon," she says. "My dad's coming to pick me up in twenty minutes, and I haven't finished packing."

"Yeah," I say. "We should go."

"You sure?"

"Yeah, let's go."

"Okay, let's go."

We stare at each other for five, ten, fifteen seconds. All of a sudden, I get a surging adrenaline rush, and I hear a voice in my head. *Kiss her. This is your last chance. Kiss her.*

Without giving myself time to hesitate, I lean over and kiss her— a quick peck in the middle of her left cheek. Her face flushes bright red. She smiles, showing every one of her teeth. We both look behind us, making sure no RAs are around to give us the four reprimands we just earned, and then we look back at each other.

"Now we really should go," she says.

"Yeah, we should."

We stand up from our bench. She runs her fingers through her hair, and I tie my shoe. I take her hand in mine, and we head back down the mountain, saying nothing the whole way.

Beauty for Ashes

Four months to the day after arriving at Liberty, I take my New Testament final, the second-to-last exam of my semester. It goes well. I stumble on a few questions about the book of Revelation, but I breeze through a section on the letters of Paul, and everything else is fairly straightforward. After I plunk my completed test down on the professor's desk, I feel a sort of nerdy euphoria. I did it! I passed a course on a very important book I used to know nothing about. As I walk out of the classroom, my step has a little more spring than usual.

After the exam, I spend an hour or two tying up loose ends—paying outstanding parking tickets, putting in my official withdrawal forms with the registrar, buying Liberty memorabilia at the bookstore. Then, after checking off everything on my to-do list, I head back to Dorm 22 to finish packing my bags.

I'm met at the door by a worried-looking Stubbs.

"Hall meeting in my room," he says. "Right now."

"What happened?" I ask.

He closes his eyes and shakes his head. "Just go to my room . . . now."

Confused, I put my backpack down and walk down the hall to his room. Inside, fifteen of my hallmates are seated on the floor. After a few more file in, Stubbs turns to James Powell.

"Powell has something to say, guys."

Dabbing a film of sweat from his forehead, Powell begins to speak: "I was sitting on the Mansion lawn with friends just now, hanging out and talking," he says. "All of a sudden, Jonathan Falwell walked into the Mansion really fast, talking on his phone. He looked terribly panicked. Right after that, some other administrators sprinted in. A couple of campus police officers went in, then the rescue squad, then an ambulance pulled up, and then a fire truck. We had no idea what was going on, so we just watched. Jonathan Falwell ran out of the Mansion screaming, "Get everybody out of here!" I asked a police officer what we could do. And he said, 'Pray. Pray really hard. It's really serious.'"

"He didn't say what it was?" asks Brad Miller.

"No."

"But we're assuming it's Jerry?"

"Yeah. What else could it be?"

Everyone looks at each other in taut silence.

"Guys, let's pray for this situation," says Stubbs. "Even if it's not Dr. Falwell who's in trouble."

Powell begins the prayers. "We have no idea how to pray, Lord, but help us to realize that your hand is over this. Give the doctors wisdom if it's a medical problem. Be with Dr. Falwell if he's involved. Give him strength, Lord."

Brad prays next. "We're assuming that it's Dr. Falwell, Father, but we don't know. We submit ourselves to you as creator to work a miracle today. I know, God, that you will do what you will do, but I also know that you listen to the hearts and the words of your people. If it is Dr. Falwell and if his life is at stake, please leave him here with us."

Stubbs speaks up, his voice cracking slightly. "As a group of brothers, we pray on behalf of this situation, in the holy and precious name of Jesus Christ."

We glance around the room. Should we go on with our lives? What else is there to do?

"Guys, let's go to lunch," Stubbs says. "As a hall."

We all file down the hall and out the doors in silence. Outside, we pass a male student holding his phone a few inches away from his ear.

"It's him!" he yells to everyone in earshot. "Dr. Falwell's in the hospital! My mom just saw it on the news! They found him unconscious in his office!"

"*Is he dead?*" someone yells back from across the street.

"No! Just unconscious! They're . . . trying to . . . it doesn't look good!"

By the time we get to the dining hall, hundreds of Liberty students have already assembled a corporate prayer session for Dr. Falwell. They're clasping hands around the long tables while the dining-hall manager prays out loud.

"Dear God, please help Dr. Falwell. Please, God, please help him, please, God."

Dr. Falwell's health has always been an issue of concern at Liberty. Two years ago, he was admitted to the hospital in critical condition for breathing problems stemming from a bout of viral pneumonia. He recovered and was quickly discharged, but ever since then, the prospect of another death scare has haunted this campus.

Much breath is spent arguing about what will happen to Liberty when Dr. Falwell dies. Some of my friends think classes will be cancelled for a month. Others think the university will go into a tailspin. Donations will dry up, they say, and without the draw of a celebrity leader, enrollment will plummet and the school will eventually be forced to fold. I've heard some people say that without its founder, Liberty is doomed.

Dr. Falwell has always reassured Liberty students that he has no plans to leave the school hanging. He often speaks about a biblical prophet named Hezekiah who prayed to God for fifteen more years of life. God granted Hezekiah's prayer, and Dr. Falwell expects an even bigger measure of grace. "I'm going to live to be 115," he said in one interview. "And I'll be giving the ACLU the devil when I'm a hundred. So just mark it down. I'm here to stay."

On my way back to the dorm after lunch, I pass the prayer garden, a small, hedged-in area in front of Dr. Falwell's office. A group of Liberty maintenance workers are gathered in a circle in their work uniforms, holding hands and praying, their bodies rocking back and forth. One worker, a stout, mustachioed man, wipes his eye with his sleeve.

I climb the steps to my hall, walk to my room, and open the door. Eric is standing in the middle of the room in his gym clothes, blanched and wide-eyed.

"He's dead, dude."

Three of my hallmates are crowded around Eric's TV, watching the news reports pour in. Luke clutches his head with both hands as Eric clicks through the channels.

". . . A native of Lynchburg, Virginia, Falwell started the Thomas Road Baptist Church there in 1956 and Liberty University in 1971. When he founded the Moral Majority eight years later, it marked the first concerted campaign in the media age to enshrine the tenets of evangelical . . ."

". . . A preacher by trade, Rev. Falwell used television as his pulpit and the Moral Majority as his vehicle to spread the evangelical gospel to voters, but also to lawmakers. Aides found Falwell in his office at Liberty University this morning."

"This can't be happening," Luke says. "This is a joke."

Eric navigates over to CNN.com. A bright yellow banner at the top of the page announces:

REV. JERRY FALWELL DEAD AT 73.

He clicks to other websites looking for something that corrects the mistake. But every site reads alike:

AP -- REV. JERRY FALWELL HAS DIED
REV. JERRY FALWELL, MORAL MAJORITY FOUNDER, DIES

"Are you kidding me?" Luke says, his voice climbing an octave. "You're freaking kidding me!"

From outside my window comes a piercing yell: *"Jerry's dead!!! Jerry Falwell is dead!!!"*

In a panic, I race out of the dorm. The chaos outside is unlike anything I've ever seen. Students are sprinting between buildings, shrieking hysterically into their cell phones, huddling in place to pray. Two female professors stand next to a lamppost, crying into the crooks of their arms.

In front of the bookstore, I spot a girl from my New Testament class, a curly-haired senior named Jessica. She's slumped against the wall, one hand holding back her hair, the other clutching a cell phone, head bobbing with each sob.

"Mom!" she wails. "He's not going to be at my graduation! I've been waiting to shake his hand since I was a little girl!"

No. No. This can't be happening. Jerry Falwell can't be dead. I just saw him two days ago. He saw me in the hall of Thomas Road Baptist Church and came over to congratulate me on the article I wrote about him. He said, "That was very fine work, Kevin," and then he shook my hand. His handshake was firm, healthy, robust. Just last week, in a convocation sermon, he told us, "God's man is indestructible until he has finished the work God has called him to do."

That's what he said. God's man is indestructible. And yet, at the moment, everything seems terribly wrong, almost post-apocalyptic. Professors are sprinting through the corridors of DeMoss Hall, ties and lab coats flapping behind them, emitting bloodcurdling yells.

"*There will be an emergency meeting for all students and faculty at Thomas Road, immediately!*"

In a daze, I walk the half mile to Thomas Road, where a lone spotlight is shining in Dr. Falwell's usual place at the pulpit. The church pianist plays a soft, sparse melody while hordes of shrieking, distraught people flood in. Dorm 22 gathers in a single row of seats near the middle.

Paul Maddox is staring blankly ahead, backpack hanging from his shoulder.

"I never thought . . ."

"I know," Zipper says. "I can't believe this is happening."

Over the next twenty minutes, thousands of members of the Liberty community pile into the sanctuary. Professors in suits sit next to varsity athletes in uniform, all of them picking liberally from the tissue boxes being passed around the rows like collection plates. When the sanctuary reaches capacity, Ron Godwin, the university's executive vice president, steps to the pulpit.

"This morning at about ten to seven," Godwin says, "I received my usual wake-up call—Dr. Falwell confirming when he wants to have breakfast. Today, Dr. Falwell and I had breakfast at Bob Evans. It was breakfast as usual, filled with vision, plans for the future, and joy. . . . Dr. Falwell's staff entered the office this morning and found him unconscious. Resuscitation was attempted there and was unsuccessful."

He steps back from the pulpit, composes himself, and returns.

"Staff, faculty, students . . . a giant has fallen. Dr. Falwell was pronounced dead at 12:40 PM today. He is with the Lord."

A Thomas Road associate pastor steps to the pulpit. "Take the hand of the person next to you," he says, "and let's pray together for the next few moments."

Paul clasps my hand tightly. As we pray, I look up at the mourners around me, more despondent than any group of people I've ever seen. Men are baldly weeping, women are flailing and howling. This is the kind of guttural, last-ditch grief I've only seen on the evening news from tornado survivors or parents who have lost their children. These are the tears of people with no contingency plan.

"Father," prays the pastor, "on rare occasions in history, you choose to raise up giants. Men and women of unusual vision, of unusual compassion, with a love for humankind that transcends that which is normal. Lord, we thank you today that we've been able to walk in the shadow of such a man. We know, Father, that Dr. Falwell has been faithful and he is with you in paradise . . . May we carry forward the unfinished work that Dr. Falwell so nobly began."

In the near silence of the sanctuary, I sit in my seat trembling, pulse resonating in my chest cavity. This wasn't supposed to happen. I was supposed to leave Liberty tomorrow, right after my Theology exam, and drive back to my old life. My bags were packed, my gas tank was full. Everything was tidy and neatly wrapped. Everything was done.

*   *   *

After the service, students and faculty are ricocheting around Thomas Road's lobby, sobbing and holding each other and giving teary interviews to the local media, who arrived several minutes ago and who seem to be taking quotes from all warm bodies. I push through the press line ("Excuse me young man! Do you attend Liberty University? Do you have any thoughts on Rev. Falwell's death?") and start the walk back to campus with my hallmates.

"It still hasn't sunk in for me," says Paul, walking across the parking lot. "Like, he's gone."

"It doesn't make any sense," says Zipper.

"Do you remember his last convo speech?" says Lucas, a junior on the hall. "Where he was talking about God's man being indestructible until he has finished the work God wants him to do?"

"Ugh," says Paul. "This is so crazy."

Back in my room, I glance at my cell phone. I'd left it on my desk during the service. I have twelve new voicemails, which I scan quickly.

"Kevin, Aunt Deborah here. What's going on down there?"

"Kevin, it's Mom. Did you hear what happened?"

"Oh my God, dude. This is unreal. Did you get his last interview?"

I open my e-mail—thirty-seven new messages. I click the first two and am shocked by what I see.

> This is Annie Scranton with MSNBC. I'm writing to you to see if you might be available to do a quick three-minute phone interview with us regarding the Rev. Jerry Falwell.
>
> Please call me as soon as you get this.

> We would be interested in speaking with you if possible.
> Todd Starnes
> News Anchor
> Fox News Radio

Eric comes into the room. "Hey, man, some guy from ABC News just called the hall phone looking for you. He said it's about your article on Falwell. I told him you'd call back."

I can't call back. I can't answer any media requests, in fact. How could I ever act as a Liberty spokesperson for a national audience? No, it's too stressful. For the next few hours, I sit in my room cowering in my chair as the phone calls and e-mails pour in. Many of my secular friends are overjoyed about Dr. Falwell's death, and they assume I am, too. They leave voicemails saying things like, "I am dancing in the streets right now" and "I don't want to express joy at someone's death, but . . . it's Jerry Falwell." One friend forwards an article titled "Ding Dong, Falwell's Dead."

What can I tell these people that will make any sense? I'm not celebrating Dr. Falwell's death, but I'm not exactly distraught, either. I haven't gotten much past shock, to be honest. What the hell is going on? Did Jerry Falwell really die on the next-to-last day of my Liberty semester? Did I really get the last interview of his life? If God really did make all this happen, the guy has a macabre sense of humor.

By nightfall on the day of Dr. Falwell's death, Liberty barely resembles itself. Satellite-topped news trucks form a half-mile line along the entrance road to campus, and swarms of microphone-swinging reporters make undisturbed passage between parts of campus nearly impossible. My friends and I have been cooped up in Dorm 22, watching the TV coverage of Dr. Falwell's death and avoiding the media outside. I'm in SLD Jake's room with Paul Maddox and Aaron McClain, a senior who lives down the hall.

"I was just out for dinner with my girlfriend," says Jake, "and there were probably ten times when one of us just stopped talking and said, 'Jerry Falwell's freaking . . . dead.'"

"It's not going to sink in until next year," says Paul. "Not until the first convocation."

Dr. Falwell's death might not sink in until next year, but the response from Liberty students has been quick and heavy. Dozens of freshly minted Facebook groups pay tribute to the founder—"Champions trained by Jerry," "Students Mourning Jerry Falwell," "Jerry Falwell WE WILL MISS YOU." Several students painted the spirit rock, a large boulder near the basketball arena, to read: "In Loving Memory of

Dr. Jerry Falwell: Fought the fight, finished the course, kept the faith." Other students decorated his reserved parking space with flowers and cards.

Obviously, Liberty's reaction is very different from the outside world's reaction. All day, we've watched as national news outlets have summarized Dr. Falwell's life as "controversial" and "provocative," and that's the positive stuff. The National Gay and Lesbian Task Force released a statement that read, "We will always remember him as . . . someone who demonized and vilified us for political gain and someone who used religion to divide rather than unite our nation." The atheist kingpin Christopher Hitchens went on CNN an hour ago to denounce Dr. Falwell, calling him an "ugly little charlatan" and saying "I think it's a pity there isn't a hell for him to go to."

"There hasn't been that much respect paid to Dr. Falwell today," Jake says, twirling a pencil in his fingers. "I mean, they're talking about how he blamed 9/11 on gay people. And yeah, he said some real bad stuff, nobody disagrees about that. But they never mention Liberty or Thomas Road or any of the good stuff."

"Yeah, I thought they might pay a little bit of respect to a man's life, even if they don't respect what he did," says McClain.

"Guys," says Jake after a long silence, "Liberty is never going to be the same."

Tomorrow is technically the last day of school, but Liberty has given us all the option of remaining in the dorms until Dr. Falwell's funeral, which is slated for a week from today. I decide to stay the extra week, if only because I'm too stunned to go anywhere. Dr. Falwell died, the doctors say, of a heart attack that capped years of persistent cardiac problems. Which means, I suppose, that when we had our interview less than two weeks ago, he wasn't simply tired from overwork—he was nearly dead. That realization, along with every other emotional shock of the past twelve hours, has put me in a state of semi-paralysis.

Before going to bed tonight, I brush my teeth, set my alarm, and check Facebook one last time. There, on the most tragic day in the thirty-six year history of this university, a student has added a new item to the list, "You Know You Went to Liberty If . . .":

Today was the hardest day of your year, and it had nothing to do with exams.

Over the next two days, Liberty's campus is overrun with tens of thousands of evangelical Christians who have flocked to Lynchburg to pay tribute to the fallen chancellor. Those of us who live here full-time have been giving directions to pastors from Peoria, electricians from Nevada, and homemakers from Little Rock (one of whom told me, upon walking around Liberty for a few hours, that "someone should write a book about this place").

On Thursday, Dr. Falwell's body is brought to the atrium of DeMoss Hall for an open-casket viewing. I wait in a two-hour line to pay my last respects, and when I finally make it up to the front, I see Dr. Falwell lying there in his black suit and red tie, a leather Bible clutched to his chest, his casket surrounded by two armed policemen. I've only been to one other open-casket viewing, and I forgot how expressionless and waxy a dead man looks. I stand there for a few minutes, next to an elderly Christian lady who is weeping quietly and whispering, "Praise God, praise God."

On my way out of the atrium, I run into Johnny Hager, the managing editor of the *Liberty Champion*.

"Kevin!" he says. "Oh my gosh, it's so good to see you."

Johnny and I got to know each other while I was working on my Falwell article. He's a bright, sweet-natured guy with a stocky build and a sparse goatee. When I ask him how he's holding up, he shakes his head.

"I never thought my last week at Liberty would be like this," he says. "It hit me about an hour ago. I was there, looking at Dr. Falwell, and then all of a sudden, I realized that he's actually gone forever. I just started to cry."

Johnny and the rest of the *Champion*'s editors decided to reprint my article in a special memorial edition they're putting out later this week. As I suspected, my interview with Dr. Falwell was the final print interview of his life (not the last interview altogether, though, since he gave an interview to CNN after we met), and the response has been overwhelming. Since Tuesday, I've gotten scores of e-mails from Falwell supporters, who tell me things like "I am sorry for your loss" and "Thank you for this article about a wonderful man who is surely today with Our Lord. He will truly be missed."

I'm having conflicted feelings about the article I wrote for the *Champion*. On one hand, I'm glad to have met Dr. Falwell. It gave me a glimpse of a side of him that has been largely ignored in the reports of his death, which have focused almost exclusively on his moments of political buffoonery. At the same time, all the Falwell-related coverage has made me question my willingness to excuse him for his sins. Did I really have a good time interviewing a guy who once called gay people "brute beasts," who protested the Civil Rights Act and called the Prophet Muhammad a terrorist? And if I did, what does that say about me? Can't I call evil by its proper name? Has this semester made me a moral milksop?

I will stand by one thing I wrote: like him or hate him, Dr. Falwell was no phony. All week, I've watched as liberal commentators and op-ed columnists have placed Dr. Falwell in a category of deceitful charlatans alongside Jim Bakker and Ted Haggard. And while I understand the urge to do so, it's wrong. Not only is it wrong, it's dangerous. If you chalk Dr. Falwell's entire career up to a charade, you risk obscuring the fact that there are *millions* of Americans, Liberty students and alumni included, who believe the same things he believed. Dr. Falwell may have used manipulative tactics to get his message across, and he may have abused his bully pulpit, but he was hardly a lone voice, and that's a much harsher reality to process.

In a way, Dr. Falwell's sincerity has also made me feel a bit—a *tiny* bit—bad for him. I remember something he told me during our interview, when I asked him what his biggest wish for this year's graduating Liberty seniors was. He responded, "I hope that they're spiritually ready for the greatest challenge any American graduating class has ever faced. Islamic terrorism is out of control, and we're at war, and America doesn't seem to have the necessary resolve to be able to win. It's going to be, in my opinion, a very long war. I think it's going to go on a hundred years. And it's going to take resolve or we won't win. I pray that our graduates will go out and turn the country around."

At the time, it struck me as an uncharacteristic moment of insecurity on his part. This war is going to go on for a hundred years? Isn't this the guy who used to say that America could be restored to its full greatness within his lifetime?

But since Dr. Falwell's death, I've read a number of statements he made in which he seemed less than confident about the success of the Religious Right's agenda. Like when he told *Christianity Today* in 2004 that he thought it would take "at least another forty years" to overturn *Roe v. Wade*, or when he told the *Washington Post* that he wasn't happy about the Republican candidates in the 2008 election, saying, "There are no Ronald Reagans out there."

Dr. Falwell has always claimed that the Moral Majority was a success. And politically, he may be right. His efforts turned millions of evangelical Christians into ballot-punching Republicans, and the presidential elections of the 1980s were altered significantly by the presence of a huge new voting bloc. But what does the Moral Majority have to crow about today? Look around. *Roe v. Wade* hasn't been overturned. Homosexuality is becoming more culturally benign every day. The tenets of feminism have become enshrined in much of America's social landscape, and pornography is more widely available than ever before. If Dr. Falwell had been a simple huckster, none of this would have bothered him. But I think he was in it to win. I think he wanted America to be saved, and I suspect it was painful for him to see his dream slipping away.

Dr. Falwell, as many in the media have noted this week, was an old lion of American evangelism. Religious leaders all over the country have expressed their sadness at his passing and their appreciation for his historical legacy, but buried in the subtext of those comments is always the notion that Dr. Falwell, and the brash, bulldoggish Christianity he pioneered, is largely a thing of the past. In 2005, *Time* magazine ran a cover story on the twenty-five most influential evangelicals in America. Dr. Falwell didn't make the list. A 2006 Pew Poll pegged his approval rating at 44 percent—among *evangelicals*. Near the end of his life, the man who had been the public face of American evangelicalism for almost two decades had been ceremonially put out to pasture by his descendants, many of whom favor a kinder, gentler approach to spreading the gospel. America's Christians have moved on from the Moral Majority's agenda, and I have no doubt that the evangelical church will survive Dr. Falwell's passing.

As for Liberty, I'm not so sure.

This year's commencement took place in Liberty's football stadium on Saturday, although I'm not even sure the 2,500 graduating seniors wanted to be there. Former House Speaker Newt Gingrich had the unenviable task of addressing the class of 2007 five days after the spiritual foundation of their school was ripped out from under them, and while everyone tried their hardest to make the occasion enjoyable—there were even some antics involving Silly String—it was pretty obvious that any joy in that stadium was merely window dressing. Before the degrees were conferred, a ten-minute video montage of Dr. Falwell's life was shown on the giant screens, leaving very few dry eyes and even fewer people who felt like celebrating. Administrators eulogized the Chancellor, the university's flags were lowered to half mast, and the top of one graduate's cap read, "I LOVE YOU, JERRY." One of my hallmates called it a funeral with diplomas.

The next day, Thomas Road Baptist Church held its first Sunday service without its founding pastor. Dr. Falwell's youngest son Jonathan, heir apparent to the Thomas Road pulpit, gave an emotionally charged sermon comparing the church's situation to the scenario that faced Israel after the passing of its leader.

"After Moses died," he said, "God gave Joshua, Moses' assistant, the instructions to cross the Jordan River into the land he had promised them. Today, Thomas Road, we are all Joshua. We must carry on the vision my father had fifty-one years ago for this church. We must cross this Jordan."

After church, I followed several thousand Thomas Roaders out to the parking lot, where we waited for Dr. Falwell's casket to be brought— in a horse-drawn carriage flanked by a squadron of police cars—into the church sanctuary, where it would lie in repose for two more days. As we waited, a few members of the congregation began to gossip about Dr. Falwell's upcoming funeral.

"I hear President Bush is making a surprise appearance."

"I heard Mel Gibson is coming in his private plane."

"Wow. You think he'll sign autographs?"

"I'm not sure. But I heard the prime minister of Israel is coming, too."

"We're going to have to camp out in line overnight to get a seat."

Most of my friends have gone home for the summer. The university gave us all the option of staying an extra week, but I was one of only four or five Dorm 22 residents to take them up on it. For the past six days, I've been living in solitude in an empty dorm room on an empty hall, speaking to no one, and not really doing much of anything, all because I wanted to attend Dr. Falwell's funeral tomorrow. I'm beginning to wish I had left with everyone else.

Part of what's bothering me about the grief-laden exercises of this week is that I'm not actually sure what the object of my grief is. I feel emotionally low, but when I try to match my state of mind to an external factor, I always come up short. Am I sad because Dr. Falwell died? Sort of, but I was much sadder to see my grandmother go, and I didn't mourn her death nearly as intensely. Am I feeling guilty because I was the last person to interview Dr. Falwell at length? Sure, but I've assuaged my guilt with the fact that for a final print interview, mine was pretty charitable, especially compared to the hammering he's gotten from the mainstream media this week.

My dad called me today. I've been avoiding my phone all week, but I was feeling so moody and homesick that I picked up. We ended up talking for almost an hour. I told him all the stories of the past week, from the death announcement at Thomas Road to the horse-drawn carriage to the spectacularly overshadowed commencement exercises, and when I finished, he asked me, "So, how do you feel about Jerry Falwell?"

For me, this is the hardest question he could have asked. Because when my dad asks it, he doesn't just mean, "How do you feel about Jerry Falwell?" By extension, he's also asking, "How do you feel about Liberty?" and "How do you feel about evangelicalism?" and "How do you feel about the time you've spent there?" I still don't feel totally equipped to answer any of those questions. Not even remotely. But since tomorrow marks the end of my semester, I suppose I should try my best. So here goes.

The things I hated about Dr. Falwell are the things lots of people hated about him. I hated his intolerance, his quickness to judge and caricature. I hated the way he invented outside threats to fuel his own ministry, and I hated his anti-intellectualism. I hated that unlike some of my friends at Liberty, who have never met any gay people, Dr. Falwell was fully aware of how homophobia operates and what its effects are, and he exploited it anyway.

What did I like about Dr. Falwell? Well, I liked his compassion among his people. I liked his Wonka-esque whimsy and his prankster streak, and I appreciated him as a talented pastor. But more than that, what I liked about Dr. Falwell was that he made me question my own assumptions. I sat in the Thomas Road choir loft week after week, listening to him preach to his congregation, and the more I heard, the less angry I became about the fact that any of this existed. In a way, I think Dr. Falwell functioned for me as a sort of human Rorschach test. Over the course of the semester, as my thoughts about faith and people of faith became more nuanced, so did my opinion of Dr. Falwell. I could appreciate his love for his flock in large part because I had learned to love them myself. And at the beginning of the semester, when all I saw in Dr. Falwell was hatred, I may have been saying more about my own heart than his.

The only solid Falwell-related conclusion I've found this week came from Valentina, a girl from my Daytona Beach evangelism trip. I had dinner with her a few days ago, and afterward, we sat in my parked car, having the "I can't believe he's dead" conversation that has been on infinite loop around here. At one point, after trying to condense her own opinions about Dr. Falwell and failing, Valentina looked out my passenger-side window and said, "Think about it: if it hadn't been for Jerry Falwell, this school wouldn't be here. I wouldn't have met my friends. I wouldn't be the person I am now."

That's all I can say today. Whatever Jerry Falwell has been to the world, however he'll be remembered, I have to acknowledge that if it weren't for him, I wouldn't have come to Liberty at all. I wouldn't have met Valentina or Jersey Jocy or Paul Maddox or Pastor Seth or Zipper or Anna. For better or worse—and I'm not quite sure which it is yet—the man changed my life.

Meanwhile, my dad is still waiting for an answer to his question: what do I think of Jerry Falwell?

"He was a complicated guy," I say.

"That's it?" my dad says. "A complicated guy?"

"Yep. That's it."

He'll never understand.

I refuse to camp out overnight for a funeral. Camping out in line should be reserved for U2 concert tickets and newly released video game systems, not remembrances of the dead, even if that dead is a major American religious and political figure. So on Tuesday, the day of Dr. Falwell's funeral, when several thousand people were waiting outside the doors of the Thomas Road Baptist Church, clamoring for seats to the most high-profile event in this city's history, I take the opportunity to sleep in.

At noon, and not a moment before, I shower, shave, comb my hair, change into my one and only suit, and walk over to Liberty's basketball arena, where Dr. Falwell's funeral is being shown via simulcast. I take a seat in one of the middle rows, next to a family of four from Charlottesville, all dressed in their Sunday best. I've always thought it was weird that people dress up for funerals the same way they dress up for weddings—after all, the person in the casket can't see what you're wearing—but it's doubly weird when the funeral you're watching is being projected on a Jumbotron screen from a half mile away. I do notice that the element of distance has made this basketball arena a more relaxed environment than over at the church. A few rows away, while waiting for the service to begin, an elderly female attendee breaks out her knitting needles.

Technically, I could have gotten into the service at Thomas Road even without waiting in line overnight. I could have asked to sing in the church choir, which has been asked to sing the "Hallelujah" chorus at the end of the service. But I couldn't. I already feel duplicitous enough. Yesterday, I learned that the special edition of the *Liberty Champion*, the one with my article reprinted inside, is being handed out at Dr. Falwell's funeral, meaning that thousands upon thousands of people are processing their grief over his death, at least in part, through something I wrote. If that weren't enough, I then got a call from a *Champion* staffer who told me that the Jerry Falwell Museum is planning to add my article to its permanent collection. I managed to wait until the phone call was over to scream.

At 1:00 PM, Dr. Falwell's funeral begins. Few of the rumored luminaries showed up, but a representative from the Oval Office is on hand, and several evangelical celebrities like Pat Robertson and former Christian Coalition leader Ralph Reed made the trek. The funeral itself is a beautiful, touching service. Franklin Graham, son of Rev. Billy Graham and a Liberty parent, gives a stirring tribute to Dr. Falwell's ministerial legacy. Dr. Falwell's daughter Jeannie eulogizes her father with words that would mist the eyes of anyone with a pulse. Charles Billingsley, the velvet-voiced Thomas Road soloist, sings Dr. Falwell's favorite song, a Bill Gaither gospel number called "Going Home."

> *Many times in my childhood*
> *when we'd traveled so far,*
> *By nightfall how weary I'd grow;*
> *Father's arm would slip 'round me,*
> *So gently he'd say,*
> *"My child, we're going home."*
>
> *Going home, I'm going home,*
> *There's nothing to hold me here;*
> *Well, I've caught a glimpse of that heavenly land,*
> *Praise God, I'm going home.*

Everyone around me in the arena is crying, and to be honest, I don't know why I'm not. Maybe I spent all my sadness already. Maybe I'm too consumed with terrible, skin-crawling guilt. I might be half a mile away from the funeral, but I feel like I'm wrapped up in the middle of all of this. During "Going Home," the camera panned across a row of seats in Thomas Road's sanctuary, and I flinched when I saw that a lady in the row had a copy of the *Liberty Champion* in her lap, opened to my article.

Is God punishing me for meddling in other people's affairs? Is that what this is? A divine comeuppance? Did some cosmic thug bring me to Liberty knowing that I'd end up this way? I don't think so. I don't. But at the moment, I'm not quite sure what the purpose of all this is. I'm not sure if I should apologize, or for what, or to whom. Right now, I just want to leave.

After the choir sings a tear-filled "Hallelujah" chorus, after the pastor gives the final amen, I walk across campus to my car. I unlock it, and I toss my funeral program in the backseat. I take off my tie, I start the engine, and I drive away from Liberty's campus. The sun is shining. I open my window and let the hot wind wallop my face. Praise God, I'm going home.

Epilogue

I t's midnight at Brown University, and I'm kneeling on the floor of my dorm room, praying.

I've been back at secular college for almost a year now, and I still pray a few times every week. In fact, that's about the only thing my life today has in common with the life I led at Liberty. I don't follow a nightly curfew, I don't avoid R-rated movies, and Lord knows I don't go to Bible study on Friday nights. In fact, I'm not sure when the last time I cracked open a Bible was, but it must have been at least a couple months ago.

If I seem detached from my Liberty persona, it's a recent development. When I first arrived back at Brown, I was culture clashing all over the place. My re-entry shock came in two forms. First, I'd be surprised by something I experienced—an English professor who began the first day of class without leading prayer, or a boozy frat party, or the presence of actual, non-closeted gay couples—and then I'd be surprised that I was surprised. Wasn't this *normal*? Had Liberty really screwed my perspective up that badly?

Happily, no. After a few weeks of wide-eyed readjustment, I settled back in at Brown. My friends dragged me out to parties and my professors got me up to speed on my secular studies, and eventually, I felt it all coming back. By Halloween or so, I was able to forget, for brief periods of time, that I ever went to Liberty. I'd land on a Thomas Road Baptist Church sermon while flipping channels on a Sunday morning, and I'd think: *did I really do that?* It seemed utterly foreign, and I was surprised—and a little embarrassed—that I had once felt so comfortable there.

I think of Liberty frequently and with great fondness. I don't remember everything I learned in my courses, but a fair amount of theological arcana stuck around, and every time the Bible comes up in one of my Brown classes, I'm transported in a flash back to DeMoss Hall. (After my final exams at Liberty, if you're curious, I ended up with four Bs and two As). I've been able to keep abreast of Liberty happenings through Facebook, and just a few minutes ago, I glanced at the photograph I keep on my desk, a shot of my Dorm 22 intramural softball team. We're on the field celebrating a play-off win, and right in front, wearing under-eye war paint and sticking out his tongue, is Jersey Joey.

Joey still calls me every few weeks, both to tell me about his exploits at Liberty and, I suspect, to experience secular college life vicariously through me. (He began one check-in by asking, "Rooster, you got any loose broads up there?") By Liberty standards, Joey's not doing very well these days. As he predicted, his efforts at personal reform failed, and he's now committing regular acts of actual rebellion. Recently, he told me about sneaking out after curfew, taking up a smoking habit, and spending a sinful spring break in Florida. Joey's stories always come packaged with a tiny bit of remorse, but mostly, he sounds excited to be getting away with it all.

"I'm livin' large, Rooster," he says. "Larger than this place, that's for sure."

Paul Maddox has had a rough-and-tumble year since I left. During the summer, Paul went to visit his girlfriend Lauren, met her parents, and ended up asking for—and receiving—their permission to seek Lauren's hand in marriage. "I just think it's the right thing," he told me. "I know it was a quick decision, but I feel like it's going to work out." It didn't. He proposed, she accepted, and a month later, Lauren broke up with him, saying that she needed to wait until after college to get married. Paul spent months in a heartbroken slump, and briefly considered dropping out of Liberty. Then, in the spring, he dug himself out. He refocused on his academics and his faith and even tried out for the Liberty football team again. Against all odds, he made the varsity squad.

"Will I get any playing time?" he said. "Maybe. It doesn't matter, really. I'm just blessed to be out there."

Updates from the rest of my Liberty friends come through the grapevine in bits and pieces. James Powell, the new RA on Dorm 22, has proven himself to be a capable leader, and most of the guys seem to think the hall is in good hands. Zipper, my former next-door neighbor, moved across campus to take a position as the Spiritual Life Director on another hall and is going through training to become an RA next year. Max Carter, Liberty's student body president, was admitted to the University of Virginia law school, where he'll matriculate next fall. Travis, Jersey Joey's roommate, accepted Jesus as his savior last September, in part due to the influence of a Christian girl he wanted to date. Eric, my old roommate, is planning to go to seminary after college, and he still sees Henry, our third roommate, walking around campus sometimes. Anna, my Christian crush, left Liberty after the fall semester. She returned home to Delaware, where she's been taking classes at a medium-size state school. "I liked Liberty's Christian atmosphere," she told me, "but there weren't enough free-thinkers there. I was toughing it out, and I don't think college is something you should tough out. I want to enjoy myself."

Overall, Liberty seems to be doing quite well these days. After Dr. Falwell's death, his sons, Jerry Jr. and Jonathan, took over the helms of Liberty and Thomas Road, respectively. Their ascendancy worried many of the Lynchburg faithful, and some predicted a quick downfall for the Falwell empire. But today, both the school and the church are thriving. Unbeknownst to many Liberty students, Dr. Falwell carried more than $30 million in life insurance policies, the dividends from which went to Liberty's general fund upon his death. For the first time in history, Liberty is a debt-free school. Enrollment is up 10 percent from last year, new buildings are sprouting up every day, and student morale is at an all-time high. Thomas Road, too, is experiencing unprecedented growth, adding 1,200 new members to its ranks in the months following Jonathan Falwell's installation as senior pastor.

There are people, of course, who say that Liberty will never be as good as it was, that Dr. Falwell's death spelled the end of Liberty's glory days. But almost every Liberty student I've talked to reports that while adjusting to new leadership has been difficult, the transition has been largely positive. Under Dr. Falwell's guidance, Liberty was frozen in place by a half-century of ideological inertia, and his passing has freed the school from its bindings. Jerry Falwell, Jr. is just as conservative on social and theological issues as his father was, and from all reports, he intends to keep Liberty headed a few miles to the right of center, but the younger Falwells belong to a different generation of evangelicals, and the difference on campus is palpable.

For one, seeds of ideological diversity are sprouting. New Facebook groups created since I left include "Good Stewardship of the Earth and its Creatures Is a Biblical Mandate Not a Leftist Sentiment," "College Democrats of Liberty," and "God Is Not a Republican" (which put my jaw on the floor). For another, campus culture is moving even more quickly toward the mainstream. Liberty students tell me excitedly about the relaxed hair code for men (locks that come over the ears are now legal), and there's talk of a new, loosened alcohol policy that allows students one booze-related indiscretion before they're expelled. Fox, my old RA, described this year's campus atmosphere to me this way: "I don't know exactly how to express it, but there's a new electricity at Liberty. It's not just the rules changing. I think this school is changing a lot. People are trying new things. God is moving in different ways."

As for Dr. Falwell, his memory still hovers low over Liberty's day-to-day operation. At the first convocation of the fall semester, Jerry Falwell, Jr. chose to replay one of his father's old speeches on the Jumbotrons. The younger Falwell has been easing into his role as Liberty's chancellor, but no one seems to think he has filled Dr. Falwell's shoes entirely. Today, I went on Liberty's website to check out the campus happenings, and as always, I was astounded by the amount of attention paid to the deceased founder, and how odd that attention can appear to the outside world. On the front page, I saw a picture of Dr. Falwell's completed headstone, located at his burial spot, just outside his office on the Mansion lawn. The headstone took the shape of a ten-foot limestone cross, topped with an eternal flame powered by a propane feed.

I shook my head in amazement. Really? A former segregationist, and the way you memorialize him is by erecting a burning cross?

A few days after I left Liberty for the last time, I tried to peel the silver Jesus fish emblem off the bumper of my Honda. The metal part came off easily, but a brown fish-shaped residue remained on the bumper, and no amount of scrubbing or scraping could get it off. I appreciated this on two levels. First, it meant that when I gave the car back to my dad—I had borrowed it from him for the semester—he was forced to drive around our ultra-liberal college town with the outline of a Jesus fish on his car, drawing worried stares from our friends and neighbors.

Second, the indelible Jesus fish provided me with the world's easiest metaphor to describe my transition from Liberty back to the secular world. Namely, no matter how hard I tried, I couldn't quite scrape it away. Even when I was back at Brown full-time, caught up once again in the flood of papers and seminars and parties on the weekend, something about Liberty kept nagging at me. I kept having flashbacks of my time there—my Sundays in the Thomas Road choir loft, my History of Life class, my prayer chapel session with Zipper—and each memory was followed by a rush of guilt.

For almost a year after I left Lynchburg I had kept up my pretense about my Liberty semester. I still hadn't told any of my friends there that I had come to Liberty, in effect, to write about them. My reluctance to reveal myself was completely selfish: I just didn't want to be a villain. How could I tell Jersey Joey that I had been hiding a huge part of myself from him for an entire year? How could I explain to Zipper that I wasn't saved? It would be better for everyone, I thought, if Liberty heard about my book another way. Maybe someone would put the puzzle together on their own. Maybe my publisher could send a nice letter.

But in April, eleven months after I left Liberty, I decided I needed to go back and tell them myself. If my semester at Bible Boot Camp taught me one thing, it's the freedom of conscience that comes with confession. I realized that the only way to get rid of my emotional burden would be to confront it head-on. And so, stomach in knots, I made the twelve-hour drive to Lynchburg.

The first person I saw was Jersey Joey.

"Rooster!" he said, pulling me in for a hug. "Good to see you, ya friggin' queer."

Joey and I went out for dinner on the first night of my visit, where we spent a solid hour catching up, talking, laughing. He told me about some of his exploits, like a non-Christian girl he had recently begun to date. The girl is a waitress at a Lynchburg restaurant, and several weeks before my visit, Joey slipped her his phone number. She called, they hit it off, and before long, he was smitten.

"This girl is danger," Joey reported. "She's not into religion, but she's real pretty, and she's got these huge knockers. Huge, Rooster. Double Ds. I can barely get my hands around 'em."

Joey promised that he was carefully guarding his virginity, but he wasn't sure how long he could hold out.

After a few more stories, I looked him in the eye.

"Joey, there's something I need to tell you."

He deadpanned, "Let me guess . . . you're gay."

"No."

Deep breath.

"I wrote a book about us, Joey. I came to Liberty to write about the school. I'm a writer. And after I left, I turned my life—our lives—into a book."

Joey squinted at the sky. He flicked his cigarette, sending embers flying.

"Rooster, are you serious?"

"Yeah. I am."

He looked at me. Now, he was breaking into a sly smile.

"You little bastard! I knew it!" He laughed for thirty seconds straight, coughing out spidery wisps of smoke. "You were always doing weird crap! Taking notes in church, asking weird-ass questions, always wanting to know everything about everybody. I knew something was off about you."

Joey and I spent the next two hours in the restaurant parking lot, sitting on a ledge and talking about my book. He wanted to know everything: how I'd decided to come, what I thought about Liberty, what the best and worst parts of my semester were. We laughed about the time he had almost caught me, when he asked if I was working for *Rolling Stone*. I showed him proofs of the cover design my publisher had drawn up. He liked it, though he pointed out that my author photo looked "gayer than gay, but what would I expect from the Rooster?"

I was blown away. Why wasn't he yelling at me? A year and a half of secrecy, and he makes gay jokes? Didn't he think I was satanic?

"This blows my mind, to be honest," he said. "But I'm not mad. I think it's pretty cool actually. I'm happy for you. I haven't read a book in six, seven years. But I might read this one."

I thought Joey's reaction was a fluke. He was my best friend at Liberty, after all. Surely, other people wouldn't respond so warmly. But I was wrong. Over the course of the weekend, I told twenty of my closest Liberty friends about my book—including Paul, Zipper, Pastor Seth, and Eric—and the strangest thing happened: everyone forgave me. In fact, the reactions I got surpassed even the best-case scenarios I had drawn up in my mind before my trip. After I reassured people that I hadn't come to Liberty to disparage it, and after I said that I had changed their names and identifying details, everyone was excited to read my take. They wanted to know what the book was called and where they could buy it. But for whatever reason, they weren't mad. My roommate Eric, upon hearing my news, apologized to me.

"Wait, why are *you* sorry?" I asked. "I'm the one who was hiding things from you."

"I know," he said. "But if I had known who you were, I would have tried to show you a better picture of myself."

I reminded Eric that I had come to Liberty to get the real story of Liberty life, not an airbrushed façade.

"I know," he said. "But I still wish I had acted better toward Henry and stuff. I guess it's a good lesson for me."

People even seemed to understand why I had gone incognito. "You would have had a totally different semester if we had known you weren't a Christian," said James Powell. "I don't think you would have gotten the real story."

This part of my confession—the news that I wasn't an evangelical—was the only part that was met with anything less than excitement. When I told Zipper about my Quaker roots, he gazed at the floor.

"So, does this mean you're not saved?" he asked.

I wanted to give Zipper the spiel I had concocted in my mind since leaving Liberty—about how although I had stopped short of getting saved, I had experienced immense spiritual growth at Liberty. I wanted to tell him that his warmth toward me, and the warmth of my other Liberty friends had been a better apologetic device than all the Way of the Master routines and History of Life classes combined. But I knew what he meant. Zipper wanted to know if I had prayed the Sinner's Prayer, if I had gotten down on my knees and asked Christ to be my personal savior. And I had to tell him that I hadn't.

"Wow," he said. "Well . . . wow."

The news that I wasn't an evangelical confused Zipper, and it confused many more of my Liberty friends that weekend. In their mental categories of saved and unsaved, what I told them took me out of the saved category, but it didn't put me fully in the category of unsaved, either. For a Liberty student, an unsaved person is someone who doesn't get it, who doesn't know how to quote C. S. Lewis or sing "Jesus Paid It All" without looking at the words. And for them, the fact that I *did* know these things, that I had gone through the same Christian gauntlet as them, made my story all the more confusing and all the more heartbreaking. My news would have been easier to swallow if I had been a Jew or a Muslim or a steadfast atheist. But to be *this* close to Christianity for an entire semester and not have accepted Christ? It killed them.

"It's such a shame, man," said Rodrigo, my hallmate from Mexico City. "Think about it: you had *every chance.*"

So they prayed for me. In the weeks following my Liberty visit, I was the subject of one-on-one prayers, group prayers, even long-distance prayers. James Powell sent me a text message two days after I left that read, "Hey buddy. Just wanted to let you know that I'm praying for you this week. Let me know if there's anything I can do for you."

A few weeks later, I made the hardest confession of all. I called Anna to tell her, at long last, why I had been so hesitant to get involved with her at Liberty. Fists clenched, I told her my secret, and like everyone else, she reacted extremely well. She was relieved to know that I had a valid reason for snubbing her after our series of dates, although she called me a "borderline pansy" for not asking her out anyway. We spend almost an hour laughing and reminiscing about our semester-long quasi-romance, and at the end of our conversation, we said a tender goodbye and promised to keep in touch.

After telling my Liberty friends about myself, I felt the burden of a year and a half's worth of white lies and equivocation lift off my shoulders. I was finally free to be myself. I could talk to Zipper on the phone without pretending that my world was being rocked by God like his was. I could talk to Anna without any fear that I was leading her on under false pretenses. Everything I did, even at Brown, took on a new aura of openness. I began to tell everyone in my life exactly how I felt about them at all times. I poured my heart out at every available opportunity. I grabbed at transparency like an addict grabs at a crack pipe.

And over time, I found that the distance separating my two worlds all but collapsed. Having thrown off the yoke of exaggeration and half truth, I was now free to be the same guy—the exact same guy—when talking to my Liberty friends and my Brown friends alike. I somehow thought this synthesis of personalities would be greeted with fanfare or celebration, but it passed more or less unnoticed. A few of my Brown friends noticed a new streak of earnestness (one friend began calling me "Hallmark"), but the people at Liberty were almost completely unfazed. They saw me for who I am, and even though I'm sure they're not completely happy with it—I'm guessing they'd like me to curse a little less and pray a little more—they didn't seem altogether shocked or dismayed that I was living on my own terms, at my own pace. The conversion attempts I got eventually slowed to a trickle, and when that happened, my Dorm 22 hallmates and I were left yammering on about our grades, our career anxieties, our families, our love lives. Finally, we were friends, with nothing left in the way.

Did my semester at Liberty bridge the God Divide? Of course not. It would be asinine to cue up the triumphal music now, as I claim some diplomatic victory or other for myself. At the end of the day, the two sides of this culture war still have glaring differences, and those differences are likely to continue to define the relationship between the evangelical community and America at large for decades to come. Humans have always quarreled over their beliefs, and I suppose they always will. But judging from my post-Liberty experience, this particular religious conflict isn't built around a hundred-foot brick wall. If anything, it's built around a flimsy piece of cardboard, held in place on both sides by paranoia and lack of exposure. It's there, no doubt, but it's hardly forbidding. And more important, it's hardly soundproof. Religious conflict might be a basic human instinct, but I have faith, now more than ever before, that we can subvert that instinct for long enough to listen to each other.

Earlier tonight, I got a distressed call from Jersey Joey. The girl he's dating, the non-Christian waitress, has been hinting strongly that she wants to have sex with him. Joey, who has never considered the prospect of premarital sex all that terrifying, is still trying to make up his mind.

"I mean, I know I shouldn't," he said. "But man, Rooster, I really want to. I don't want to wait until I'm freaking married to lose my virginity. That could be five, ten years from now."

I told Joey that I'd respect him no matter what he did, that he didn't need to apologize to me if he went through with the deed.

"Tell you what," he said, "if I lose my virginity to this girl, you'll be the first to know. Wish me luck, Rooster."

We laughed and said our goodbyes, and after hanging up, I went straight to my knees. If that's not worth praying for, I don't know what is.

ACKNOWLEDGMENTS

It takes a village to raise a child, but it takes something much bigger to guide a child through his first book. A tri-county area? A city-state? I'm not quite sure.

In any case, I was nineteen when I began writing this book, and while I may not have been a child in the legal sense, I certainly felt like one. The book-writing process is more daunting and byzantine than I ever could have imagined, and I wouldn't have gotten past the first page had a great number of people not stepped in to offer their guidance and wisdom.

I'm thankful, first and foremost, to my editor at Grand Central Publishing, Ben Greenberg. Ben provided witty insight and a probing editorial pen when I needed it most. His faith in this book borders on hard-line fundamentalism, and his patience with me is bottomless. Every writer should be so lucky.

A million thanks to my wonderful agent, Kate Lee at ICM, whose thoughtfulness and tenacity are miracles of the highest order. Another million to A. J. Jacobs, who took me under his wing three years ago and turned me, almost single-handedly, into a writer. His sage advice, inexhaustible generosity, and sheer big-heartedness are the reasons this book exists at all.

I'm also grateful for Jamie Raab and the rest of the Grand Central Publishing crew for helping this book along from proposal to publication. Tanisha Christie (publicist nonpareil), Nick Small, Peggy Boelke, Kallie Shimek, Valerie Russo, and Flag Tonuzi were especially great to work with. Thanks to Jeremiah Guelzo at Stone Blue Productions for taking the photograph that appears on this book's front cover, to Larissa Silva for her cheerful assistance, and to Big Tam for his expert video work.

All my thanks to the folks who read this manuscript in various stages of completion and gave me valuable feedback. Andrew Marantz edited many, many versions of these pages, worked his magic every time, and is responsible for most of the good stuff in here by now. Jon Margolick, Ariel Werner, Rhoda Flaxman, Scott Poulson-Bryant, Chris Unseth, Deborah Roose, and David Snyder all lent their eyes to the effort. Pastor Mike Wessells and the Reverend Jon Huyck fixed my theological mistakes, and three Brown University faculty members—Ross Kraemer, Doug Brown, and the Reverend Janet Cooper-Nelson—steered me to deeper analytical waters. And speaking of Brown, I'd be remiss if I didn't thank the deans and faculty members there who helped me jump through bureaucratic hoops before and after my semester "abroad." Without their support and flexibility, I'd almost certainly be kicked out by now.

I'm indebted to my family members, of course, for their unswerving love and loyalty. My parents were wonderful throughout this moderately traumatic process. Ken and Gretchen Roose and Warren Wickes, my grandparents, supported me even when it hurt. My aunts Tina and Teresa went miles beyond the call of duty. My cousin Beirne and cousin-in-law Adam came through in the clutch for me, and my big brother Carl kept me afloat.

Many other friends supported this project in ways big and small. Robert Smith III lent me a "What Would Jesus Do?" book from his childhood; Jimmy Lowe transcribed interviews like a champ; David Leipziger did a mitzvah by flying down to Lynchburg for a visit; and Laura Bitner deserves a heavenly reward for her Bible tutoring sessions (among many other things). Huge thanks to the Temple family for keeping me well-fed while I wrote at their house, to Mary Meadows for her books and sermons, and to Jacqui Friedman for, well, everything.

Of course, there is one group of people I could never thank enough, no matter how much space I devote to the attempt. Namely, the students, faculty, and administrators of Liberty University. When I arrived on campus in January of 2007, I never thought that the world's largest evangelical university would feel like home, or even a home away from home. But by experiencing your warmth, your vigorous generosity of spirit, and your deep complexity, I was ultimately convinced—not that you were right, necessarily, but that I had been wrong. Thank you for the lessons you taught me, even when you didn't know you were teaching them at all.

SELECTED BIBLIOGRAPHY

I found the following books helpful during my semester at Liberty. To see a list of my class readings while there, and to test your own Bible knowledge on actual Liberty University exams, visit www.kevinroose.com.

Adams, Marc. *The Preacher's Son.* Seattle: Window Books, 1996.

Armstrong, Karen. *The Battle for God: A History of Fundamentalism.* New York: Random House, 2000.

Arterburn, Stephen, and Kenny Luck. *Every Young Man, God's Man.* Colorado Springs: WaterBrook, 2005.

Balmer, Randall. *Mine Eyes Have Seen the Glory: A Journey into the Evangelical Subculture in America.* Oxford: Oxford University Press, 2006.

Bell, Rob. *Sex God: Exploring the Endless Connections Between Sexuality and Spirituality.* Grand Rapids: Zondervan, 2007.

———. *Velvet Elvis: Repainting the Christian Faith.* Grand Rapids: Zondervan, 2005.

Bentley, Michael L. "Creationism Through the Back Door: The Case of Liberty Baptist College." *Science, Technology, & Human Values* 9, no. 4 (1984): 49–53.

Budziszewski, J. *How to Stay Christian in College.* Colorado Springs: Th1nk Books, 2004.

Campolo, Tony. *Letters to a Young Evangelical.* New York: Basic Books, 2006.

Chambers, Oswald. *My Utmost for His Highest.* New York: Dodd, Mead, and Company, 1935.

Cherry, Conrad, Betty A. DeBerg, and Amanda Porterfield. *Religion on Campus.* Chapel Hill: University of North Carolina Press, 2001.

Comfort, Ray, and Kirk Cameron. *The Way of the Master: How to Share Your Faith Simply, Effectively, Biblically—the Way Jesus Did.* Wheaton: Tyndale House, 2004.

Durkheim, Émile. *The Elementary Forms of Religious Life.* Translated by Carol Cosman. Oxford: Oxford University Press, 2001.

Ehrman, Bart D. *God's Problem: How the Bible Fails to Answer Our Most Important Question—Why We Suffer.* New York: HarperOne, 2008.

Falwell, Jerry. *Building Dynamic Faith.* Nashville: World Publishing, 2005.

———. *Falwell: An Autobiography.* Lynchburg: Liberty House, 1997.

———. *Listen, America!* New York: Doubleday, 1980.

Falwell, Jerry, and Elmer Towns. *Church Aflame.* Nashville: Impact Books, 1971.

FitzGerald, Frances. "A Disciplined, Charging Army." *The New Yorker,* May 18, 1981.

Harding, Susan Friend. *The Book of Jerry Falwell: Fundamentalist Language and Politics.* Princeton: Princeton University Press, 2000.

Harrington, Walt. "What Hath Falwell Wrought?" *The Washington Post Magazine,* July 24, 1988: W19.

Harris, Harriet A. *Fundamentalism and Evangelicals.* Oxford: Oxford University Press, 1998.

Harris, Joshua. *I Kissed Dating Goodbye.* Colorado Springs: Multnomah, 1997.

Hawthorne, Nathaniel. *The Blithedale Romance.* New York: Penguin Classics, 1986.

Holmes, Arthur F. *The Idea of a Christian College.* Grand Rapids: Eerdmans, 1975.

Jacobs, A. J. *The Year of Living Biblically: One Man's Humble Quest to Follow the Bible as Literally as Possible.* New York: Simon & Schuster, 2007.

James, William. *The Varieties of Religious Experience*. New York: Modern Library, 2002.

Kinnaman, David. *unChristian: What a New Generation Really Thinks about Christianity*. Grand Rapids: BakerBooks, 2007.

LaHaye, Tim, and Jerry B. Jenkins. *Left Behind*. Wheaton: Tyndale House, 1996.

Lamott, Anne. *Plan B: Further Thoughts on Faith*. New York: Riverhead, 2005.

Lewis, C. S. *Mere Christianity*. New York: HarperCollins, 1952.

————. *The Problem of Pain*. New York: HarperOne, 1940.

McLaren, Brian D. *Everything Must Change: Jesus, Global Crises, and a Revolution of Hope*. Nashville: Thomas Nelson, 2007.

Miller, Donald. *Blue Like Jazz*. Nashville: Thomas Nelson, 2003.

Mooney, Margarita. "Religion, College Grades, and Satisfaction Among Students at Elite Colleges and Universities." Paper presented at the 2006 Annual Meetings of the Association for the Sociology of Religion. Revised paper obtained from the author on December 1, 2008.

Noll, Mark A. *The Scandal of the Evangelical Mind*. Grand Rapids: Eerdmans, 1994.

Penning, James M., and Corwin E. Smidt. *Evangelicalism: The Next Generation*. Grand Rapids: Baker Academic, 2002.

Perrotta, Tom. *The Abstinence Teacher*. New York: St. Martin's Press, 2007.

Radosh, Daniel. *Rapture Ready!* New York: Scribner, 2008.

Riley, Naomi Schaefer. *God on the Quad*. New York: St. Martin's Press, 2005.

Rosin, Hanna. *God's Harvard: A Christian College on a Mission to Save America*. New York: Harcourt, 2007.

Sandler, Lauren. *Righteous: Dispatches from the Evangelical Youth Movement*. New York: Viking, 2006.

Schaeffer, Frank. *Crazy for God*. New York: Carroll & Graf, 2007.

Sheler, Jeffery L. *Believers*. New York: Viking, 2006.

Snowball, David. *Continuity and Change in the Rhetoric of the Moral Majority*. New York: Praeger, 1991.

Strobel, Lee. *The Case for Faith*. Grand Rapids: Zondervan, 2000.

Strober, Jerry, and Ruth Tomczak. *Jerry Falwell: Aflame for God*. Nashville: Thomas Nelson, 1979.

Thomas, Cal, and Ed Dobson. *Blinded by Might*. Grand Rapids: Zondervan, 1999.

White, Mel. *Religion Gone Bad: The Hidden Dangers of the Christian Right*. New York: Tarcher, 2006.

Wilcox, Clyde. *God's Warriors: The Christian Right in Twentieth-Century America*. Baltimore: The Johns Hopkins University Press, 1992.

ABOUT THE AUTHOR

KEVIN ROOSE is a senior at Brown University, where he studies English and writes regular columns for the *Brown Daily Herald*. His work has been featured in *Esquire, Spin, mental_floss,* and other publications. For more information, visit his website at www.kevinroose.com.